SHAPING A GLOBAL THEOLOGICAL MIND

Theological thinkers are placed into contexts which inform their theological tasks but that context is usually limited to a European or North American centre, usually ignoring minorities and lesser mainstream theologies even in that context. This work focuses on the shift of Christian theological thinking from the North Atlantic to the Global South, even within the North Atlantic Church and Academy. It gives a Global perspective on theological work, method and context. Theologians from North America, Great Britain and Europe, Africa, Asia, Central and South America comment on how their specific context and methodology manifests, organizes and is prioritized in their thought so as to make Christian theology relevant to their community. By placing the Global South alongside the newly emerging presence of non-traditional Western forms such as Pentecostal, Aboriginal, and Hispanic theologies and theologians a clearer picture of how Christian theology is both enculturated and still familial is offered.

For Alexander and Beatrice

Shaping a Global Theological Mind

Edited by

DARREN C. MARKS
Huron University College at the University of Western Ontario, Canada

ASHGATE

Published by
Ashgate Publishing Limited
Gower House
Croft Road
Aldershot
Hampshire GU11 3HR
England

Ashgate Publishing Company
Suite 420
101 Cherry Street
Burlington, VT 05401-4405
USA

Ashgate website: http://www.ashgate.com

British Library Cataloguing in Publication Data
Marks, Darren C.
   Shaping the global theological mind
   1. Globalization – Religious aspects – Christianity 2. Theology, Doctrinal
   I. Marks, Darren C.
   230'.09

Library of Congress Cataloging-in-Publication Data
Marks Darren C.
   Shaping a global theological mind
      p. cm.
   ISBN-13: 978-0-7546-6003-3(hardcover : alk. paper)
   ISBN-13: 978-0-7546-6006-4 (pbk. : alk. paper)
   1. Theology, Doctrinal. 2. Globalization – Religious aspects – Christianity.
   I. Marks, Darren C.

   BT10.S42 2007
   230.09 – dc22

2007036258

ISBN: 978-0-7546-6003-3 (Hbk)
ISBN: 978-0-7546-6006-4 (Pbk)

Printed and bound in Great Britain by TJ International Ltd, Padstow, Cornwall

Contents

Notes on Contributors   *vii*
Preface   *xi*

1   Living in a Global World and in a Global *Theological* World   1
    Darren C. Marks

2   A Christology from Advaita Vedanta of India   9
    K.P. Aleaz

3   Theological *Popevki*: Of the Fathers, Liturgy and Music   15
    Bishop Hilarion Alfeyev

4   The Missionary Enterprise in Cross-Cultural Perspective:
    With Particular Focus on Madagascar   27
    Carl E. Braaten

5   Constructing a South African Theological Mind   35
    John W. DeGruchy

6   Globalization, Religion and Embodiment:
    Latin American Feminist Perspectives   41
    Wanda Deifelt

7   A Chicano Theological Mind   51
    Andrés Quetzalcóatl Guerrero

8   The Gospel is the Power of God for the Salvation of Everyone
    who Believes   65
    Hwa Yung

9   *Mujerista* Theology: A Praxis of Liberation – My Story   77
    Ada María Isasi-Díaz

10   A Tale of Many Stories   89
    Emmanuel Katongole

11   Indigenous Peoples in Asia: Theological Trends and Challenges   95
    Wati Longchar

12   Global Warming: A Theological Problem and Paradigm   109
     Sallie McFague

13   Beyond Suffering and Lament: Theology of Hope and Life   113
     Nyambura J. Njoroge

14   Method and Context: How and Where Theology Works in Africa   121
     Agbonkhianmeghe E. Orobator, S.J.

15   My Theological Pilgrimage   127
     C. René Padilla

16   A Life Story Intertwined with Theology   139
     Andrew Sung Park

17   To Give an Account of Hope   145
     Gerhard Sauter

18   On Belonging: Doing Theology Together   153
     Dirkie Smit

19   Catching the Post or How I Became an Accidental Theorist   163
     R.S. Sugirtharajah

20   On Being Radical and Hopefully Orthodox   177
     Graham Ward

21   Between the Local and the Global: Autobiographical Reflections
     on the Emergence of the Global Theological Mind   187
     Amos Yong

Index   *195*

Notes on Contributors

K.P. Aleaz is Professor of Religions at Bishop's College as well as Professor and Dean of Doctoral Program of North India Institute of Post-Graduate Theological Studies in Kolkata, India and South Asia Theological Research Institute, Bangalore, India. Author of 20 books and more than 100 articles, he was William Patron Fellow of the Selly Oak Colleges, Birmingham (1997), Visiting Professor at Hartford Seminary, USA and University of South Africa, Pretoria (2002), and Teape Lecturer in the Universities of Cambridge, Birmingham, Bristol and Edinburgh (2005).

Hilarion Alfeyev is Bishop of Vienna and Austria for the Russian Orthodox Church. He was ordained priest in 1987, and served in Lithuania until 1991, when he was appointed Lecturer at the Moscow Theological Seminary. In 1995 he began his work at the Department for External Church Relations of the Moscow Patriarchate, and from 1997 to December 2001 served as secretary for Inter-Christian Affairs of the Russian Orthodox Church. Bishop Hilarion holds the degrees of Doctor of Philosophy from the University of Oxford and of Doctor of Theology from St Sergius Theological Institute in Paris. He is the author of more than 600 publications, including 20 theological books in Russian, English, French, German, Italian and Finnish.

Carl E. Braaten is an ordained minister of the Evangelical Lutheran Church in America. He doctored in theology at Harvard Divinity School and has studied at the Universities of Paris, Heidelberg, and Oxford. He taught Systematic Theology for a generation at the Lutheran School of Theology at Chicago. He was founding editor of the theological journal Dialog. He was the founder of the Center for Catholic and Evangelical Theology, served as its executive director and editor of its journal *Pro Ecclesia*. He is the author and editor of 40 books and over 200 articles and chapters in various periodicals. He resides in Sun City West, Arizona, with his wife LaVonne.

John W. DeGruchy is Emeritus Professor of Christian Studies at the University of Cape Town where he taught from 1973–2003, and where he is currently a Senior Research Scholar. He is also an Extraordinary Professor at the University of Stellenbosch.

Wanda Deifelt is Associate Professor of Religion at Luther College, in Decorah (Iowa), USA. Formerly she held the Chair of Feminist Theology at *Escola Superior de Teologia* in Sao Leopoldo, Brazil, where she was also Dean of Graduate Studies.

Andrés Quetzalcóatl Guerrero is Professor of Mexican-American Studies and Spanish at AIMS Community College in Colorado. A graduate of Harvard, he is the author of *A Chicano Theology* (1987) and has worked in numerous educational institutions in the USA and abroad.

Hwa Yung is the Bishop of the Methodist Church in Malaysia. He was formerly the Principal of the Malaysia Theological Seminary, and then the Director, Centre for the Study of Christianity in Asia, Trinity Theological College, Singapore.

Ada María Isasi-Díaz is Professor of Christian Ethics and Theology at Drew University in Madison, New Jersey, USA. She has lectured and taught in several countries for the last 30 years and is writing her 6th book, *Justice: A Reconciliatory Praxis of Care and Tenderness*, to be published in 2009.

Emmanuel Katongole is Research Professor of Theology and World Christianity and the co-director for the Center for Reconciliation at Duke Divinity School. He is a Roman Catholic priest trained in Uganda and the author of numerous books and articles, including *Beyond Universal Reason; The Relation Between Religion and Ethics in the Work of Stanley Hauerwas* (2000), *African Theology Today* (2002), and more recently, *A Future for Africa* (2005).

Wati Longchar served as Consultant on Ecumenical Theological Education for Asia and Pacific – WCC and CCA. He was formerly Professor of Christian Theology at Eastern Theological College, Jorhat, Assam, India.

Darren C. Marks is Assistant Professor of Theology and Religion at Huron University College, University of Western Ontario, London, Canada. He is the author/editor of numerous books/articles on systematic theology, including *7 Theological Ideas* (2007), *Blackwell Companion to Protestantism* (2004) and the first volume of this series, *Shaping a Theological Mind*.

Sallie McFague is Distinguished Theologian in Residence at the Vancouver School of Theology. Prior to emigrating to Canada in 2000 she taught theology at the Vanderbilt University Divinity School in Nashville, TN. She is the author of several books in the area of religion and ecology, the most recent being *A New Climate for Theology: God, the World, and Global Warming*.

Nyambura J. Njoroge is the co-ordinator of World Council of Churches – Ecumenical HIV and AIDS Initiative in Africa (WCC–EHAIA), based in Geneva, Switzerland and formerly the global co-ordinator of WCC Ecumenical Theological Education (WCC – ETE) Program.

Agbonkhianmeghe E. Orobator, S.J., is a Jesuit priest from Nigeria. He teaches theology and religious studies at Hekima College, the Jesuit School of Theology and Peace Studies, Nairobi (Kenya), where he is also the Rector.

C. René Padilla is Director of *Ediciones Kairos* in Buenos Aires, Argentina, and President of the Micah Network. He was formerly General Secretary of the Latin American Theological Fellowship.

Gerhard Sauter is Professor of Systematic and Ecumenical Theology and Director Emeritus of the Ecumenical Institute at the University of Bonn, Germany. He has written a number of major articles in encyclopedias and theological journals and is the author of many books in German, Polish, and English, including *What Dare We Hope?* (1999), *Gateways to Dogmatics* (2003) and most recently *Protestant Theology at the Crossroads* (2007).

Dirkie Smit teaches systematic theology at Stellenbosch in South Africa. He actively serves the local and ecumenical church and supervised many postgraduate students now teaching at different institutions in Nigeria, Ghana, Kenya, Namibia, Zimbabwe and South Africa. His publications, mostly in Afrikaans, include *Neem, lees!* (2006) and *Essays in Public Theology* (2007).

R.S. Sugirtharajah is Professor of Biblical Hermeneutics at the University of Birmingham, UK. He is the author of *The Bible and Empire* (2005), *Postcolonial Reconfigurations: An Alternative way of reading the Bible and doing theology* (2003), *Postcolonial Criticism and Biblical Interpretation* (2002) and many other books and articles.

Andrew Sung Park is Professor of Theology at United Theological Seminary in Ohio. He previously taught at Claremont School of Theology, CA. His publications include *The Wounded Heart of God: The Asian Concept of Han and the Christian Doctrine of Sin* and *From Hurt To Healing: A Theology of the Wounded*.

Graham Ward is Professor of Contextual Theology and Ethics and Head of the School of Art, Histories and Culture at the University of Manchester, UK. His publications include *Cities of God* (2000), *True Religion* (2002) and more recently *Christ and Culture* (2005). He remains active in the Radical Orthodoxy movement and is editor of several book series including Christian Theology in Context (OUP) and Religion and Theory (Blackwell).

Amos Yong is Associate Research Professor of Theology, Regent University School of Divinity. He also acts as editor for *PNEUMA:The Journal of the Society for Pentecostal Studies*, review editor for the *Journal of Religion, Disability & Health* and is the Evangelical Theology editor for *Religious Studies Review*. He is the author of numerous articles and books on systematic theology, specializing in Pentecostal studies.

Preface

As a younger theologian, I invited some of my 'heroes' to participate in a little project entitled *Shaping a Theological Mind* (Ashgate, 2002). Being freshly minted as a theologian from Oxford, that book, as critics rightly pointed out, was largely Euro and Anglocentric in its presentation. Over the past few years, I have become increasingly aware of different voices and perspectives in Christian theology and have wanted to return to that original project, hoping to learn what constitutes a theological mind in those climes. Thus, the idea for this *Shaping a **Global** Theological Mind* text was born.

But I wanted to avoid what I perceive as a problem, which is the continued relegation of 'Western' and 'Global' in terms of West and 'third-world', 'two-thirds world' or 'Global South'. This is not so much because it smacks of paternalism (although it does indeed) but because 'global' means so much more than merely location. Instead, as I argue in my opening essay, 'global' is a reality into which everyone now is initiated and as such 'global theologies' are present in the West and indeed everywhere. Global theologies are not merely theologies that deal with the problems of the 'anthropological', issues such as real poverty, colonialism and pluralism in some 10°/40° window, but theologies that ask the same questions, giving different answers indeed in the Colonial Fatherlands themselves. Thus, I invite North American Pentecostal scholars, Chicano/a scholars and so forth to participate alongside more distant and identified 'global theologians' from Asia, Africa and Latin America. In addition, and, perhaps surprisingly, I still invited Western scholars from the 'old school' (and new school of postmodernism) to speak of 'global theology'. A global theological mind is, therefore, any mind operating in the present Christian time in response to the pressures and issues of this global world with all of its 'scapes' and integration/fragmentation. This mind can be that of an Orthodox bishop in Europe or an Evangelical leader in South America, as readily as it can be a liberation theologian or indigenized African or Asian theologian.

To contributors I owe a tremendous debt for their willingness to participate and for the excellence in the essays. Each work has been a learning experience for me, contributing to what I call in my essay in *Shaping a Theological Mind* a Christian *habitus*. There are some who wished to participate but for personal or professional reasons fell aside, and to them I am also grateful and wish time and circumstance could have allowed participation. Of course, no one person is the repository of the sum of Christian theological scholarship and there were many who recommended the scholars in this book: Simon Chan, Vinoth Ramachandra, Andrew Louth, Isabel Phiri, Mercy Oduyoye, John Mbiti, Walter Dunphy and Laurenti Magesa all gave the gift of a few moments of time to assist me in identifying the best possible list of contributors. I am grateful to each of them. I am also grateful to my students in the graduate program at the University of Western Ontario. I have the privilege of seeing a global theological mind opened in them each year in seminars as they read many of the contributors of this volume. Thanks also to Dana Van Allan for her work on the index.

Finally, I dedicate this book to two children born into my life in 2006 and therefore into a global world, and I hope a global Church. I pray that my godson, Alexander Miller, and my daughter, Beatrice, are raised in a C/church that is truly global in its vision of how its Lord *is* transforming lives, giving hope and humanity to a world in its birth pains awaiting the kingdom of God's completion (Mk 3). I pray the future portrayed in these essays is in their own experience of Christ and, in that sense, each author is godparent/parent to them as well.

Darren C Marks
Stratford, On
St Ignatius Loyola Day (July 31, 2007)

Chapter 1

Living in a Global World and in a Global *Theological* World

Darren C. Marks

It has become almost too trite to speak of living in a global world. As in many other slogans of the *Zeitgeist*, the meaning is both clear and unclear. It is clear that living in a global world means that persons, things and ideas are now easily mobile and thus one is aware of analogues with, differences from, and so forth in places other than 'here'. For some this means that living in a global world is a phenomenon of a largely disposable, multi-complex, and inter-related historical place of 'now'. For others, it is about finding a buttress or fortress in the sea of changes caused by a 'them' whose consumption, presumption and assumption of power is an inevitable juggernaut. Whatever 'global' means, it rides the coattails of a long sixteenth century of Western modernity and scholars, usually sociologists (for they are the last of the truly grand systematizers/metaphysicians allowed in the *wissenschaftliche* academy), offering competing visions of this new borderless world.

Perhaps the most common definition of 'global' is actually a misconstrual of the term, being 'globalization'. Globalization, given its best articulation by the political theorist Francis Fukayama,[1] is the economic reality of the free market arising out of the European seventeenth-century and the rise of capitalism.[2] It is the true triumph of the free Cartesian/Kantian West, namely a choice on whether one drinks 'Coca-cola' or 'Pepsi', complete with the moral arguments for why one should or shouldn't. The argument is that the market in its desire to provide choice, and here what is really meant is a 'dis-embedding' of human need from the local, necessarily created a new abstract space from which now local-global actors do business. It is an abstract space in that globalized agents – law, governance bodies – or the 'experts' are everywhere and nowhere at the same time. Take, for example, any trade organization – it clearly has a 'headquarters' but is also enacted in all locations. It may have traders in, and all working under, a common charter but with applications or amendments configured by the local situation. This 'glocalization'[3]

---

[1]   See, for example, Francis Fukuyama, *The End of History and the Last Man* (Penguin, 1992).

[2]   Karl Polanyi's *The Great Transformation* (Beacon, [1944]2001) remains the best analysis of the free market and its dis-embedding of economics from the local to the abstract international.

[3]   A term employed by Frank Lechner and John Boli to reflect the constructive and reflexive rather than determinative and merely reactive nature of global culture on local

is a nexus of determination and cooperation between the abstract centre and realized points on the circle. In any event, globalization is understood in the economic sense as the abuse of the new 'nation-states' of international corporations. However, there is another dimension to this globalization and abstract space. Just as the older nation-states, as in Hobbes' *Leviathan* (1651), treated all subjects (and places) as a uniform Euclidean world regardless of difference (if only for the purposes of taxation), the multinational corporation acts likewise, treating all peoples and places as the same. The global world for the multinational corporation, according to John Law and John Urry,[4] is the largest abstract Euclidean container ever imaginable – it treats everyone the same, at least in terms of the corporate goals, and offers the choice to opt into the program as it were. This choice is ironically called the 'golden straitjacket'.[5]

Anthony Giddens extends this idea more fully when he argued that globalization is actually the world phenomenon of Western modernity extended to the remainder of the world.[6] Giddens predicted that the response of such a mode of cultural and economic imperialism would be a series of defensive reactions or fundamentalisms. In particular, as in the work of Samuel Huntington and others,[7] those cultures which are especially impervious to Western modern ideas of deliberative, rational and disembodied public spheres as an extension of the self (see, for example, J.J. Rousseau) are going to be hotspots of dissent. 'Embattled traditions', 'fundamentalisms' are then to be expected in the runaway world of the Western juggernaut. Of course, this includes the usual suspects, rife with Said's Orientalism, of so-called pre-modern or 'axial' societies connected with Islam or those groups bearing general uncertainty or anxiety in and towards the West. Utilizing Jaspers' motif of modernity as a new axial age – an age in which there is a threat of collapse of the old order[8] – theorists can connect fundamentalisms in the Islamic non-Western world with Western fundamentalists in that both are reacting to change and both harken to a pre-cataclysmic vision of order in their traditions. In an axial age such as ours, the traditional 'order of things' is represented by a new theocratic aristocracy of priests and mediators.[9] This ontotheological abuse is the rise of fundamentalisms or religious extremists. Religion, in the Marxist-sense, functions to sooth the rumblings of modernity and market but does so in a naïve, retrograde and repressive manner. Of course, what is operative is the tacit assumption that whatever modernity *is*, it is essentially correct and the equally tacit idea that eventually the rest of the world will come of age and embrace the same movements, including the religiously-inclined. The global world is then a series of dialogues or interactions with a dominant centre and defensive or reactive margins that reject, modify or succumb according to the author.

bodies. See, their *World Culture: Origins and Consequences* (Blackwell, 2005).

[4]   J. Law and J. Urry, 'Enacting the Social', *Economy and Society* 2004, 33(3): 399.

[5]   Thomas Friedman, *The Lexus and the Olive Tree* (Farrar, 1999), p. 87.

[6]   Anthony Giddens, *The Consequences of Modernity* (Stanford University Press, 1990).

[7]   S. Huntington, *The Clash of Civilizations and the remaking of World Order* (Simon and Schuster, 1996); N. Chomsky, *Hegemony or Survival: America's Quest for Global Dominance* (Holt, 2003); and R. Robertson, *Globalization: Social Theory and Global Culture* (Sage, 1992) are but a few of this ilk.

[8]   K. Jaspers, *The Origin and Goal of History* (Yale University Press, 1953).

[9]   S. Eisenstadt, *The Origin and Diversity of Axial-Age Civilizations* (SUNY, 1986).

In this instance of dominant centre and reactive margins many consider that what is occurring is exactly a rehearsal of old modes replaced by new actors in the network. Instead of abstract and (apparently) uniform intentional actors in nation-states, a globalized world has new and equally abstract and (apparently) uniform actors in corporations, NGOS, and associations or 'denominations'/networks. This shift occurs in multiple ways, on new 'landscapes' (or rather vast vistas) of ethnicity, finance, media, technology and finally ideology.[10] Each of these interpenetrate the others and like the 'butterfly effect' of quantum mechanics, a shift in one alters the others so that the old order, birthed in modernity, is by-passed, weakened and altered by the far-away, near and complex.[11] The modern reflective autarkic monadic culture (although it never really existed) is displaced by the reflexive combinard *bricolage* postmodern 'scapes. The world-machine is less and less sensible, functioning in an imagined community, and expects that this fluid container hold all of the waves of as many voices and 'scapes as possible. Of course, this means a new and almost by definition ahierarchial authority structure must be the new global agent(s). It is not 'there' or even 'here and now'; nor is it a visible body with representational authority that is the engine in a globalized world. Instead, before a 'we' creating a 'here' positing a 'now' and selecting a 'there'; what exists in the globalized world is the great *theological* conundrum – an 'I' living in isolation from God and thus from humanity and creation.

Thus, in a very real sense, the globalized world is treated as a collection of de-subjectivized, incoherent 'I's' and this reality stumbles into our collective experience while we try to raise the dead in a myriad of 'Zombie categories' in order to order the an-archic 'I'.[12] And so, theory-in-hand, new battlegrounds are envisioned for the global world: ideological in terms of materialism, racism, sexism and nationalism, and ontological or institutionalist in terms of formal representative bodies as the only legitimate actors.[13] Thus, the world-culture is a grand museum from which the local is able to select and organize the various exhibits which is useful to it. However, and centrally, there is again a *theological* problem in such a conception of the world regardless of how optimistic (and most remain pessimistic) this kind of transposition or interaction can be. Connecting the ideological and the institutional, however that latter category is conceived, is the invisible *educational*. Institutions run, as Immanuel Wallenstein correctly hits upon in every one of his texts, on the fuel of ideas, commitments, values, and these are 'taught' in the execution of culture. Just as, he points out, one needs a 'French Revolution' to centrist Liberalism in order to have a capitalist system, so the market (our great educator) teaches in all its myriad ways that this is the normative vista of human life. This is education, formally and

---

[10]   A. Appadurai, *Modernity at Large: Cultural Dimensions of Globalization* (University of Minneapolis Press, 1996). Also see Peter Berger's 'faces' in market, faculty-club of liberalism, pop-culture and religious faces in his 'Four Faces of Global Culture', *National Interest* 49 (1997): 23–9.

[11]   M. Castells, *The Power of Identity* (Blackwell, 1997).

[12]   There is no better thinker on this point that Ulrich Beck. See his *Individualization* (Sage, 2001).

[13]   See Lechner and Boli's analysis in *World Culture* pp. 29–60.

informally in the 'scapes of technology, media and even in order to simply exist (cf. Rev 13:17). John Meyer argues in his work[14] that the formal systems, actual educational institutes (in complete concordance with the initial Western desire to educate for good *peaceable/conforming* citizens) are the most important place of enculturation or rejection. In educational structures – a real ontological entity with its own life and rules etc. – occur the attempts for global peaceable citizenship with its assumption of isomorphism while giving lip-service to exomorphism.

So what then is the *theological* problem in the global world? I intimated two in the preceding paragraphs, but there are many more and many of these are themes recurrent in the essays of the theologians and Christian leaders/thinkers that follow. Clearly the two easiest, if I have argued well, are the tacit stresses on the 'I' before a 'We' and the competition of a new idol to God in capitalism and its near cousin of progressive liberalism reinforced informally in the 'scapes of technology/media and formally taught in the educational institutions of the world, underpinned by the desire of the governments to have *peaceable/conforming* citizens. In the case of the former, the Christian Church, transtemporally and translocally, is not an 'I' (or at least that 'I' is Christ) but always a 'We'. In the case of the latter, not only does it mean that much of the global Christian is in a virulent and necessary denouncement of an idol, but also that the global Christian is in a virulent and necessary denouncement of its mouthpiece – literally Balaam's ass for many – of *theological education* which imposed, imposes and silences in favor of the idol. This not only rejects the assumptions and method(s) of largely Western Protestant theology and spirituality, but also church organization, experiences (spirituality) and even to the secular itself. Global Christians, I repeatedly need to point out to my students, are not exactly enamored with their governments and tend to be suspicious of them and often heroic in opposition. Even in the West, for example, Christians ought to be creation-centered, and this 'green' space is clearly against industry and government. Further, Global Christians tend to 'find God' in their mission and often in ways that fit poorly or create anxiety for their Western counterparts whether they be of the 'John Hick' or 'Jerry Falwell' brand. Why, as Philip Jenkins points out so cogently,[15] they even have the audacity to read the Bible differently!

Overcoming Globalization: A Theological Proposal

The essays in this book are all, in their own ways, about overcoming globalization in the sense outlined above. What they ask for and engage in are two major critiques and with several developments, although one needs to be careful to equate development with novelty for it may be both a rehearsal of something older in the Christian tradition and a new dialogue with another religion, culture or even need. We must remember

---

[14]   Like Wallenstein, he is prolific on a central point on the exportation of a Western mode of education writ large as normative in order to promulgate ideology. Among his more important works is *School Knowledge for the Masses: World Models and National Curricula in the Twentieth Century* (Falmer, 1992) with D. Kamens and A. Benavot.

[15]   See his *The New Faces of Christianity: Believing the Bible in the Global South* (Oxford University Press, 2006).

that Christianity, despite Jasper's 'axial age model', was born in a dialogue with Judaism, itself in dialogue with ancient near eastern religions, and then spread by engaging the multifaceted Hellenistic and Roman worlds, eventually spreading into the frontiers of Europe and Asia with their unique cultural combinations. In short, there has never been an unambiguous Christian place. Christianity, or Christians living out their theology, has always been a theological Creole from Jesus to the present day. But this engaged nature is not the same as declaring it without a centre or without an origin, for God is the centre and origin of the Church.

The first theological critique is what I identify as a critique of modernity and specifically modernity's twins in market-capitalism and liberalism (or neo-liberalism and liberalism as some like to call them). The global theological account has to address Western modernity's basic categories, categories which treat people as products or consumers, creation as an expendable resource and culture as a battleground of colonial or imperialist ideology. Global theologians ask the question of this *anthropological and creation impoverishment*, or how it is possible to speak of God to a world made scarcely human(e) because of the imposition of an idol in Western Imperialism and all its legacies. This involves a recasting of many of modernity's precious icons – namely the autonomous and reflective self ('I') as the arbitrator of reality and Western culture's preoccupation with the individual as critical, essential and normative. In the multiplex of the global Christian, such decisions and preoccupations are the root of much of what impacts, on a daily level, the lives of countless people, destroys creation and marginalizes culture. The theological question to be asked is not merely how did we get here (and there are a myriad suggestions from scholars) but more importantly to ask how idolatrous, God-forsaken, such assumptions are and what in the Christian theological toolbox can be used in order to recognize 'the other'. One dominant theme in the global theological toolbox is pneumatology. If one aspect, but not the *only* aspect, of pneumatology is the recognition of the Spirit in another or culture or place, then the profound proliferation of pneumatology as a, if not *the*, theological category is to be expected in global theology and so it is in reality. Global theologies are highly interested in the Spirit because in pneumatology there is a promise of finding God's fore-coming for mission and disclosure for critique with its assumption of unity in Spirit. This is nothing short of *contextual theology,* making explicit the Gospel mission for this people here and now. Thus, in the essays that follow we see scholars engaged with essential questions of critique but mainly from the perspective of promise and hope, the fruit of the Spirit, and a confidence that such a hope can indeed be manifest when Christians indeed live in their witness. Of course, it must also be said that Congar's slogan 'no Christology without pneumatology, no pneumatology with Christology' demands pneumatology be rooted in Christological and Trinitarian framing lest it become a kind of process Spirit. Global theologians may name this differently – adaptionism, incarnationalism or translation – but it is a response to the 'Yes' of God for an identity that works God's purposes for that people.

But this leads to another critique found in the essays, and again intimated in the preceding paragraphs, but not unrelated to the proliferation of pneumatology as a theological concern. This is a theological critique of Western theological training and assumptions which, as amply demonstrated, are full of Imperialism, Orientalism and suffer from a preoccupation on abstract epistemological or existential axes. The history of why theological thought and training has undergone this alteration is well-traveled ground in Western scholarship and the general consensus is that Christian theology and education have suffered a double complex. In the first instance, Christian theology, as famously argued by the 'Crisis' theologians, has far too often been more interested in an apologia to the Western *wissenschaftliche* academy and now that the academy itself is revealed to be as biased as that which it claimed to rescue, the crisis theologians seem more correct than ever in their assessment. But, perhaps more insidious is the 'professionalization' of clergy and the role theologians have readily taken to assist that performance. As most ably argued by Edward Farley throughout the late twentieth-century, but largely falling on deaf ears, theological education in the Western context is divorced from congregational life.[16] Clergy and faculty largely work in isolation, refusing to connect, except in abstract and culturally-driven manners, to the challenges facing Western Christians. When the practical and theoretical do intersect, often the difference between the surrounding culture and the Church is so negligible that it is hard to think other than that a backwards institution is indeed catching up, maturing or even finally accommodating to the modern world. Clergy look like social workers, speak a pop psychology and more to the point, as raised in the following essays, act as agents of the culture because they, and the Church itself, is not so different after all. However, as the global essays remind us, is the Church the same as its leadership? What is observed in the global theological situation is that the Church is the work of the Spirit and it is the *people* of God who *as a people* are asked by the Spirit to ask some 'dangerous perhapses' to their culture – on poverty, justice, equality and so forth. This is not merely that the global situation often has a different starting point from the Western situation, in which it is tacitly assumed that Western culture and Christian life are wholly compatible, that the 'city of God' and 'city of man' are form and shadow because of the idol of the freedom of religion. No, that is not at all what is observed; instead there is a willingness to do a truly theological account of reality in the global situation. True, more often than not the state and culture are neutral or hostile to Christian perspectives, but it is also that Christian theology is tethered not only to praxis (a misused term if ever there was one) but to the life of the people of God.

What can be observed in the essays that follow is not a form of fideism or naiveté but rather a theological account of reality that starts from more concrete embodied theologies. Be it 'water-buffalo theology', 'shade-tree theology', '*lo cotidiano* theology' or 'anti-apartheid theology', most global theologians have opted to start from a different place than an abstract 'possibility of talk of God' or what Eberhardt Jüngel calls the initiation of the 'unthinkability of God' (not to be confused with *Nachdenken*). They instead embrace a theology which starts from the concrete and everyday with the expectation of hope therein. Given that the seminary in the West is more concerned with the 'professionalization' of clergy – giving them a position analogous (but far worse in training) to glorified social workers or life coaches – and that the theological academy is concerned with justifying itself as *wissenschaftliche*,

---

[16]   See, Edward Farley, *Theologia: The Fragmentation and Unity of Theological Education* (Fortress, 1983).

it is no wonder that global theologians think seminary and academy as exported both irrelevant. Education, as it stands in the Western academy, is viewed with some suspicion for it severs the people of God from the necessity of Christian life this day. And this, of course, does not even take into account that the actual physical structure/time and academic prerequisites of theological training itself may not be easily transferable.

There is no more powerful example of this than the use of the Bible in global theology. Global theologians use the Bible in an astoundingly, at least for the Western practitioner, simplistic manner. They 'proof-text' ideas, ask grandmothers, women and common, usually poor, folk what a text means and are not at all interested in the historical forms that influence so much Western study. As Andrés Guerrero argues in his essay in this volume, there is the assumption of a different kind of intelligence and understanding, one sharpened by the skills of living in *this* place so that to speak of God in *this* place requires, by definition, reading the Bible *as this* person or this community. Likewise, texts become a communal phenomenon or *Wirkunggeschichte* – evaluated not as *Lebenspraxis* in the Protestant sense as what is important to me and then to others by extension – but rather as 'wild spaces' (borrowing from McFague) that grab the community and direct it to its theological life and mission (see, for example, Sugirtharajah's essay). Those 'wild spaces' are not the individualized reading of the Bible and interiority associated with Western Christianity and its analogues in the choosing of a 'like' congregation, but instead involve an ecclesiological reading. Engaging in ecclesiological reading is a curious idea for Westerners and, in particular, for Western-trained scholars and clergy in that one basic assumption is that the Church is indeed *permixtum* not in the sense of saint and sinner (although that is indeed true) but in the sense that the Church is trying to sort out its 'Creolization' or mission and this indeed will involve error and truth as lived aside 'traditional religion' and 'traditional culture'. This is a communal and ecumenical event. Global theologians read their communities reading the Bible and interacting with Christian traditions given to them in their missionary past ancient and near.

The Challenges of Global Theology

If my sense is correct that global theology has two primary theological tasks in pneumatology and missiology, then it follows that both of these areas are places of challenge. In terms of pneumatology, the above reference to Congar is critical as global theology seeks to ask how the Spirit in its midst is indeed the Spirit of Christ rather than the Spirit of the 'Age' (1 Cor 2:6). It is often declared that the West needs the global South, but this is too strong as the global South also needs the West, not to correct or instruct *per se*, but to dialogue with. Karl Barth remarked in his work on (largely) liberal Protestantism which he rejected so strongly: 'God is the Lord of the Church. He is also the Lord of theology. We cannot anticipate which of our fellow-workers from the past are welcome in our work and which are not . . . . We are *with* them in the Church.'[17] The future of pneumatology is a future of both 'faces' of the Church and thus is to be 'ecumenical' in terms of tradition and location.

Related, and subsistent in the above, is a missiology that turns more to an ecclesiology rather than a social scientific account of religious pluralism or identity. Global theologians may, in their haste to leave the epistemological and philosophical behind, pick up another 'Western' idol in the social sciences as the means to analyze mission and content. It seems not enough to be ever 'reforming' its mission but global theology must also be conscious of developing an 'ecclesiology' from that mission so as not to reduce the Church to another manifestation of human ideals. This, I think, introduces two more important challenges. The first is to develop an eschatology or sense of hope in their witness that is clearly different from liberative praxis associated with Marxism or other Western 'isms' in that orbit.[18] If Hans Urs von Balthasar is indeed correct that eschatology, Christian hope, is indeed the storm front of theological investigation in that it declares *who* and *what* God is for, then it seems prudent to ask global theologians to develop in this direction.[19] The second challenge in helping move from a missiology to an ecclesiology is to consider, particularly in more Protestant-flavored theologies, exactly a theology of Scripture which is, in fact, a theology itself. This involves, as Gerhard Sauter argues, a 'faithfulness to Scripture and not a Scripture principle' and is a truly important theological work to be done.[20] What this can bring to fruition is the avoidance of that which global theologies recognize so clearly in the Western imposition on them – a translation of Scripture merely along cultural norms so that God's 'making present' is actually cultural reinforcement. Of course, for more sacramental traditions, there is work to be done in a like manner. What I am arguing is simple: while mission is the lifeblood of the Church, it is still true that the Church fulfills mission, and thus it falls to global theologians to work towards a theology of the Church in its fullest possible expression as this will prove the fruit of the mission itself.

The promise of global theology, at least in my reading and understanding, is its hope that God is indeed active in the world and that the Church is invited, in divine freedom and mystery, to participate in witnessing to that event of hope – 'He who testifies to these things says, "Yes, I am coming soon." Amen. Come, Lord Jesus' (Rev 22:20).

---

[17] Karl Barth, *Protestant Theology in the Nineteenth Century: New Edition* (trans. B. Cozans) (Eerdmans, 2002) pp. 3 and 10.

[18] This has already been undertaken by Jose Miguez Bonino, *Christians and Marxists: The Mutual Challenge to Revolution* (Eerdmans, 1976) but more work is needed.

[19] Hans Urs von Balthasar, '*Eschatologie*' in (eds. J Feiner et al.), *Fragen der Theologie heute* (Benziger, 1957) pp. 403–21.

[20] See Sauter's *Gateways to Dogmatics: Reasoning Theological for the Life of the Church* (Eerdmans, 2003) pp. 211–28.

Chapter 2

A Christology from Advaita Vedanta of India

K.P. Aleaz

There is a possibility today for any faith-experience or tradition to receive insights from sister faith-experiences or traditions and grow in its content. This can be termed as 'thinking together' and it is a multi-faith process. In fact, for the last thirty years in a modest way I have been involved in such a multi-faith process, focusing specially on Hindu-Christian studies, and more than sixteen of my books may bear witness to this 'thinking together'. The purpose of this paper is to indicate a glimpse of the outcome of such an Indian theological endeavour.

A Perspective for Thinking Together

My 'thinking together' as an Indian Christian was mainly in the company of Advaita Vedantins, and advaitic experience in terms of a perspective in theology of religions I have called 'Pluralistic Inclusivism' (see my 1993 work, *Harmony of Religions. The Relevance of Swami Vivekananda* and 1998's *Theology of Religions. Birmingham Papers and Other Essays*). 'Pluralistic Inclusivism' is an approach that is totally open to receive insights from other religious experiences and theologies. In order to go beyond a comparative approach to an inter-relational approach, as religious traditions are not static finished products but rather dynamic inter-related experiences of growth, 'Pluralistic Inclusivism' stands for dialogical theologies that encourage the relational convergence of religions.

It conceives, on the one hand, the diverse religious resources of the world as the common property of humanity and, on the other hand, a possible growth in the richness of each of the religious experiences through mutual inter-relation. 'Pluralistic Inclusivism' as related to Christian thought is an attempt to make Christian faith pluralistically inclusive so that the content of the revelation of God in Jesus Christ is to become truly pluralistic through other faiths contributing to it as per the requirement of different places and times. It is through such pluralistic understanding of the gospel that its true inclusivism is to shine forth. Here pluralism transforms itself to focus on its center, which is God as God in the universally conceived Jesus and inclusivism transforms itself to bear witness to the fulfilment of the Christian understanding of Christ in and through theological contributions from people of other faiths. The basic affirmation is that there is a possibility for the fulfilment of the theological and spiritual contents of one's own faith in and through the contributions of other living faiths.

For an Indian Christian, and perhaps for all Christians, there is a possibility of the fulfilment of the theological and spiritual contents of his/her faith in and through the contributions of Advaitic experience. Advaitic experience becomes a major hermeneutical context for India and Indian Christians. As the gospel is always in the process of formulation in terms of one's hermeneutical context, there is always the emergence of the new. And for the Indian Christian, this must be a dialogue with the Advaitic experiences of India. We cannot accept some timeless interpretation from somewhere and make it applicable to our context. Understanding and interpretation belong exclusively to us and to our context, and there is the possibility for the emergence of new meanings in the process. Knowledge of anything is an immediate existential knowledge formulated in the very knowing-process. In our knowing-process then there exists nothing externally 'ready-made' that can be adapted, indigenised, incultured or contextualised. 'Adaptation', 'Indigenisation', 'Inculturation' or 'Contextualisation' of the gospel therefore is an unreality; in fact, what really happens is its opposite in the 'gospelization' of the hermeneutical context or experiencing the emerging gospel from within a hermeneutical context. Such an idea I argued in my 1994 work *The Gospel of Indian Culture*.

In my Indian context, Advaitic experience presents an ideal, integral, God–world–human relationship: God as our and the rest of creation's 'Innermost Reality' (*Atman*) simultaneously is the 'Supreme Reality' (*Brahman*). According to Adi Sankara (birth unknown and in dispute between the 5th and 9th centuries CE), an important exponent of Advaita, creation, which includes humans, is the effect, name and form, and extrinsic denominator of *Brahman-Atman*. The *Atman* pervades, illumines and unifies the whole world, the whole of history and the entire human personality. The reality of humans and the world is totally derived from the Supreme *Atman*. In Advaita, the between *Brahman-Atman* and creation, which includes individual beings, is total and it is this relation which gives meaning to human life and fulfilment to creation (see my 1996 *The Relevance of Relation in Sankara's Advaita Vedanta*). Such an Advaitic experience in my work is a hermeneutical context of an Indian Christian experience. There is a possibility of the fulfilment of the theological and spiritual contents of the Christian faith in and through the contributions of such a school of thought of Hinduism as Advaita Vedanta.

An Indian Jesus from Advitic Experience

It is my contention that an interpretation of the person and function of Jesus is possible from within Advaita Vedanta that enriches Christian experience, and I attempted in 1997's *An Indian Jesus from Sankara's Thought* to mount an elaborate discussion on this point. In it the significance of Jesus lay in his denial of any significance for himself through complete self-sacrifice and I argued that Advaita Vedanta provides a theological basis for this self-sacrifice of Jesus and thus explains his meaning for us: It is Being Himself/Herself who is perceived in a form other than His/Her own; namely, Jesus and hence we should not make any assumption of anything other than Being at any time or place. As in the Advaita Vedanta teaching that for those who know the real character of the rope and clay, the name and idea of serpent and jar cease, in the same manner for those who know the real character of Being, the name and idea of Jesus cease. The total sacrifice of Jesus is the total affirmation of Being. We have to sacrifice ourselves as Jesus did to discover our reality as Being. Our interpretation of Jesus as the extrinsic denominator *(upadhi)*, name and form *(namarupa)* and effect *(karya)* of Brahman affirms this relation of total dependence on the part of Jesus upon Brahman.

In Advaita Vedanta creation is considered as the extrinsic denominator *(upadhi)* of *Brahman*. The difference between Jesus and the Supreme *Atman* is a creation of the extrinsic denominator like body etc. constituted by name and form; the difference is not from the supreme standpoint. Jesus in his person is able to identify the Supreme Being through the denial of his own person, which is the extrinsic denominator of *Brahman*. *Brahman* as related to the names and forms of the bodies which form *Brahman*'s extrinsic denominator, are the *jives* (living beings) and it is this *jiva*-Brahman relation that is explained by Sankara through the comparisons of pot-space *(ghatakasah)* and Cosmic Space *(mahakasah)* and the reflections *(abhasah)* of sun or moon or human person. This relation is applicable to Jesus as well. Jesus is the reflection of *Brahman*. If *Brahman* is the total space then Jesus is the space inside a pot.

Further, as in Advaita Vendanta, creation is again understood as the name and form *(namarupa)* of *Brahman*. Therefore, Jesus can also be conceived as the name and form of *Brahman*. *Brahman*'s becoming Jesus does not mean becoming something extraneous to His/Her own essence as one does by begetting a son. Jesus is only the manifestation of name and form that is latent in the *Atman* into all the states by retaining its own nature as the *Atman* and remaining indistinguishable from *Brahman* in time and space. The symbol 'son' cannot express the depth of the relation between Jesus and *Brahman/Atman*; name and form would be a better symbol and India suggests this through Sankara's Advaita Vedanta.

As creation is the effect *(karya)* of *Brahman*, Jesus also can be conceived as the effect of *Brahman*. Despite the non-otherness *(ananyatva)* between *Brahman* and Jesus, *Brahman* or the 'Cause' as cause is ontologically superior and anterior to Jesus, the effect *as* effect. Jesus is non-other than *Brahman* as his internal reality-providing 'Cause'; whereas, Jesus is not non-other than Brahman as his efficient 'Cause'. The relation between Jesus and Brahman is *tadatmya* or non-reciprocal dependence relation. Jesus, the name and form in all his states, has his *Atman* in *Brahman* alone, but *Brahman* does not have Jesus as *Brahman*'s *Atman*. The entire body of effects including Jesus has no existence apart from *Brahman*. *Brahman* as 'Cause' is the root, support, repository, upholder, controller and director of Jesus the effect.

I argue that an understanding of the function of Jesus as emerging from Advaita Vedanta goes beyond the atonement theories through which the Christian church has tried to understand it. The alternative understanding of the function of Jesus is that he re-presents the all-pervasive, illuminative and unificatory power of the Supreme *Atman*; he re-presents to us the Supreme *Brahman* who is 'Pure Consciousness as the Witness and Atman of all'; and thus he re-presents to us the eternally present human liberation.

The function of Jesus is to show us the Supreme *Brahman* who in turn is 'Pure Consciousness' as the Witness and *Atman* of all' and Jesus bears witness that 'Pure Consciousness' is *Brahman*'s own form; that the *Atman* should be realised in one form only – as homogenous 'Pure Consciousness'. He further reveals that *Brahman* being eternal Consciousness is the 'Witness of all'. The life of Jesus tells us that unless there be some principle running through everything and abiding through all the three periods of time or some unchanging witness of all, there can be no human dealing involving remembrance, recognition etc., and *that* principle is the *Atman* who is *Brahman*.

Jesus proclaims the gospel that the Supreme *Atman* pervades everything, everywhere, for all times; being all-pervasive like space, *Brahman* can very well dwell inside everything. For example, I argue that the implantation of the *Atman* in the five sheaths of human person (physical, vital, mental, intelligent and blissful) as well as innermost to all of them is identified in the life and work of Jesus. The *Atman* as witness pervades the sight, hearing, thought and knowledge of Jesus and us. The elements related to Jesus (and us) perform their activity through the pervasive presence of *Brahman-Atman*. Jesus points to the fact that the effect is pervaded and held together by its cause and the 'Supreme Cause', *Brahman-Atman*, pervades and holds together everything, though at the same time totally different from all His/Her effects.

The life and work of Jesus also proclaims that, as an emerald or any other gem dropped for testing into milk imparts its luster to them, the luminous *Atman* unifies and integrates the intellect and all other organs within the human body and imparts His/Her luster to them. The *jivatman* of the human representative Jesus is the reflection of the Supreme *Atman* in his body, senses, vital force, mind, intellect and ego. The representative intellect of Jesus, which is not conscious by itself, being transparent and next to the *Atman* easily becomes the reflection of the light of the 'Consciousness of the *Atman*'. Next comes the mind of Jesus, which catches the effulgence of the Consciousness through the intellect, and then the organs of Jesus, through contact with his mind, and lastly the body of Jesus through his organs reflecting the light of the 'Consciousness of the *Atman*'. Thus Jesus witnesses to the gospel that the *Atman* pervades, illumines and unifies everything by means of His/Her reflection.

The *Atman*, in my dialogue with Christian – Advaita Vedanta faiths, unifies all and everything in Him/Her as His/Her homogeneous essence. Jesus stands out in history proclaiming the gospel that the *Atman* is the common referent of the universe, its origin and its end and that all things are unified in *Brahman* because the varieties of genus and particulars are not different from Him/Her. Jesus is the visible manifestation of the *Atman*'s identification with everything; he reminds us that the *Atman* cannot be taken apart from anything else. The life and work of Jesus proclaims the unification of the elements, organs, objects, mind, intellect and vital force in the *Atman*. The general functions of the organs of action are again nothing but the vital forces of Jesus, which in turn is only 'Pure Consciousness'.

The life and work of Jesus re-presents the eternally present human liberation (*nityasiddhasvabhavam*) as well. It is the witness of Jesus that liberation is an ever-attained fact. Liberation is the cessation of bondage and not the production of any fresh result; it is simultaneous with the rise of complete illumination and it is a matter of immediate direct result in which the result of knowledge is a matter of direct experience. Liberation, as we experience in Jesus, is the removal of ignorance and the affirmation of one's own real nature, which is the *Atman* who is beyond acceptance and rejection. The life of Jesus affirms that the knowledge of the innermost *Atman* becomes possible for the whole humanity when the ego vanishes; when the identification of other things as *Atman* is destroyed, the experience of the *Atman* as one's own *Atman* which is natural alone will remain. A life centred on our innermost Reality *Atman*, consequently, is the liberated life as proclaimed by Jesus.

Conclusion

Thinking together with Advaita Vedanta, the theme of my theological career and writings, can thus give birth to a novel understanding and experience of the person and function of Jesus. This thinking together need not be limited to a Christology alone. It can continue in other areas such as epistemology, and works such as my 1991 *The Role of Pramanas in Hindu-Christian Epistemology* offers such a convergence while my study of Advaita Vedanta and Eastern Christian thought (2000, *A convergence of Advaita Vedanta and Eastern Christian Thought*) provides a context for elaboration of these and other areas in the future. 'Pluralistic Inclusivism' with Advaita Vedanta as Indian Christian context opens horizons for a truly global theology.

Chapter 3

Theological *Popevki*:
Of the Fathers, Liturgy and Music

Bishop Hilarion Alfeyev

My first formation was not theological. For about twelve years, from early childhood, I studied music – first violin, then also piano and composition. However, from the age of 13 I began to read theological literature (whatever was available in the officially atheist Soviet Union), and at the age of 15 I knew that I would dedicate my life to the Church. When I turned 20, I abandoned music, entered a monastery and soon became a priest.

My theological formation was not very systematic, a series of fragments woven together in a harmony. I graduated by correspondence from the Moscow Theological Seminary and Academy, and then did my doctorate at Oxford. By that time my main theological interest was the writings of the Church Fathers, which I read, in large quantities, first in my native Russian, and then in Greek or Syriac.

My doctoral thesis at Oxford was dedicated to St Symeon the New Theologian (949–1022 CE), one of three such theologians given the title 'Theologian' in the Orthodox tradition. On the basis of this eleventh-century Byzantine mystical theologian I tried to understand what constitutes the core of Orthodox theological tradition. Symeon's case illustrates, in a very striking manner, that the foundation-stone of tradition is nothing else but an experience of the direct relationship between God and the human person, the experience of immediacy with God, which is commonly designated as 'mystical.' This implies that *true* tradition is unimaginable unless mystical experience stands behind it. Those who try to oppose a formal and rationalistic 'tradition' to an enthusiastic and inspired 'mysticism' fall into the mistake of misunderstanding what tradition is. If ever the tradition becomes deprived of its mystical and prophetic core, it tends to be transformed into its own antipode.

My conclusion concerning the nature of mysticism within the Christian Church was analogous to this: true mysticism is unimaginable and impossible outside of tradition. The true mystic is not one who places personal experience above tradition, but, on the contrary, one whose experience is in agreement with the experience of the Church in general and its greatest representatives in particular. The historical role of the great mystics of the Church is very often the role of defenders of tradition and renewers of the ideal of living according to the Gospel: this is why they are usually maximalists and radicals. But it is precisely their maximalism which inspires thousands of ordinary Christians and keeps, for example, the Orthodox tradition alive. In every age mystics emerge, or rather they are granted to the Church, so as to transmit their heritage to their contemporaries and to following generations, keeping the golden chain of sanctity unbroken. After Symeon the New Theologian, I studied St. Isaac of Nineveh, a Syrian mystical writer of the seventh century, and then turned to other Church Fathers, such as Gregory Nazianzen, John Damascene and Maximus the Confessor.

A Patristic Faith

But why the Fathers, one may ask? What do they have to do with our modern life? And why is the Orthodox Church so persistent in referring to the authority of the Fathers?

St. John Damascene defined the Tradition of the Church as the 'boundaries put up by our Fathers.'[1] Before him, St. Athanasius of Alexandria spoke of the 'Tradition from the beginning' and of the 'faith of the Universal Church, which the Lord gave, the apostles preached and the Fathers preserved.'[2] These words express the essence of our faith as 'apostolic,' 'Patristic' and 'Orthodox,'[3] a faith rooted in Holy Scripture and Holy Tradition, an inseparable component of which are the works of the holy Fathers.

It is more or less obvious why Christian faith should be 'apostolic' and 'Orthodox.' But why should it be 'Patristic'? Does this imply that Orthodoxy must be necessarily styled as in the 'patriarchal days of old'? Or is it that, as Christians, we should always be turned towards the past instead of living in the present or working for the future? Should perhaps some 'golden age' in which the great Fathers of the Church lived, the fourth-century for instance, be our ideal and a bearing to guide us? Or, finally, could this imply that the formation of our theological and ecclesial tradition saw its completion during the 'Patristic era,' and that, subsequently, nothing new could unfold in Orthodox theology and Orthodox church life in general?

If this were so – and there are many who think exactly in this way – it would mean that our principal task is to watch over what remains of the Byzantine and Russian legacy, and vigilantly guard Orthodoxy against the infectious trends of modern times. Some act in precisely this way: fearfully rejecting the challenges of modernity, they dedicate all their time to preserving what they perceive as the traditional teaching of the Orthodox Church, explaining that in the present time of 'universal apostasy' there is no place for any creative understanding of Tradition, since everything had been clarified by the Fathers centuries earlier. Such supporters of 'protective Orthodoxy' prefer, as a rule, to refer to the 'teachings of the holy Fathers.' Yet in reality many of them do not know Patristic doctrine: they make use of isolated notions to justify their own theories and ideas without studying Patristic theology in all its pluriform fullness.

No one will challenge the need for preserving the Patristic legacy. The 'protective' element is emphasized in the words of St. Athanasius quoted above: the Fathers have *preserved* Holy Tradition for us. But have they preserved this treasure for it to wither away, like the talent buried in the ground, unearthed from time to time to establish whether it has corroded from so long a lack of use? Did the Fathers write books for

---

[1]   *Third Apology against Those Who Decry Holy Images*, PG 94, 1356 C.
[2]   *Letter to Serapion* I, 28.
[3]   *Synodicon*, Sunday of Orthodoxy.

us to keep on shelves, dusting them from time to time and ever so rarely consulting them for that obligatory quote?

Were we to concentrate our energies solely on preserving the accumulated wisdom of past Fathers, then things would be quite simple. If, however, our vocation is to *invest* the talent of the Patristic legacy, we would find ourselves confronted by a tremendous task indeed, not only one that would include study of works of the Fathers, but also their interpretation in the light of contemporary experience. Similarly, it would require an interpretation of our own contemporary experience in the light of Patristic teaching. This evaluation does not only mean studying the Fathers; the task before us is also to think and to live in a Patristic way. We shall never be able to understand the Fathers if we do not share, at least to some degree, in their experience and endeavours.

This is a tremendous and inspiring task; and it is also quite hazardous. Just as no financial investor is immune from bankruptcy, neither is a theologian who approaches the Patristic legacy in a creative way preserved from error. The distance - in time, culture, and spirituality – between the Fathers and us is too great; it would seem to be impossible to surmount the obstacles that confound our attempts to penetrate the mind of the Fathers. Yet so long as we fail to overcome them, we shall never be able to fulfil the mission entrusted to us by the modern age. This mission consists in possessing the capacity not only to make our faith truly 'Patristic,' but also to express it in a language accessible to twenty-first century men and women.

The *oeuvre* of the Fathers is no mere museum exhibit, neither is the 'Patristic faith' simply a legacy of the past. The opinion that the holy Fathers are *only* the theologians of *earlier* times is widely held. The 'past' itself is defined in varying ways. According to some, the Patristic age ends in the eighth-century with St. John Damascene's *Exact Exposition of the Orthodox Faith*, which epitomises several centuries of theological dispute. Others define its end in the eleventh-century with the final schism between the first and the second Rome, or midway through the fifteenth-century, when the second Rome, Constantinople, fell, or in 1917 CE, with the fall of the 'third Rome,' Moscow, as the last capital of an Orthodox empire. Consequently, a return to 'Patristic roots' is conceived as step back to the past, the restoration of one of different centuries' spirituality.

This point of view must be rejected. In the opinion of Fr. Georges Florovsky, 'the Church is still fully authoritative as she has been in the ages past, since the Spirit of Truth quickens her now no less effectively than in the ancient times.' It is not possible, therefore, to limit the 'Patristic age' to one or other historic era.[4] A well-known contemporary theologian, Bishop Kallistos (Ware) of Diokleia, states, 'An Orthodox must not simply know and quote the Fathers, he must enter into the spirit of the Fathers and acquire a "Patristic mind." He must treat the Fathers not merely as relics from the past, but as living witnesses and contemporaries.' Bishop Kallistos does not consider the Patristic age to have ended in the fifth or eighth century; the Patristic era of the Church continues to this day. 'Indeed, it is dangerous to look on

---

[4] Cf. 'St. Gregory Palamas and the Tradition of the Fathers,' in *The Collected Works of Georges Florovsky,* vol. I: *Bible, Church, Tradition: An Eastern Orthodox View* (Vaduz, 1987), pp. 105–20.

"the Fathers" as a closed cycle of writings belonging to a bygone age, for might not our own epoch produce a new Basil or Athanasius? To say that there can be no more Fathers is to suggest that the Holy Spirit has deserted the Church.'[5]

Hence the confession of a 'Patristic faith' not only implies the study of Patristic writings and the attempt to bring the legacy of the Fathers to life, but also the belief that our era is no less 'Patristic' than any other. The 'golden age' inaugurated by Christ, the apostles and the early Fathers endure in the works of the Church Fathers of our days, to last for as long as the Church of Christ will stand on this earth and for as long as the Holy Spirit will inspire it.

The Contextual Reading of the Fathers: A New Catholicity

Russian twentieth-century theology paid much attention to the Patristic legacy. Systematic study of the works of the holy Fathers, which began in Russia in the first half of the nineteenth-century and reached its climax in the early twentieth-century, was continued after the 1917 revolution by theologians of the Russian emigration. At the St. Sergius Theological Institute in Paris, the works of such scholars as Archimandrite Cyprian (Kern), Archpriests Serge Bulgakov, Georges Florovsky and John Meyendorff, as well as the lay theologian Vladimir Lossky and others, paved the way for the further examination of the Fathers. Florovsky was to be the chief impetus behind the 'Patristic renaissance' in Russian theology: his were the key concepts for the interpretation of the Patristic legacy, in particular the idea of the 'neo-Patristic synthesis.' The latter, according to Florovsky, 'should be more than just a collection of Patristic sayings or statements; it must truly be a *synthesis*, a creative reassessment of those insights which were granted to the holy men of old. It must be *Patristic*, faithful to the spirit and vision of the Fathers, *ad mentem Patrum*. Yet it also must be *neo*-Patristic, since it is to be addressed to the new age, with its own problems and queries.'[6]

The past century has contributed much to the study of the Patristic legacy, thanks to new critical editions of the works of the Fathers and to scholarly studies produced by the above-mentioned scholars. But has the 'neo-Patristic synthesis' of which Florovsky dreamt been achieved? I do not think so. There was an objective reason for this: in the past century the time for such a synthesis had not yet come. It may yet be achieved if we do not abandon the way outlined by the theologians of the past century. They achieved a mighty, qualitative leap forward and succeeded in breaking down the wall between the Christian East and West, laying the foundations for a truly 'Catholic' theology (meaning a theology which, following Fr. John Meyendorff, includes and organically assimilates the theological heritage of East and West in all its diversity). But another qualitative leap forward is needed in order to build the neo-Patristic synthesis upon this foundation, a leap that we, who have entered the twenty-first century, can make.

---

    [5]   Bishop Kallistos Ware, *The Orthodox Church* (London, 1992), p. 212.

    [6]   Andrew Blane (ed.), *Georges Florovsky: Russian Intellectual and Orthodox Churchman* (St. Vladimar's Press, 1993), p. 154.

It is necessary to find a new approach to the Fathers, one which would allow us to see the Patristic heritage more comprehensively. I am deeply convinced that a fundamental and indispensable element of such a new approach should be the logically consistent use of a *contextual* method of Patristic reading. Allow me to deliberate on the main characteristics of this method in more detail.

The contextual method presumes that one takes as a starting point the fact that the Fathers of the Church lived and wrote in different ecclesial, theological, cultural, historical and linguistic contexts. The Patristic tradition is not one single 'patch' on which the Fathers worked. It has many poles and comprises many historical, linguistic and cultural layers. As far as dogma is concerned, for instance, the Greek and Latin traditions were already quite different from one another in the third-century (it is sufficient to compare Origen's and Tertullian's teachings on the Trinity to confirm this). Differences deepened in the next centuries (compare the Trinitarian theology of the Great Cappadocians and of St. Augustine). Several centuries later, significant divergence in the field of ascetic practice and in mysticism became apparent (compare Symeon the New Theologian with Francis of Assisi, or Gregory Palamas with Ignatius Loyola). The impression received is that the two traditions were predestined from the very outset to develop along different lines. This is, however, not the same as saying that the eleventh-century schism between East and West was altogether unavoidable; remember, for an entire millennium, both traditions had lived side by side within the bosom of the one Church.

A particular place belongs to the different national traditions of Patristic writing be they Syriac, Ethiopian, Coptic, Arabic, Armenian or Georgian. Comparing the theological thinking and language of Ephrem the Syrian and Gregory of Nyssa, two representatives of the same faith, sharing the same spirituality, and near contemporaries yet living in totally different cultural and linguistic contexts, we cannot but notice the enormous difference between them. Gregory's language and manner of thinking turn towards Greek culture; Ephrem, on the other hand, lives in the world of Semitic Christianity; Gregory expresses the richness and diversity of Christian Tradition in the figurative categories of Greek mythology, whilst Ephrem appeals to the characteristic imagery of the Palestinian-Aramaic tradition. As befits a Greek, Gregory is more rational and disposed to definitions, while Ephrem is more emotional and expressive.

It is important to remember that there were no strong channels of communication between the different theological traditions. Aside from some rare exceptions, theologians from one tradition neither knew nor understood the exponents of other traditions. In the first millennium, Latin authors were virtually unknown to the Hellenic East; and, in the West, only a selected number of Greek authors (in particular Dionysius the Areopagite) were read. Neither East nor West knew the Syriac tradition (except for one or two writers such as Ephrem the Syrian and Isaac of Nineveh). The situation differed for those who had received Christianity together with a fully-shaped theological system, such as the Slavs, who from the very beginning were oriented towards Greek Patristic writings. Even here, however, we can speak more of a *transplantation* of Greek culture to Russian soil rather than *relationship* between two independent traditions or their interpenetration.

Until the modern world, the world was disposed in such a way that only very few people succeeded in breaking free from the limits of their own linguistic and cultural contexts. Comparative or cross-contextual study was beyond the reach of the ancients. Indeed, aside from some extremely rare exceptions, the early Fathers were scarcely able to experience fields of learning other than their own theological, linguistic and cultural context. Phenomena that were proper to other theological systems' traditions were judged through the parameters of one's own tradition; there was no all-encompassing vision. Now, however, we have the luxury of understanding contextually and thus from a perspective that may be truly neo-Patristic, standing on the shoulders of the Fathers and those Orthodox theologians who redressed them to their and now our age in the hope of the unity of God's catholicity.

Liturgical Texts as a School of Theology

The school of Orthodox theology that formed my theological thinking was not so much a theological seminary, academy or university but the *Divine Liturgy* and other services. The liturgical texts of the Orthodox Church penetrated my mind and heart so deeply that they became, along with the Gospel and the writings of the Church Fathers, the main criteria of theological truth, an inexhaustible source of knowledge about God, Christ, the world, Church and salvation.

As a fifteen-year old boy I first entered the sanctuary, and from that time became an active participant in the divine services. Although I had regularly attended church beforehand, listened to the words of the services, confessed, and received Holy Communion, it was only after my entrance into the altar that the *theourgia*, the mystery, and 'banquet of faith' began, which continues to this very day. After my ordination, I saw my destiny and main calling in serving the *Divine Liturgy*. Indeed, everything else, such as sermons, pastoral care and theological scholarship were centred round the main focal point of my life, the Liturgy.

Orthodox divine services are characterized by inner integrity and astounding beauty. From the priest's exclamation at the very beginning, we are immersed in an atmosphere of uninterrupted prayer, in which psalms, litanies, hymns, prayers and the celebrating priest's invocations follow one another in a continuous stream. The entire service is conducted as if in one breath, in one rhythm, like an ever-unfolding mystery in which nothing distracts one from prayer. Byzantine liturgical texts filled with profound theological and mystical content alternate with the prayerful incantation of the psalms, whose every word resonates in the hearts of the faithful. Even the elements of 'choreography' characteristic of Orthodox services, such as solemn entries and exits, prostrations and censing, are not intended to distract the faithful from prayer but, on the contrary, to put them in a prayerful disposition and draw them into the *theourgia* in which, according to the teaching of the Fathers, not only the Church on earth, but also the heavenly Church, including the angels and the saints, participate.

In my view, liturgical texts are for Orthodox Christians an incontestable doctrinal authority, whose theological irreproachability is second only to Scripture. Liturgical texts are not simply the works of outstanding theologians and poets, but also the fruits of the prayerful experience of those who have attained sanctity and *theosis*. The theological authority of liturgical texts is, in my opinion, higher than that of the works of the Fathers of the Church, for not everything in the works of the latter is of equal theological value and not everything has been accepted by the fullness of the Church. Liturgical texts, on the contrary, have been accepted by the *whole* Church as a 'rule of faith' (*kanon pisteos*), for they have been read and sung everywhere in Orthodox churches over many centuries. Throughout this time, any erroneous ideas foreign to Orthodoxy that might have crept in either through misunderstanding or oversight were eliminated by Tradition itself, leaving only pure and authoritative doctrine clothed by the poetic forms of the Church's hymns.

Liturgical texts are not simply a commentary on the Gospels, since they often speak of that which the Gospels pass over in silence. I would like to give an example from the Nativity service. The Gospel reading (from Matthew's Gospel) speaks very briefly of Christ's birth and Joseph's initial decision to put Mary away in secret (Mt. 1:18-19). Much that happened has remained hidden from us. For example, the narrative is silent about Joseph's personal drama and we can only guess about his feelings and doubts, as well as about the words he uttered to his betrothed when he learned of her pregnancy. However, Orthodox liturgical texts attempt to recreate in poetic form a dialogue between Joseph and Mary:

> When Joseph, O Virgin, was wounded by sorrow while going to Bethlehem, Thou didst cry unto him: why art Thou languishing in sorrow and confused, not knowing that all that has happened to me is part of the fearful mystery? But now lay aside all fear, knowing of the most glorious events, for in His mercy God hast descended to earth and is now in my womb, taking on flesh. When thou shalt see Him born, as He has willed, thou shalt be filled with joy and worship Him as thy Creator.

One may refer to such texts as 'poetic invention' or 'Church rhetoric,' or one may see in them something more – namely, a perceptive understanding of the feelings and experiences of those whose lives form Sacred History. Byzantine hymnographers made use of an extremely rich array of literary techniques since they spoke about that which 'the eye has not beheld, the ear has not heard and has not entered the heart of man' (1 Cor 2:9), about mysteries beyond the limits of human reason, but grasped only by faith. There are many mystical truths in Christianity which, being difficult to explain in prose, are better served by poetry to help the faithful to understand.

The Divine Liturgy

The *Divine Liturgy*, or the Eucharist, stands in the very centre of an Orthodox theologian's spiritual life. From the Orthodox point of view, no theology is possible without participating in the Liturgy. Theology is considered as a continuation of the Liturgy, as its extension.

Some of my non-Orthodox friends complain that the Orthodox Liturgy is too long, saying 'why do you have to stretch out the Eucharist when you can serve it in half an hour?' My experience of the Liturgy is altogether different: two hours are never sufficient for me, since the time goes by so quickly and the dismissal comes too soon. It is always difficult to leave the altar and to descend from the heavens to earth, from the experience of the sublime to the cares of this world. There is a story about a nineteenth-century priest in St. Petersburg who had a small room above the church's sanctuary. After serving Liturgy he would climb into this room by means of a ladder and after two or three hours only then would he return to the church to talk with people. Although the majority of clergy in the twenty-first century cannot allow themselves this luxury, the reasons for this priest's desire to prolong the sweetness of communion with God and the unearthly stillness and calm which enter the soul while serving the Liturgy are wholly understandable.

The Liturgy is a 'common act,' and without doubt demands the presence and active participation of the laity. Orthodox practice knows of no private Liturgies which priests might serve by themselves (as is very widespread in the Catholic Church). The entire structure of the Liturgy also presupposes the presence of a congregation which, together with the priest, is also a celebrant of the Liturgy. This is a congregation not of spectators, but of participants, who join in communion of the Mysteries of Christ.

I wholly agree with those who support the revival of ancient church practice whereby lay people commune at every Liturgy. Moreover, the guidelines for preparing for Holy Communion should be the same for both clergy and laity. It seems unfair and contradictory to the meaning of the Liturgy that different rules are laid down for clergy and laity. At the Liturgy everyone – bishops, priests and laity – stands before God with the same dignity, or rather with the same unworthiness, for 'nobody attached to fleshly desires and delights is worthy to come near or approach' the communion of Christ's Holy Mysteries.

The active participation of lay people in the Liturgy presupposes the possibility of their responding to the exclamations of the priest and hearing the so-called 'secret' prayers. In contemporary church practice these prayers, as a rule, are read by the priest silently, which creates an additional barrier between the priest and his flock. More importantly, this habit deprives the faithful since the main point of the Liturgy passes them by. I have heard many arguments in favour of the practice of silent prayers, but none has seemed convincing to me. The so-called 'silent' prayers were originally read aloud by the celebrating clergy. I think that in our time the faithful should have the opportunity to hear these prayers in their entirety, not only their concluding subordinate clauses (these signify that the prayers have been read but do not give the least notion of their content). At least, the prayer of the *anaphora*, which summarizes the essence of the Liturgy, should be read aloud.

The celebration of the Liturgy is a creative act in which the fullness of the Church is involved. The text of the Liturgy is always the same, but each Liturgy grants us the opportunity to experience the mystery in a new light, renewing our encounter with the living God.

Much in the celebration of the Liturgy depends on the clergy. Very frequently the worship is 'stolen' from the faithful by hurried or careless serving. The celebration of the Liturgy, whether by a bishop in cathedral or by a village priest, must be unhurried and dignified, and all words should be read as carefully and distinctly as possible. It is very important that the priest pray together with the congregation; he should not mechanically utter words that have long since lost their freshness. It is inadmissible to make the Liturgy a matter of habit or perceive it as something ordinary, even if it is served daily.

Theatricality, acting and artificiality in the serving of the Liturgy are unacceptable. The clergy should not openly express their emotions or draw attention to themselves by their manner of celebration. The congregation's attention must be focused not on them, but on the Celebrator of the Liturgy – Christ Himself. This also holds true for the deacons, who in some cases turn the services into a theatre by exploiting all of their vocal and artistic abilities to make as strong an impression as possible. The role of the deacon is extremely important: he calls the faithful to prayer and is therefore obliged to create a prayerful atmosphere, not ruin it.

Having made mention of the diaconate, it is valuable to note a special characteristic of the Orthodox Liturgy. At its celebration, a warm, trusting relationship is established between the president of the Eucharistic celebration, whether he be a bishop or priest, and the deacon. The deacon repeatedly addresses the celebrant with the words 'Pray for me, holy master,' 'Remember me, holy master,' to which the latter answers: 'May the Lord guide thy steps,' 'May the Lord remember thee in His Kingdom.' Whether taking a blessing from the celebrant or handing him the liturgical vessels, the deacon always kisses his hand; before and after every liturgical action the deacon bows to him. These motions are not just vestiges of ancient church 'etiquette.' They also have an iconic dimension, symbolizing the relationship of absolute trust and love that exists between people in the Heavenly Kingdom and that should exist between those who live in God. Moreover, these actions stress the hierarchical nature of the Church, in which, according to Dionysius the Areopagite, divine 'emanations' (*proodoi*) and 'flows of light' pass from the higher orders to the lower: from angels to humans, from priests to deacons, from the clergy to the laity. Finally, the respect shown during services to the officiating clergyman as the celebrant of the Eucharist who, as it were, represents Christ Himself, is similar to that given to sacred images, for the honour rendered to the icon or type (celebrant) ascends to the Prototype – Christ.

If we can call the services of the Orthodox Church a school of theology, then the *Divine Liturgy* is this school *par excellence*. It teaches us about the mysteries of the Heavenly Kingdom because it itself is an icon of this Kingdom, the most complete, perfect reflection of the heavenly reality in our earthly conditions, a revelation of the transcendent through the immanent. In the Kingdom of God all symbols shall pass away, and only the heavenly reality will remain. There we will not commune of the Body and Blood of Christ in the form of bread and wine, but in a more perfect way we shall be united with Christ Himself, the Source of life and immortality. If the manner of our communion with God will change, its essence will remain the same – always a personal encounter with God, not of isolated people, but of people in communion with each other. In this sense it is correctly said that the Liturgy served on earth is but a part of the incessant Liturgy celebrated by people and angels in the Heavenly Kingdom.

Church Singing

Some years ago I visited the Valaam Monastery of the Transfiguration, where I served an all-night vigil and *Divine Liturgy* in the monastery's main church. The services there struck me by their prayerfulness, harmony, simplicity and grandeur. The monastic singing and Valaam chant used during the services made an especially strong impression.

Valaam chant is a form of ancient Russian Znamenny chant, which itself absorbed the main characteristics of Byzantine church music. It is known that Byzantine chant was brought to Kievan Rus' already during the time of Yaroslav the Wise. The 'Book of Degrees' (*Stepennaya Kniga*, 1563) mentions that it was during this time that three Greek chanters came to Rus' from Constantinople, bringing with them 'special eight-tone, sweet, three-component, and most beautiful extended singing to praise and glorify God.' The word 'three-component' has been subject to various interpretations by musicologists and theologians. In any case, it refers not to three-voiced, but to unison singing. One could suppose that the word 'three-component' points to the three dimensions of ancient church chant: the musical, verbal and spiritual (through which it differed from secular singing, which had only two: verbal and musical).

Being composed of these three aspects, both Russian Znamenny chant and Byzantine singing are phenomena of the same order (in the Western tradition Gregorian chant is the closest phenomenon). They are characterized by a spirituality that is lacking not only in many works of secular music, but also in the contemporary Western-style church singing, which is composed according to principles totally different from those of ancient chant. It is no secret that the concert-like, 'Italianate' singing performed in many Russian churches does not correspond to the spirit of the traditional liturgical texts to which they were written. The main aim of such music is to give pleasure to the ear, while the aim of true church singing is to help the faithful immerse themselves in the prayerful experience of the mysteries of the faith.

The structure and musical characteristics of ancient Russian singing are also entirely different from those of Western-style singing. Znamenny chant was not written by composers but rather compiled from an already existing collection of canonical musical fragments, just like ancient mosaics were pieced together from a collection of stones of various colours. It is not easy for modern man to appreciate ancient chant, and just as difficult to 'lay aside all earthly cares' and enter the depths of prayerful contemplation. But only this and similar singing is truly canonical and corresponds best to the spirit of Orthodox divine services.

At present, ancient Russian chant is becoming better and better known. Just as ancient Russian icons, once-forgotten but relatively recently (at the beginning of the twentieth-century) now restored to their original splendour, Znamenny chant is now being revived by masters skilful at reading its 'hook notation.' In my opinion, the restoration of Orthodox liturgical culture to its original beauty, grandeur and instructiveness is unthinkable without the revival of canonical church singing, which for the Russian Church is prayerful Znamenny chant.

Even the so-called '*popevki*' (canonical musical fragments), the main building components of Znamenny chant, are nothing other than a musical reflection of various prayerful movements of the soul. Moreover, each musical fragment has its own theological basis. If ancient Russian icons are said to be 'theology in colours,' then ancient Russian chant can be considered 'theology in music'. And if Western-style church singing, like the Russian 'academic' paintings on religious themes, is at best a school of piety, then monophonic Znamenny chant can be regarded as a school of prayer *and* theology.

Non-Liturgical Music

Having abandoned musical composition at the age of 20, I did not return to it for 20 more years. During all this time I believed that the musical page of my life was over. And yet, a few days before my fortieth birthday I began to compose music. I started with the full setting of the *Divine Liturgy*. I then composed the *All-Night Vigil* (or Vespers). Both compositions were intended for church services.

Then, however, I composed something more substantial, and not for church use. The inspiration came out of the blue as I was driving from Vienna to Budapest on the 19th of August 2006, the feast of the Holy Transfiguration according to the Julian calendar. I suddenly thought that I should write a musical composition on the Passion story and that this music should be based on the Orthodox liturgical texts from the Passion Week. The title '*St. Matthew Passion*' also came immediately and I had no doubt that I should use St. Matthew's account of the Passion. By choosing this title I also wanted to declare my indebtedness to J.S. Bach.

In Budapest I celebrated the service dedicated to St. Stephen of Hungary, and on the 21st of August I drove back to Vienna. As I was driving, the first melodies began to come, and I began to record them in my memory. As soon as I arrived, I started to put them on paper. I then worked very hard for about three weeks. I cancelled one or two international trips, I almost did not respond to phone calls and e-mails, and I could not sleep during nights, because melodies continued to come to my mind even at 3 o'clock in the morning. On 10 September the main bulk of work was finished. Then I left music aside for a couple of months, and then returned to it again in order to make sufficient revisions and to compose new movements instead of some of the original ones which I decided to remove.

It turned out to be a composition consisting of 48 pieces and lasting for more than two hours. This story is divided into 16 parts and performed in Russian in the style usually adopted for the reading of the Gospel in Orthodox churches. Excerpts from the Gospel are interspersed with music – recitative, choral sections and arias – the text of which is mostly taken from the services held by Orthodox Christians during Holy Week.

Orthodox understanding of the Passion is significantly different from that of that of the Catholic or Protestant Churches. In Western religious art, especially in Renaissance poetry and painting, the Passion has often been represented with an emphasis on its emotional, almost heart-rending nature. Artists have stressed the reality of Christ's suffering, portraying his agony on the Cross, trying to convey as realistically as possible the human pain and horror of the tragedy on Golgotha.

Canonical Orthodox icons of the Crucifixion, on the other hand, have never shown Christ suffering. The Savior is always shown already dead, with His eyes closed. The torment of the last moments of His life on earth remains, as it were, off stage. This is not because icon painters have been unable to convey His suffering but because they have consciously avoided this kind of realism. Contemplating the crucified Christ, an Orthodox Christian sees not only the suffering of humanity, but also God in unchanging and eternal glory; as God-made-human, accepting death for the salvation of all humankind.

This same understanding is reflected in the liturgical texts of Holy Week which form the basis of '*The Passion*' and which have determined its general mood. The lyrical, emotional element is subordinate to a prayerful sympathy with the suffering Christ and spiritual contemplation of the crucifixion of God-made-human. This is the essence of my music, which reflects a very Orthodox reading of the story of Christ's suffering. Being based on the Orthodox liturgical texts and inspired by the Orthodox Church singing, my music is as much about despair as about hope; as much about suffering as about redemption; as much about death as about resurrection.

Bringing Together

The school of the Patristic Fathers, and living in their inspiration and the inspiration of the same living God, life in the liturgy and the mysticism of music all form me as a Bishop in the Orthodox Church. Being a bishop in the Orthodox Church, I spend much time celebrating divine services, which continues to be for me a source of spiritual and theological inspiration. I do not have much time for scholarly work, though I try to steal some hours from my busy schedule to write on one theological subject or another. I continue to compose music: my most recent composition is '*Christmas Oratorio*'. All this – scholarship, liturgical common life and music – shapes my theological mind, and I consider all this activity as a theology, either in words, or in prayer, or in music.

Chapter 4

The Missionary Enterprise in Cross-Cultural Perspective: With Particular Focus on Madagascar

Carl E. Braaten

Introduction: A Personal Odyssey

My interest in the theme of this book stems from my childhood experience of growing up a son of Lutheran missionaries in Madagascar – an island off the southeast coast of Africa with a totally different culture and one of the poorest and most primitive places in the world. My father and mother, Torstein Folkvard and Clara Agnes Braaten, were called and sent to serve as foreign missionaries by the Norwegian Lutheran Church in America. I was a year old when I arrived in Madagascar in 1930 and seventeen when I left for the United States in 1946. Twenty-eight years later I returned to Madagascar, accompanied by my wife LaVonne. I was undertaking a year-long sabbatical project to visit mission fields and to speak at seminaries in various parts of the world – Japan, Hong Kong, Singapore, India, Kenya, Tanzania, Peru, Chile, Argentina, and Brazil. Its purpose was to reflect on the question whether the missionary enterprise carried out by European and American Christianity – Protestant and Catholic – was a success or failure.

Why should that even be a question? It had become commonplace in the academic community to criticize the missionary enterprise as an accompaniment of Western colonial exploitation, cultural supremacy, and imperial expansionism. The missionary movement was held up to ridicule, expressed in an often-quoted pithy statement by an African leader: 'When the missionaries came to Africa they had the Bible and we had the land. They said, "Let us pray." We closed our eyes. When we opened them we had the Bible and they had the land.' Popular movies like *Hawaii* portrayed missionaries in a very negative light. Two other developments contributed to such hyper-critical views of missions. By 1970 African Churches were calling for a missionary moratorium and in response the mainline churches slashed their support for missions in terms of money and personnel. In Europe and North America (e.g., John Hick and Paul Knitter) the pluralistic theory that holds that all religions are more or less equal, pray to the same God, and receive the same salvation was no longer merely an academic proposition but was becoming operational policy of mission boards. Why missions, if they are no longer wanted or needed?

My trip to Madagascar in 1974 confirmed that the deepest roots of my faith and outlook were embedded in the missionary experience of going with the Gospel to people who have never heard, so that they might believe and be baptized into the body of Christ. The Christian life is a pilgrimage! The missionaries were not on a metaphorical pilgrimage; they experienced literally what it meant to be pilgrims, to be aliens in a foreign land. As a result of growing up in such a missionary milieu I have found it quite natural to identify with the biblical paradigm of exodus and exile, of being a sojourner in a strange land, of feeling that home lies not here but elsewhere. I was returning now to Madagascar with questions about the entire missionary enterprise to which my parents had devoted their lives.

I discovered on this sabbatical project that, if I had any doubts about the missionary endeavor, they were not in fact very deep, but formed only a thin outer layer of my mind that had during the intervening decades become preoccupied with the problematic(s) of Western academic theology – demythologizing, hermeneutics, etc. Somewhat to my surprise, revisiting my boyhood haunts in south Madagascar felt like a homecoming. There was the same old missionary children's home and schoolhouse. There we learned the four R's. The fourth was religion. We studied the Bible, no, we memorized it, lots and lots of it. The Bible was treated not so much as the final authority but as the primal source. I later became grateful that this pietistic community of Evangelical Lutherans never laid on me heavy theories about biblical origins, inspiration, inerrancy, and the like. Our pietistic teachers were not biblical scholars; they could not teach us all about the Bible, only what the Bible was all about. Consequently, I was later spared the anguish of many Lutherans in walking through the fires of biblical criticism. Connected with such a narrow parochial base was the inevitable exposure to other cultures, languages, and religions. Growing up amidst Malagasy, French, Métis, Chinese, Indians, Arabs, Norwegians and Americans proved the making of a global multi-cultural perspective without any special effort on our part.

During the twenty-eight years away from Madagascar I did not spend much time thinking about the worldwide mission of the Church. I was more engaged with the prior question, whether Christianity is true. As a philosophy major in college the question of truth became all-consuming for me. If I could not get over the hump on this question, the relevance of the Christian mission would become moot. At the University of Paris I studied phenomenology (Merleau Ponty) and existentialism (Jean Wahl); at the University of Minnesota I encountered logical positivism in full force (Herbert Feigl); at the University of Heidelberg I wrestled with the issue of demythologizing raised by Rudolf Bultmann; and at the University of Oxford Ludwig Wittgenstein and the Philosophy of Linguistic Analysis were all the rage. What do all these matters of epistemology have to do with my roots of origin on the mission field? Not much! But I could not begin to undertake a theology of the Christian mission until I had first come to terms with what seemed to me the prior matters of theological methodology. As a student of Paul Tillich I was convinced that theology cannot go solo, without dealing with philosophical questions. In fact, I still prefer Tillich's question and answer way of relating philosophy and theology to its alternatives; philosophy asks the question to which theology provides an answer. What convinced me more than anything else is that this method is best able to pass the praxeological test in the missionary situation.

Missionary Theology

At the end of my sabbatical travels I wrote my first book on a theology of the Christian mission, which I entitled (1977) *The Flaming Center*. The flaming center of missionary practice is the scriptural witness to Christ. For Lutheran missionaries the hermeneutical principle of biblical interpretation is simply expressed by Luther's phrase '*was Christum treibt.*' And for them theology was not a speculative exercise of abstract thought but ongoing reflection at the ground level of missionary praxis. This view of theology was nicely captured in a slogan coined by Martin Kähler: 'Mission is the mother of Christian theology.'[1] This kind of Christocentric theology that the missionaries left behind is now being taught and practiced by native theologians, pastors, evangelists, and catechists.

In this section I will deal with some of the emphases and challenges of the missionary theology typical of the younger churches founded by the missionaries.

Karl Barth and Paul Tillich were my leading theological influences. They placed theology within the context of the Church or the University. Barth put theology at the service of understanding faith (*fides quaerens intellectum*); Tillich gave theology the task of answering the world's questions. The two approaches have proved to be very fruitful in their different ways. But there is a third way, and that is how theology originated in the missionary situation of apostolic Christianity, in the course of spreading the Gospel in obedience to the Great Commission. The New Testament is a book of the missionary writings of the early Christian community. The Church of the apostles was spreading the flame of the Gospel throughout the world, from Jerusalem to the farthest corners of the earth.

For missionary theology the Gospel is the root from which the Church and its theology grow, and without the mission they will bear no fruit. The younger churches in Africa and Madagascar have the missionary idea in their DNA. Just as Western missionaries were sent to them, they are now returning the favor and sending missionaries to the secularized and neo-pagan nations of Western Europe. Philip Jenkins has written about the prospect of churches and Christians in the Global South converting or re-Christianizing the North.[2] It is already happening, but the point is: whereas the older churches of Europe and North America barely pay lip-service to the missionary idea, the younger churches of the Global South have it in their blood, and they got it from the missionaries. For them mission belongs to the essence of Christianity because the Gospel it preaches is a message of salvation rooted in a divine commission. This is a far cry from cultural propaganda or colonial ideology, as the hyper-critics of the missionary enterprise falsely claim. If, as Ernst Troeltsch believed, Christianity in the end is viewed merely as the religion of Europe and America, and not a gospel of divine redemption uniquely and universally valid, there is no good reason why it should enter the battle of the religions, inviting people to place their trust in the Triune God of the Bible and loyalty to the Christian faith.

---

[1]   Martin Kähler, 'Die Mission - ist sie ein unentbehrlicher Zug am Christentum?' *Schriften zu Christologie und Mission* (Kaiser Verlag, 1971), p. 190.

[2]   Philip Jenkins, *The Next Christendom. The Coming of Global Christianity* (Oxford University Press, 2002), pp. 204–9.

The Bible is the chief and almost the only document used by the Protestant missionaries in Madagascar, and the same could be said for other mission fields in Africa and Asia. The Bible was the first book translated into the Malagasy language by the British missionaries in the nineteenth-century. Soon after there followed a book of worship and hymns in the native language. Lutheran missionaries translated Luther's *Small Catechism* for the instruction of pastors and catechists, and that was about it. Not much of a theological library. The missionaries, of course, brought their own favorite devotional books, biblical commentaries, and dogmatic texts that they had used in seminary, and these supplied the Christian substance of what they transmitted to the Malagasy people. As theology it amounted to second and third generation Lutheran Pietism, which originated in the Awakening Movements that swept across Europe in the late nineteenth-century and from there made its way with the immigrants to America. They brought with them a Bible, a hymn book, and Luther's *Small Catechism*.

After the missionaries left the island, all theological instruction in the Malagasy Lutheran Church, its seminaries, and Bible schools was eventually taken over by indigenous pastors and teachers of Bible and doctrine, some of whom had gone abroad for postgraduate studies in theology. Now that the Malagasy teachers are free to read the Bible with their own eyes, unconstrained by the 'commonsense realism' of the missionaries, a whole new outlook is beginning to emerge. Although the missionaries were Pietists, they received their education in post-Enlightenment institutions of higher learning. This means that willy-nilly they were inoculated to some degree by Western Rationalism with its roots in ancient Greece (Plato and Aristotle). It is difficult to exaggerate the combined impact on the Western mind, no matter what one's ethnic or religious identity, of the seismic movements of Hellenization, the Renaissance, the Reformation, the Enlightenment, and the rise of modern science.

Missionaries were not exempt from these various influences as to how they read and interpreted the Bible. Although the Bible is rife with stories about dreams and visions, prophecies and speaking in tongues, exorcisms and miracles, demons and evil spirits, sacrifices and offerings, the missionaries at that time were not into any of those things.[3] They did not drive out demons, they did not perform miracles of healing, and they did not speak in tongues. They spoke many languages but not in tongues; they practiced the arts of healing but according to the methods of modern medicine. But the Malagasy people are culturally disposed to believing and practicing the very things the missionaries neglected. After all, even the witch doctors were exorcists and healers. Malagasy Christians feel like they are virtual contemporaries of the biblical personalities and don't ask for a lot of fancy hermeneutics to take the biblical accounts literally. They love the Old Testament in particular, because there are many points of convergence between the ancient Hebrew culture and traditional Malagasy culture. The worldview is felt to be similar, and the social, agricultural, and ritual symbols are readily translatable.

---

[3]   After World War II a number of younger Lutheran missionaries, influenced by the charismatic movement in the United States, arrived in Madagascar predisposed to such phenomena as demon exorcism, speaking in tongues, healing miracles, and the like.

How to Deal with Syncretism

When the Christian Church is planted in a new culture, the question arises as to whether syncretism is inevitable or how to deal with it. Two observations will help to highlight the problem.[4] The Malagasy Lutheran Church is experiencing a religious revival, due to the evangelistic activity of a lay woman prophetess, whose name is *Nenilava* (Tall Mother). She was born in 1918 of non-Christian parents. Her father was a tribal chief, a famous healer and diviner. At age 10 she began to see visions and hear voices. She married a Lutheran catechist who taught her Luther's *Small Catechism*, and baptized her. She came to believe that Jesus was the voice calling her name. She claimed that Jesus called her to preach the gospel of repentance and forgiveness, to drive out demons from people possessed, and to heal through prayer and the laying on of hands in the name of Jesus. All this without ever having seen how they do it on TV! Nenilava's method was to train volunteer lay persons, whom she called shepherds (*Mpiandry*), to accompany her on her travels throughout Madagascar. The response was tremendous. The revival continues after her death, with the shepherds going in pairs from village to village, preaching the biblical story of salvation. She carried on her work within the Lutheran Church, eliciting a mixed reaction from the missionaries. Many were quite baffled by her success in accomplishing what they were less able to do. Driving out demons and speaking in tongues and performing miracles like the apostles of old, those were things experientially strange to the missionaries.

A second observation has to do with the attitudes of Malagasy Christians to a traditional ancestral ceremony of 'turning the dead' (*famadihana*). The Malagasy people venerate their ancestors. They believe the ancestors have the power to affect the welfare of the living for good or bad. Ancestors are believed to be bilingual, with the ability to intermediate between the Supreme Being (*Zanahary*) and the living. The ceremony consists of exhuming the corpses, wrapping them in new shrouds, and replacing them in ancestral tombs. The ceremony lasts two or three days and is conducted at great expense, because the family is required to serve a huge meal for as many as one hundred invited guests. Animals are sacrificed to show respect for the ancestors and to gain their support for better living conditions.

At first all the churches condemned the ceremony and eradicated all traces of ancestral veneration from their worship practices. However, after the Second Vatican Council the Malagasy Roman Catholic Church changed its policy and, in the name of inculturation, incorporated the pagan ceremony into its liturgy, eliminating only those elements clearly in conflict with Catholic dogma. The aim of this shift in policy was to make the Christian faith more relevant to the daily lives of the Malagasy people. In continuity with the missionaries' opposition to syncretism the Malagasy Lutheran Church has not changed its policy and thus has to provide a theological answer to

---

[4]   For information about Nenilava's revival movement and the ancestral ceremony of 'turning the dead,' I am indebted to a doctoral thesis submitted to the University of South Africa by Georges Andrianoelina Razafindrakoto, *Old Testament Texts in Malagasy Contexts: An Analysis of the Use of the Old Testament in Three Religious Contexts in Madagascar* (June 2006).

questions people are asking: If Catholics can do it, why can't we? Don't we have the same Bible? Don't we have the same faith?

The issue raised by such a divergent response to a pagan ritual is: Can a foreign faith be inculturated or contextualized apart from falling into syncretism? Missionaries were allergic to every hint of syncretism. But was not the Christianity they transmitted itself a product of a two-thousand-year process of synthesizing the biblical message with a series of cultural forms – Greek, Roman, Teutonic, Slavic, Nordic, and so forth? Is there any such thing as a pure Gospel without being wrapped in the swaddling clothes of some culture? The Western churches have inculturated or contextualized the Gospel in their way, the African and Asian churches will inevitably do so in their way. The history of Christianity is a laboratory of creative experiments and endless debates on how to relate Christianity and culture, surveyed by H.R. Niebuhr in his classic, *Christ and Culture*.

There is no single model on how to incarnate Christian identity in a particular culture, not in the North, East, West, or South. The churches in Europe and North America are suffering profound internal divisions, some of them dying away, others on the brink of schism. The looming splits have to do with the authority and interpretation of the Bible as well as the role of traditional canons, creeds, confessions, and codes that norm Christian beliefs and practices. Christianity in the Global South will not be spared the trials and troubles that their parent churches in the North are experiencing at the present time, and that the Church has always faced, starting with the early Church councils that had to deal with conflicts arising from its relation to Judaism, Gnosticism, and Mystery Cults. I believe that what the missionaries did was basically right; they provided the new Christians and churches with the elements of the classical Christian faith – the Bible, Creeds, Catechisms, Prayer Books, Sacraments, Liturgies, and Hymnals. These are the reliable resources that have served the churches through the centuries and across the cultures and are available for use by what Philip Jenkins calls 'The Next Christendom,' arising in the Global South. Their reception in Africa and Asia are certainly undergoing transformation under the impact of taking root in cultures other than those from which they arose. Theologians and church leaders are unavoidably involved, as were all their preceding fathers and mothers in the faith, in the struggles for Christian orthodoxy and orthopraxy over against rival heresies and heterodoxies. The final test as to whether a belief is Christian is not whether it is African or American, Asian or European, traditional or contemporary, but whether it preaches the Gospel of Christ according to the Scriptures.

A Postscript on Theological Education

The title of this volume, 'Shaping a Global Theological Mind,' can be read as an *indictment* and as an *invitation*, as an *indictment* of the provincial way of teaching theology common in the West and as an *invitation* to structure a curriculum and methodology that promote a universal perspective for a mission-oriented Gospel and Church.

The scientific study of world religions and cultures has become the specialization of university Departments of Religious Studies, whereas church seminaries and divinity schools have traditionally specialized in the various disciplines of Christian theology – biblical studies, church history, dogmatics, and practical theology. The study of other religions and cultures came into play as a subspeciality of missiology, preparing candidates for overseas Christian missionary activity. I think this whole approach is wrong-headed.

When the first Christians conceptualized the faith, they inevitably contrasted it to the religions from which they were converted. Once they were Jews, now they are Christians; once they were believers in Hellenistic mysteries, now they are baptized into the body of Christ. They knew from whence they came and they could not understand their newfound faith except in terms of their former bondage from which Christ delivered them. They understood Christianity by contrast. Their previous religious experience was like living under the burden of the law, from which the Gospel of Christ set them free. The experience of the first Christians – whether Jews, Greeks, or Romans – has been replicated ever since millions of times over, whenever persons of other religions transfer their loyalty from other gods to the God of the Bible. The only ones who believe that all gods point to the same ultimate reality are a handful of post-Christians who teach that all religions are alike and that the evangelistic mission to convert people to Christ is pointless or worse.

The study of non-Christian religions and cultures should become part of the prolegomena of Christian theology, as foundational for the study of the Bible and Christian self-understanding. All religions in some way lay claim to truth and salvation, and such claims should be taken seriously. The Christian belief system should not be elaborated in isolation from competing religious claims and experiences. Apologetic theology is essential in the missionary situation, in order to answer the question whether or to what degree other religions experience the truth and power of the God whom the Bible declares to be the one and only God – Creator and Sustainer of all things. The Bible cannot be understood apart from the knowledge of the other religions existing in ancient times. Furthermore, we cannot understand the history of Christianity without knowing how it assimilated elements of truth (e.g., the idea of *Logos*) that appeared first in other religious traditions. When the missionaries in Madagascar translated the Bible, they used the Malagasy word for the Supreme Being, *Zanahary*, for the Lord God who created all things. They did not bring God to the island; God was already there and the Malagasy already knew some important things about him that the missionaries could and did baptize.

We are calling for an end to a monochromatic teaching of Christianity with reference only to itself. Karl Barth's method of writing church dogmatics that starts and ends with its own interior symbol system does not work in the missionary situation. As a theological method it works well in a situation of apostasy and amnesia, characteristic of much of Western Christianity. That is its great attraction. But once the brackets of Christendom are removed and Christianity finds itself anew in a globalized missionary situation, the factor of competition with other religious claims returns to the fore. The element of competition belongs to the very nature of the First Commandment's 'No Other God' as well as the Great Commission's 'No Other Gospel.' If these exclusive claims are not explained and defended in dialogue with the competing claims of other religions, the study of Christianity becomes a monologue.

The study of world religions is imperative for Christian theology because it is practically necessary to search for common ground in the missionary situation. The mainstream of classical Christianity, building on what the apostle Paul asserts in *Romans* 1, has always affirmed that there is divine revelation in other religions and that there is truth, goodness, and beauty to be ascertained through dialogue with people of other religions. This was most certainly true of the encounter of the Church Fathers in the ancient Church with the philosophies and religions of Greece and Rome. Call it general revelation or natural theology, the point is that there is knowledge of God through the way things are made ('orders of creation'). The missionaries in Madagascar discovered that the Malagasy people believe in a Super Being who created the world, whom they regard as father, protector, and provider of all things, and who is therefore to be worshipped and revered. He is the almighty judge who punishes evildoers and rewards those who do good. However, not for a moment did any of the missionaries draw the conclusion that such knowledge of God leads to the salvation that Christ achieved through his life, death, and resurrection. As Lutherans they were trained to observe a distinction between 'general revelation' through creation and law and 'special revelation' through Christ and the Gospel.

The proposal I am suggesting for a revision of method in theological education is a *conditio sine qua non* for shaping a global theological mind, one that I believe is essential for the sake of the worldwide Christian mission.

Chapter 5

Constructing a South African Theological Mind

John W. DeGruchy

There is no such thing as a disembodied mind, theological or otherwise. Our minds are shaped by the context in which we are nurtured during our formative years, and by those years that soon follow as we pursue our careers and callings. Let me briefly outline the context in which my theological mind was constructed so that we might share a conversation around the themes that have emerged.

A Brief Biographical Sketch

Born in 1939 in Pretoria before the outbreak of the Second World War, I was old enough to be aware of the advent of apartheid that began in earnest a decade later. This meant that my subsequent years of education, both at school and university, coincided with the growing power of the apartheid regime. Following a youthful evangelical conversion and a growing sense of calling to the ministry, I completed my theological studies in 1960 – the same year as the Sharpeville Massacre that occurred three days after my twenty-first birthday. The next year I was ordained and began my ministry in Durban. Those were tumultuous years of growing resistance and repression, of treason trials and the beginnings of the armed struggle.

During 1963–4 I studied at Chicago Theological Seminary and the University of Chicago, experiencing at first hand the Civil Rights Movement and witnessing on television the assassination of John F. Kennedy. A few years after my return to South Africa I began to work for the South African Council of Churches (SACC) from 1968–73 in Johannesburg. From the first week I was plunged into the deep end of what soon became known as the 'church struggle' against apartheid. During those years I completed my doctoral dissertation on the ecclesiology of Karl Barth and Dietrich Bonhoeffer, a topic relevant to the work I was doing, and one that profoundly influenced the subsequent development of my theological mind.

My appointment to teach in the Department of Religious Studies at the University of Cape Town followed in May 1973 where, after several years of teaching courses on the Indian Religious tradition (for which I had some training earlier in Durban), I eventually became Professor of Christian Studies. Until the ending of apartheid in the early 1990s, much of my teaching and writing in theology and Christian tradition, as well as my preaching and church involvement, inevitably impinged on issues that had to do with the church struggle against apartheid. Whether lecturing on the early 'Church Fathers', the Protestant Reformation, or contemporary developments in theology, the conversation soon turned to the significance of the material for us as Christians living in South Africa today.

After 1994, when the new democratic South Africa was born, my theological focus shifted to the issues now facing us during these years of transition, with 'democracy' and 'reconciliation' being central, and themes that had been of interest but of less apparent relevance, amongst them 'theological aesthetics'. Now, many years into the 'new South Africa', and in a world rapidly changing through globalisation, the 'war on terror', and the struggle against poverty and HIV/AIDS, there is no lack of challenge for anyone who recognises the importance of theological reflection in relation to both the intellectual and moral challenges of our time and my own particular context.

Doing Theology

The theological enterprise, as I understand it, is an ongoing conversation between contemporary faith communities, the biblical texts and the history of their interpretation, and the context in which we live. Each individual theologian, by which I mean all people of faith who think critically about what they believe, is a participant in this conversation. However, while each may engage as an individual, theology is a communal affair rather than an individual 'seeking the truth' in some abstract, academic way (important as that may be). It is a way of engaging the world from the perspective of faith in God. For this reason I prefer to speak about 'doing theology' rather than 'studying theology', and regard the preparation of a sermon or the engagement in some act of social witness as integral to the theological task.

Within this broad framework 'academic' theologians also engage in conversation with others in the discipline, both of the past and the present. In my experience, several theologians have been of particular importance, pre-eminently Dietrich Bonhoeffer. But, of course, there have been many other interlocutors with whom I have engaged – theologians of a variety of confessions, traditions and conviction, both living and dead. All have been part of the conversation that has shaped my own theological mind. And all, as I, were influenced by the context in which they lived. They have been most helpful when they have helped me respond to Bonhoeffer's perennial question: 'Who Christ really is, for us today?' This question brings together Christian tradition, existential commitment, and historical context.

The answers that we give will undoubtedly vary from one historical context to another, even though they remain grounded in the common confession of Christians through the centuries. The Christological affirmations of the canon and creeds, though open to a variety and rich range of interpretation, provide boundaries within which we explore possible contextual answers to the question. At the same time, doing theology within specific contexts, with all their ambiguity, often pushes us to transcend boundaries that might well have constricted theological reflection in the past. Let me share some of my own answers that have arisen at different moments in my journey, and even though I will not always explicitly demonstrate the Christological connections, they are certainly there.

Confronting Heresy

I was deeply influenced in the nineteen-sixties by the witness of Beyers Naudé, the South African Dutch Reformed pastor who, after the Sharpeville Massacre of March 21st in 1960, opposed his church's support for apartheid. In doing so, even though he was a distinguished leader and moderator, he was defrocked. Naudé established the Christian Institute (CI) in 1963, which I joined at the time. Deeply influenced by Bonhoeffer's theology and witness, and the church struggle in Nazi Germany, Naudé taught us – a younger generation of aspiring theologians – what it meant to confess Christ as Lord in South Africa. This was expressed, inter alia, in *The Message to the People of South Africa* (1968) jointly prepared by the SACC and CI, and eventually in the *Belhar Confession* (1984) of the Dutch Reformed Mission Church.

While the church struggle had many dimensions, one was certainly ideological. Apartheid was theologically justified by the Dutch Reformed Church in much the same way as the Reich Church gave its tacit support to Nazism. Just as the Confessing Church in Germany recognised at Barmen that such legitimation was a heresy, so we too rejected the theological justification of apartheid as heretical. Instead of proclaiming the gospel of reconciliation in Jesus Christ, theological advocates of apartheid promoted racial segregation as God's will in all spheres of life, including the church. Much of my theological energy went in to confronting this heresy, an account of which is developed historically in my *Church Struggle in South Africa* (new updated edition 2005) and theologically in *Liberating Reformed Theology* (1991). One of my present interests, not least sparked off by the post-modern respect for difference, contemporary ideological abuses of Christianity, and the current debate about the Gnostic gospels, is to rethink whether the category of heresy is still useful. I think it is, but how and why is part of my current reflection on what it means to confess Christ as Lord.

Restoring Justice

Whatever the contribution made to the struggle against apartheid and the liberation of South Africa by those engaged in the church struggle, I, along with many others, had a profound sense of accomplishment and joy when the apartheid era finally ended and the new South Africa was born. This led me to reflection on the theological significance of democracy and the specifically Christian contribution both to the shaping of democratic theory and to the role of the churches as midwives of democracy in South Africa and elsewhere. My 1995 *Christianity and Democracy* is such a theological work

But democracy in and of itself does not necessarily bring about a just social order. We soon recognised that although the apartheid regime had ended, the legacy of oppression and injustice was part of daily reality. We also knew that we could not simply brush the past under the carpet as though the wrongs done to people could be forgiven without any reparation. Such cheap reconciliation was, as Bonhoeffer taught us, the peddling of cheap grace. So the state-sponsored establishment of the Truth and Reconciliation Commission (TRC), headed by Archbishop Desmond Tutu, initiated a critical process of dealing with the past and preparing the way into the future. It was also highly significant theologically-speaking as many of its insights and discourse developed out of theological reflection. As someone involved in the process that led to the formation of the TRC, and more especially in evaluating its significance for faith communities, this influenced a great deal of my theological work during the life-span of the TRC and beyond. Central to my reflection was the connection between theological and political discourse, between personal and social reconciliation, and between reconciliation and the restoration of justice. These themes found expression in *Reconciliation: Restoring Justice* (2002).

Celebrating Freedom

The struggle against apartheid was a struggle for liberation. On the day that the new democratic South Africa was inaugurated, with Nelson Mandela as its first President, the sense of freedom was palpable. It was one of those rare events in history that some people have the privilege of experiencing during their lifetime. It was a defining moment both for the country and for one's own personal and social life. Obviously not all whites experienced it in the way I did, but by far the majority would now look back with expressions of relief that apartheid did not end in a bloody civil war. Suddenly we were able to live as world citizens instead of being part of a pariah nation, isolated by sanctions and threatened by the escalating armed struggle. Along with citizens in the former communist bloc countries of Eastern Europe, who experienced a similar liberation at that time, we began to experience both the benefits and the challenges of post-modernity and globalisation. Issues that were formerly on the sideline now became of central theological concern: multiculturalism, religious plurality; economic development being some of the major ones.

Knowing that the arts had played an important role in our liberation from apartheid, and that they were crucial for the renewal and flourishing of the new South Africa, also led me to reflect on the transforming power of art in relation to Christianity. This in turn encouraged me to engage in theological aesthetics, pondering the significance of beauty as a category that we had neglected in the struggle for truth against heresy, justice against oppression. A whole new theological horizon opened up as I reflected on Bonhoeffer's hopes expressed in his prison letters that the church itself become a 'zone of freedom' in which art, along with friendship, and much else that enhances our humanity, would flourish. I explored these issues in *Christianity, Art and Transformation* (2001), and more recently took the discussion further in an unanticipated direction that related to a final shift in my formal academic career.

Affirming Humanity

My final years at the University of Cape Town were spent as director of the Graduate School in Humanities, a position that daily brought me into direct contact with academics and graduate students across the human and social sciences, as well as the creative and performing arts. I had long been convinced that theology should be in dialogue with other disciplines. Theology had become a conversation not only with other theologians or the Christian tradition, but with many others committed to the search for truth, the struggle for justice, and the affirmation of our common humanity. It was this sense of sharing a common humanity in our intellectual and moral quest that led me back to the Christian humanist tradition that flourished during the Renaissance, but which, often by other names, has been remarkably influential in Christian history. I explored the significance of this tradition in a partly autobiographical text that was published in Britain as *Being Human* and in the United States as *Confessions of a Christian Humanist* (2006).

Confessions of a Christian Humanist documents much of my theological journey in an autobiographical way. It is a confession of faith that some might regard as too conservative and others too radical. Be that as it may, in the course of trying to sketch where I have now arrived, I also highlighted four elements that have become crucial for me. The first is the love of learning and the need for us to seek wisdom in the proper sense of that word. The second is the need for us to respect difference while standing for the truth, as we understand it. The third is the need for the development of a critical patriotism that is cosmopolitan in breadth and committed to global justice and peace. And the fourth has to do with the need to cherish beauty and encourage a creativity of the Spirit. These, so it seems to me, are critical both for the future of humanity and of Christianity.

Living in Hope

Many of my writings, lectures and sermons have, over the years, ended with a word of hope. For me, this has always been of central importance not just as a cardinal theological virtue along with faith and love, but as a way of being Christian in the world. Perhaps it became so important because, for many years, I was accustomed to hearing people around the world asking me: 'Do you have any hope for South Africa?' Some still ask that question. My answer invariably made the obvious point that for me as a Christian, hope could not be equated with optimism even though it was the primary antidote to pessimism and cynicism. Christian hope is fully aware of human frailty and sin, fully cognisant of the vagaries of history and the unravelling of social forces, and therefore realistic in its assessment of both the human condition and political realities. But it is also an affirmation of faith in the God whom we have come to know in Jesus Christ, and therefore a commitment to live in a particular way that embodies and anticipates the reign of God over all reality. To live and therefore witness in hope, I would suggest, is at the heart of our Christian confession, my answer to the question: 'Who Christ really is, for us today?'

Chapter 6

Globalization, Religion and Embodiment: Latin American Feminist Perspectives

Wanda Deifelt

The term globalization is usually employed in the context of global economy, but it is also deeply related to the role of religion – particularly Christianity – when the topic is addressed from feminist, liberationist, and post-colonial perspectives. Throughout history, adventurers, military personnel, merchants, and financiers have constantly expanded geographical and political boundaries. Such endeavors are perceived positively when history is written from the outlook of those whose territories were expanded, but that is not so from the viewpoint of those whose territory was invaded. Today, the unprecedented changes in communication, transportation, and technology give the process of social, political, financial, and cultural expansion a new impetus, leaving us with the impression that the world itself has shrunk, compressing time and space.

The enthusiasm with which such advances are received, however, is not matched by actual improvement in the lives of the socially outcast – who only benefit marginally from the results of globalization. In fact, in spite of the rhetoric of social equality (as equal opportunity), globalization perpetuates historic injustices. A theological undertaking concerned with the wellbeing of humanity and the entire planet needs to point out that the religious discourse has been historically co-opted to justify inertia and passivity towards these injustices. But such a theological undertaking needs also to move beyond denouncing social inequalities and acknowledge its own compliance with these powers. It needs to articulate theological reflections and meaning that empower believers to be full participants in this world, not jut striving to expediently reach the next one.[1] I propose that reclaiming embodiment offers such a contribution, which is also the theme of my theological work.

Both colonialism and globalization have been the focus of liberation and post-colonial analysis. However, their concrete effects on women's bodies are not always contemplated. Colonialism left its imprints by means of sexual exploitation and the objectification of women's reproductive role. The bodies of female African slaves and indigenous women, besides being exploited for their labor, were also domesticated by means of sexual violence. For women, the patterns of colonialism – which once robbed their dignity by subjection to slavery and denial of any type

---

[1]   This concern is best expressed through an ethics of care. For a complete account, read Wanda Deifelt, 'A Lutheran ethics of embodied care,' in Karen Bloomquist (ed.), *Lutheran Ethics at the Intersections of God's One World* (Lutheran World Federation, 2005), pp. 49–62.

of rights – are now carried onto a globalized economy through the new exploitation of bodies: the women working in sweatshops, in sex tourism, or in trafficking. From a Latin American feminist perspective, these concerns are expressed through a theology of embodiment.[2]

Globalization

Globalization is presented as a loose web of free economic, political, and cultural exchange. It works on the presupposition of equality and freedom of interest, where everybody can potentially be a player. Guided by the interests of progress, capital gain, investment, and profit, globalization repeats the colonial pattern of social and political exploitation. In this, it is similar to European colonial powers in their enterprises expanding the horizons of the Portuguese, Spanish, English, Dutch, French, or Belgian nations. As a result, they also expanded political and economic borders. The wealth taken from Asia, Africa, Latin America and the Caribbean came in the form of precious metals, material goods, and cheap labor.[3] Today, this expansion comes in the form of new markets, contracting, and outsourcing.

As a result, in a globalized economy, exploitation becomes more complex and subtle. The free market economy is presented as the solution for long-standing problems of poverty, starvation, genocide, wars, and ethnic disputes. This neo-liberal approach to economy, however, negatively affects the lives of those who do not come to the table to negotiate as equals. Privatization, deregulation, and trade liberalization are presented as 'modes of an efficient economy' without acknowledging that these initiatives widen the social and economic gap. In the name of development, many social programs are cut back. Globalization 'requires following neo-liberal policy prescriptions that will generate an unfettered market over against implementing economic policies that will address domestic problems and priorities.'[4] Public health, housing, and education, as well as incentives for grassroots initiatives, are perceived as backwards because they don't feed the market economy.[5] Many governments have been forced to privatize services and goods in order to comply with international monetary regulations.

Globalization widens the historical social and economic gap created by the older colonialism. Because current economic policies re-inscribe colonialism, and corporations usurp local political power, globalization is experienced as neo-colonialism.[6] As globally mobile capital reorganizes itself, it often sweeps away regulations and undermines local and national politics. It is accurate to say that globalization does create new markets and wealth, but these realities are frequently mislabeled as development. Instead, globalization most often presents opportunities

---

[2]   See, for instance, the collective publication by Brazilian feminist scholars: Marga Ströher et al. (ed.), *À Flor da Pele: Ensaios Sobre Gênero e Corporeidade* (Sinodal/CEBI, 2004).

[3]   Eduardo Galeano, *Open veins of Latin America*, trans Cedric Belfrage (Monthly Review Press, 1973).

[4]   Rebecca Todd Peters, In Search of the Good Life (Continuum, 2004) p. 55.

[5]   Jung Mo Sung, Sementes de Esperança (Vozes, 2005) pp. 98–112.

[6]   Peters, *In Search of the Good Life*, p. 143.

for local governments and elites, the same people who have been the local beneficiaries of illegal appropriation of land and material goods. Generally speaking, local populations only experience minimum benefits from such enterprises. A global economy allows for the benefit of working in sweatshops, for instance, which compared to starvation is an important – albeit relative – improvement. Globalization also causes widespread disorder, insecurity, and uneven distribution of riches. Governments in the so-called developing countries (Asia, Africa, Latin America and the Caribbean) have had to curtail social programs in order to meet the demands of international capital markets.

The widening gap between the 'haves and have-nots' particularly strikes women and children. The feminization of poverty is a well-known problem: women and children are the poorer among the poor. Most of the inhabitants of the planet do not benefit directly from the easy mode of traveling and the convenience of credit cards that are accepted all over the world. Rather, they are just trying to make ends meet. Not only are *basic* needs not met, but vaccines against common but deadly diseases, access to housing and education, or having electricity and running water in one's home, are still far from reality. Historically disadvantaged, women and children are particularly vulnerable in this situation simply because they do not comply with the model of production and consumption idealized by the globalized market. Consider this: Almost half of the world's population lives with less than two US dollars per day.

A report released by the International Labor Organization (ILO) in May of 2005 showed that there are 12.3 million people around the world working as slave laborers. Almost half of them are children. Asia and the Pacific region alone have 9.5 million slave workers. Latin America and the Caribbean come second with 1.32 million. The ILO report (*Global Alliance Against Slave Labor*) also tells us how profitable the slave business is, generating 31.6 billion US dollars per year. Despite the fact that child labor has been critiqued for years, it continues to be a common practice all over the world. It is not only children working in cocoa or coffee plantations in Africa, Bolivian mines, or sweatshops in Guatemala, El Salvador, and Pakistan. Child labor also includes child prostitution, child pornography, and the trafficking of children for sexual purposes.

In historic colonialism, sexual violence became a key aspect of the construction of patriarchy and the maintenance of asymmetric power relations.[7] Globalization perpetuates such violence, making power relations even more complex. The interconnection between gender constructions, racial identity, and class stratification finds in globalization a more nuanced way of perpetuation. Colonialism was constructed precisely on the basis of power prerogatives. It functioned under the political and ideological assumptions that affirm the superiority of white over black/ indigenous, man over woman, and rich over poor. Globalization, on the other hand, employs a neo-liberal rhetoric of the free market – one that presumes equal access and opportunities. Ultimately, however, it results in social disparity, economic inequality, and political disenfranchisement. It defuses potential conflicts on the

---

[7] For a review of current publications about gender constructions in colonial history, see Susan Midgen Socolow, 'Colonial Gender History', *Latin American Review*, 40/3 (2005): 254–265.

basis of merits and achievements, without acknowledging that not all citizens are necessarily born equal. Today, market-oriented, not people-oriented, economy leads to impoverishment, mass migration, urban and rural displacement, violence, and media manipulation.

> What we have come to call globalization is not simply a process that links together the world but also one that differentiates it. It creates new inequalities even as it brings into being new commonalities and lines of communication. And it creates new, up-to-date ways not only of connecting places but of bypassing and ignoring them (cf. Castells 1998).[8]

Globalization takes its toll on people's lives, exploiting human bodies. Paradoxically, this global economy defends consumerist values without paying attention to the social disparities and ecological disruptions over-consumption creates. By feeding a profit and market-oriented economy, healthcare, the distribution of wealth, access to land and education, or affordable housing are seen as reward to some and not a right to all. Globalization is quick to discharge those who do not produce. Human bodies, then, are the means of profit, and devoid of inherent dignity or sacredness.[9] Bodies are valued as long as they produce and consume. This economy is accompanied hand-in-hand with religious expressions that remit hope to the eschatological realm of a future place, and not to the here and now.

The Religious Underpinnings of Social Inequality

Liberation theologians were among the first to denounce the Christendom model that theologically justified colonialism and, more recently, the alienating religious practices that support globalization. The expansion of colonial powers was possible because the religious discourse upheld it, justifying, condoning, and upholding the social and economic reality as God's will. *Conquistadores* arrived in the 'New World' with the cross in one hand and the sword in the other, defending the notion of the Christian world as a form of social and economic polity. In Latin America, this concept of Christendom offered a cohesive political unity that lasted well into the twentieth century, when most countries adopted a nominal separation between Church and State. However, the fact that such theological cohesiveness was shattered did not undermine its political power. By employing a Christian rhetoric, *conquistadores* enforced the power of the imperial crown. The alliance of secular rulers and clergy led to the vision of an earthly crown with Christianity as a state religion.

Besides the economic and political motivation, the conquest of the Americas was also made possible because of its under-girding religious fervor: *conquistadores* would locate the missing tribes of Judah, find the lost paradise of Eden, or simply

---

[8]   James Ferguson, *Expectations of modernity: Myths and meanings of urban life on the Zambian Copperbelt* (University of California Press, 1999), p. 243.

[9]   Ecofeminists such as Rosemary R. Ruether, Sallie McFague, Ivone Gebara, and Karen J. Warren correctly point out that the same logic of domination which exploits people also exploits other species and earth's ecological systems.

convert heathens to Christianity.[10] Ultimately, the encounter of European Christians with indigenous populations of Africa and America was marked by a power dynamic that deemed the non-European as 'other.' As pointed out by James Axtell: 'To Europeans, "others" might appear in an infinite variety of shapes, hues, and habits, but they were always and distinctively unlike Europeans, for the most part, therefore, regarded as inferior.'[11] In contrast, for the indigenous populations, the 'other' tended to be similar. This is not that indigenous people lacked ethnocentricity, but rather that their experience was limited to encounters with other groups that largely shared comparable world visions.

For the Europeans, the pillage of the Americas and Africa was but a small reward for a greater task: that of Christianizing the world, extending the borders of Christendom. The irony of the entire enterprise can be summarized in the name of one of its leaders: Christopher Columbus. Christopher derives from Christo-pherus, the one who brings Christ. One might ask, of course, which Christ was ultimately brought to the foreign land and its peoples. Was it the 'Christ of glory,' or was it the 'Christ of the cross'? Was it the Christ who maintained the conquerors comfortably in their glory and imposed the cross (as an instrument of torture) on indigenous populations? Or was it the Christ who challenged the torture of slaves, the rape of women, and the robbing of people's land?

In its theological sense, the Christendom held by the Europeans followed the idea of *Corpus Christianum* as a society guided by Christian values in its social, political, and economic life. This notion united the Western Christian world under the Roman Catholic Church, gaining new impetus with the crusades, the fight against the Moors in Spain, and the Inquisition. These endeavors were supposed to lead to a religiously uniform community, under the *corpus iuris canonica* (body of canon law). The theological underpinning of the *Corpus Christianum*, however, did not see Christ in the 'other,' as defended by liberationist, feminist, and post-colonial theologies. To the contrary, the 'other' encountered in the indigenous, African, female body was to be conquered and, through the effort of Christianizing them, made to become more similar to the Europeans.

Following an Aristotelian logic, however, it was assumed that the 'other' would never become an equal, in spite of all efforts to turn barbarians into Christians. The classic debates between Bartolomé de Las Casas and Juan Ginés de Sepúlveda regarding the place of the indigenous people in the overall scheme of creation (whether they had souls and could actually be saved) also tells us that the Christendom model was not cohesive or monolithic. Dissonant voices, however, were not able to prevent the dissemination and perpetuation of a disembodied theology – one that denies the human body and takes pleasure in martyrdom. Ironically, the *Corpus Christianum* (the theological concept of the body of Christ manifest in church and society) would become a social body that denies embodiment, supporting dualism and hierarchy.

---

[10] Tzvetan Todorov, *The conquest of America*: *The Question of the Other* (University of Oklahoma Press, 1999).

[11] James Axtell, *Beyond 1492: Encounters in colonial North America* (Oxford University Press, 1992) pp. 31–2.

A similar problem can be identified in the last century with its missionary movements, especially those of evangelical or charismatic backgrounds. Of course, there are many noteworthy examples of missionary initiatives, promoting access to education and other means to improve the quality of life among local populations. The overall tendency, however, was proselytism and the conversion of souls. The influx of televangelism and its prosperity theology unleashed the proliferation of neo-Pentecostal churches, currently the fastest growing religious groups in Latin America.[12] Prosperity and success are interpreted as external evidence of God's favor. For the millions living outside that realm, suffering is perceived as God's punishment. Followers are led to believe that merit-making efforts, such as financial donations to the church and attending worship or prayer sessions, can ensure God's favor. The emphasis is on the individual's capacity to negotiate benefits with God, not necessarily on the life in community and the concern for the wellbeing of others.

The primary legacy of the Christendom model is its emphasis on *chronos*. Its theology focuses on either the past (the tradition) or the future (the expectation of eternal life), leaving little to be said about the present. This leads to resignation and passivity. The neo-Pentecostal model, with its prosperity theology, focuses on the *eschaton*, a reality that is elsewhere but which can be invoked in order to alter the quotidian. Since God controls the outcome of the here and now, it is necessary for the individual to engage in merit-making efforts. These initiatives have little to do with agency, transformation of the present reality, or a recognition that humans depend on God. Rather, they work as 'bribery' to achieve success and prosperity. If the attempt fails, it is due to the individual's lack of faith. In both models (Christendom and neo-Pentecostalism), faith is given no importance as a catalyst for change and source of transformation for the wider community. Neither model addresses human capacity to change reality and confront social injustices, discrimination, sexism, or violence. They share a theology that does not see the possibilities of *kairos*, the opportune moment of God's presence in history, the qualitative time of God's redemptive actions that also leads to the betterment of the here and now, extending God's grace to the entire creation.

Christianity was and still is used to justify social inequality, pre-emptive war, torture, and to curtail freedom. The religious discourse is used to deny dignity and full humanity. It is employed to lead to passivity and acquiescence. Racism, sexism, classism, militarism, earthism, and homophobia are professed as God's will. By invoking the authority of Scriptures, suffering can be imposed unto others as if it were God's wish, particularly if it is done under the rubric of 'saving souls.' The name of God is used to justify ungodly acts. But I raise alternative questions in my work: Is Christianity only concerned with salvation? Does it only refer to the spiritual realm? What does Christianity have to say about the here and now? What does Christianity have to say in terms of the wellbeing of God's creatures and the whole creation?

---

[12]   Pablo A. Deiros, 'Protestant Fundamentalism in Latin America,' in Martin Marty and Scott Appleby (eds.), *Fundamentalisms Observed*, Vol. 1 (University of Chicago Press, 1991), p. 155.

Embodiment: a Christian Tenet

Christendom, neo-Pentecostalism, and globalization have in common a disregard for human bodies. A globalized economy prioritizes profit, not people. It emphasizes *free* trade as opposed to *fair* trade. It is geared toward a consumerist society, one that does not pay attention to inhuman work conditions, rampant violence, or social injustices. In the name of capital gains, globalization exploits human bodies and lures consumers into a make-believe reality, one that compensates for personal vulnerabilities and shortcomings by buying goods. Christianity, in the Christendom model, also disregards the human body, even if it uses the nomenclature of embodiment, such as *Corpus Christianum*. With neo-Pentecostal prosperity theology, personal privileges are ascertained by negotiation with God, without affirming God's transformative actions in the wider community. Both, then, are similar to the model of globalization in which the individual's capacity is rewarded with benefits (in this case, divine ones). Hence, neither model is capable of critically addressing globalization because they share a common ideology, namely, a lack of concern for the wellbeing of bodies (the personal body, the communal body, and the body of creation).

What I am proposing, in my work, is a theology of embodiment. Embodiment is defined in the broad framework of the body and its multiple levels: the human body, the environment, and the cosmos. The house (*oikos*) we inhabit comprises our physical body, the social body of communities, and the body of the entire creation. A theology of embodiment seeks wellbeing and affirms that these bodies need to be cherished as God's gifts and cared for accordingly. A theology of embodiment draws from creation, where corporality is positively affirmed. It revisits incarnation, where God assumes a human body, becoming *totally* human. This includes interaction with other bodies, the environment, and the cosmos. It is ecclesiological, given that the church is a communal body with a cosmological vision. A theological reflection that takes embodiment as a parameter for its action and reflection must then affirm the care for bodies as a central Christian tenet. It is a theology that may start with the experience of human bodies, but it moves on to reflect on embodiment in a broader sense. The aim is not to reduce human bodies to moral conformity (generally established by classist, sexist, racist, anthropocentric, and homophobic guidelines). An embodied ethic instead reclaims the importance of bodies in the Christian tradition. It affirms a commitment for the wellbeing of the different places God has made for us to inhabit: the house that is our body, our family, our community, and our planet. Embodied theology sees bodies in all their expressions as sacred places.

Despite the negative historical examples described earlier, Christianity does have in its core an ethics of care. The Gospel promotes transformation – the transformation of individuals, institutions, and society – and leads to a deep concern for the wellbeing of self and others. A theology of embodiment, which draws from God's incarnation and perceives God as active in the love of and for creation, can foster the necessary impetus for such transformative approach. As a hermeneutic category, bodies can be both a source and reference for such reflection. The human body, for example, summarizes the negativity of a dualistic mentality. On the one hand, it suffers the impact of ideologies and bears the imprints of violent, asymmetric, and unjust social systems. On the other hand, the human body allows us to envision new possibilities.

The concept of embodiment (the human body in its totality) means to overcome the dichotomies between body and soul, reason and passion, acknowledging the integrality of human beings and their interdependence. The body becomes the *locus* of God's revelation and call for action. The same applies to all bodies we inhabit: our physical body, family, community, environment, planet, and cosmos.

Even if the eschatological dimension is one of Christianity's key components, its system of beliefs has to deal with the way we organize ourselves in society, how we relate to one another, how we make use of the material resources available to us, and how our everyday existence relates to the divine. The early Christian community, as the followers of Jesus, understood this very well and imitated his love and care for those who were socially outcast or dispossessed. To live a godly life is not reduced to the spiritual world. The here and now anticipates the reality of the Reign of God by offering glimpses of it. The theology of incarnation focuses on the immanence of the divine, one that allows us to see Christ in the neighbor. As stated by Martin Luther: 'We relate to God through faith, but we relate to our neighbor through love.'[13]

To pursue this endeavor – an embodied theology – allows us to establish ties among ourselves, as God's creatures. Unlike the theology established by the Christendom model, this experience of faith has concrete implications for the present. Unlike a theology of prosperity, which seeks individual rewards for merit-making efforts, this is a reading of the Christian faith that fosters community and a sense of solidarity. As reminder of our shared creaturehood, such ties foster commitment for the promotion of peace and justice, assuring the wellbeing of the whole creation. Furthermore, such an approach allows us to recognize the initiatives of 'globalization from below;' that is, those movements, organizations and citizen associations that, as part of civil society, offer counter-examples of the 'globalization from above' described earlier. Globalization from below is solidarity extended on a global scale.

For Christians, to assert the role of religion in a globalized age means to go back to the novelty of the Gospel of Jesus Christ. In light of the individualist, consumerist, hedonistic, and apathy-filled *mores* of globalization, Christianity reclaims the active participation of all believers in acts of transformation. It calls for active social participation, mutual accountability, and a concern for the wellbeing of the whole creation. There is a change in attitude: human arrogance is replaced by interdependence, indifference is overcome by empathy, and hatred is met by love. Such transformation is possible only once we recognize ourselves as vulnerable human beings in need of communities and networks that support one another. Following in discipleship, Christians extend solidarity to all in need.

This discipleship is not a simplistic appeal to congregational life or a plea that people abide by the social rules and norms of their churches. The goal, instead, is to promote a wider and deeper sense of what community itself is all about: a reflection of the body of Christ concerned with the wellbeing of bodies. Human beings belong to accidental communities, those maintained due to need, convenience, or nature (one's family, job environment, etc). But the body of Christ is also an intentional community. Intentional communities draw on and demand people's agency, depending on their

---

13   Martin Luther, 'The freedom of a Christian,' in J. Dillenberger (ed.), *Martin Luther: Selections from his Writings.* (Anchor, 1961) p. 79.

willingness to stay together, to work out differences, to rely on each other, and to grow together. They establish a greater awareness of our connections as human beings and our need to be informed about needs and accomplishments elsewhere, outside the immediate circle of blood relations or job networks. It also requires intentionality in reassessing our anthropocentric mode of thinking and acting in relation to our environment. Of course, accidental communities can be as empowering and rewarding as intentional communities are when one does not take them for granted and, in fact, celebrates them as gifts and opportunities of discipleship.

Intentional communities must address vulnerability. To be able to rely on others, whether for support or comfort, is a gift of community. Being able to trust is highly discouraged in our society because we operate under the general framework of taking advantage of others for our benefit. However, Jesus' model of ministry and his invitation to discipleship are based on trust, on our capacity to love and to stand in solidarity with others. Such communities are not homogeneous, in the same way human bodies are not all the same. Diversity is celebrated, not as a threat to the Gospel, but rather a manifestation of God's creative power, and is another gift we are invited to share.

To take embodiment seriously – to recognize the fundamental role of creation, incarnation, and the call to life in community – is to live out vulnerability and place ourselves under God's grace. Life itself needs to be celebrated and anything that falls short from the abundant life Jesus proclaimed denounced as contrary to God's will. To acknowledge vulnerability is to allow humans to be humans, and the divine be divine. Human vulnerability also foments creative ways of establishing global networks of solidarity and mutual empowerment. If we can recognize God at work in our midst, also in the reality of suffering and exclusion, we can address the urgent issues of our time.[14] The theological construction of ecclesiology is based, in part, on the notion that the local and the universal cannot live without each other, that we are interconnected. A globalized reality has turned us all into *glocal* citizens: global, yet local.

Religious communities, non-profit organizations, labor unions and associations, each have both a local and global dimension. Local actions have global repercussions and vice-versa. This is not new. However, even if local initiatives are all part of civil society, the interactions between them are not necessarily established. Sometimes, it takes a movement such as the World Social Forum, for instance, to gather liberationist initiatives from all over the planet to enable such exposure.[15] The motto of the World Social Forum – 'Another world is possible' – draws on a general dissatisfaction with the contemporary state of things, particularly social injustices (in their multiple manifestations), and the conviction that reality can and needs to be transformed. There is no predominance of any particular religion or political agenda. It is precisely the confluence of multiple initiatives that makes it unique.

---

[14]   Vitor Westhelle, *The Scandalous God: The Use and Abuse of the Cross* (Fortress, 2006).

[15]   The World Social Forum brings together individuals, representatives of non-profit organizations, political parties, churches, labor unions, grass-roots movements, etc., to a yearly event. The first edition of the WSF happened in Porto Alegre, Brazil in 2001, and has happened since in other continents (India and Kenya, most recently). More information: www.forumsocialmundial.org.br.

The concrete initiatives of solidarity, the works for peace and justice, the signs of hope, and the experience of life even in the midst of death are possible when theology moves away from a purely eschatological concern and focuses on the here and now. Faith is not an experience that removes us from reality but one that empowers us to be and become. By reclaiming an embodied theology, that is, a theology that takes God's yearning for the wellbeing of bodies to its final consequence, it is possible to affirm the sacredness of bodies. It allows the creation of networks that fashion a globalization from below. These are intentional communities created around the globe, where people experience that their lives are worth living, that there is dignity and purpose in their existence. This is the sense of connection and belonging Christians experience when they profess: 'In Christ there is neither Jew nor Greek, slave or free, male and female, because we are all one in Christ (Gal 3:28).

Chapter 7

A Chicano Theological Mind

Andrés Quetzalcóatl Guerrero

A Chicano Theology was written twenty years ago. The unedited version is in the Andover-Harvard Theological Library. It is my doctoral dissertation. When I told Professor Harvey Cox that I wanted to write a Chicano Theology of Liberation, he said, 'Well, you are not going to find any information in the library'. He was right. There was no information on a Chicano Theology in the libraries of the USA or anywhere else in the world for that matter. There were theologies of liberation from Latin America, Asia, Africa and the USA. *A Black Theology of Liberation* by Professor James Cone was a great inspiration to me. After I read this book, I realized that he was a half a century or more ahead of his time. He is still a half a century or more ahead of his time. The reason is because the problems addressed by that manuscript are alive and well in the USA. The power elite in the USA will not face its own problems, nor will the power elites of the world for that matter. Power is self-hating and the more power, the more self-hate they generate within themselves. That self-hate controls them and for the most part also the minds, soul and hearts of those they oppressed. The most logical solution to the problems they themselves create is self-love, but that entails letting go (S. Marie Augusta Neal). To love self for the benefit of those they oppress is the beginning of wisdom.

The problems addressed by James Cone are based on the experiences of racism by African Americans. Racism is the cornerstone of capitalism and its mother is imperialism. Hernán Cortez is the modern father of both capitalism and imperialism, and yes racism is their foundation. But the foundation of racism *et alia* 'isms' is egotism, i.e., self-hate. To maintain inhuman structures such as capitalism and imperialism, you have to establish institutions that teach self-hate instead of self-love. At the time of writing *A Chicano Theology*, I was not aware of the devastating power of self-hate. Let me explain what I mean.

Recently Pope Benedict XVI wrote an encyclical on *agape* and *eros* (*Deus Caritas Est*, 12/25/05). From what I read in his encyclical, he did not mention self-love, which is at the foundation of brotherly/sisterly love. A Chicano Theology will define self-love as *destino*. It is the destiny of all of us, especially the oppressed, to love ourselves so that the Law of Christ can be incarnated in us. In the 'Our Father' we pray, 'Thy Kingdom come, Thy Will be done on Earth as it is in Heaven'. That Kingdom and that Will is love. There is no second or third. But it has to originate from within a person. In 1918 after World War I, G.F. Nicolai wrote *The Biology of War*. In *The Biology of War*, Nicolai states: 'Only a madman can love another more than himself' (Nicolai 357). This set me to thinking on this phrase for the next thirty-one years. We were always taught the 'Golden Rule' – 'love your neighbor as you love yourself'. But it occurred to me. What if we did *not* love ourselves? What if we were being taught to hate ourselves? And then it came to me. How do we as Christians and humanists maintain dehumanizing and destructive structures like imperialism and capitalism (and now Globalism (all economic systems based on self-hate)? How do and did we come to believe in such inhumane structures and institutions that instead of uniting the children of God, we divided and divide them so that oppression and injustice can prevail? It has to be taught was my conclusion.

Martin Luther King's *Letter from the Birmingham Jail* (April 16, 1963) pointed the finger at the Catholic, Jewish and Protestant churches. They were responsible for so much hatred toward the African-American. Hate had been taught at the expense of love. Freedom was understood as freedom for white folks, but not black, red, brown people or for women. Freedom was believed and is still believed today to be brought about through a process of assimilation. But what were we assimilating into? All schools teach the process of assimilation. Reies Lopez Tijerina said it best when I interviewed him for *A Chicano Theology*, 'You teach children in a capitalist country to be good capitalists, just as you teach communist children to be good communists'. So what is the common denominator of assimilation in the USA school system?

Theologically speaking, the common denominator of this process of assimilation or rather this process of domination is the Calvinist doctrine of election which states that some are chosen and some are not. Professor James Cone highlighted this doctrine in his immortal book, *A Black theology of Liberation*. I always knew as a Chicano what I was assimilating out of, but I did not know what I was assimilating into. It took me almost all my life, but now I have discovered something. No wonder so many young people of color in the USA never finished or finish school. The process of assimilation maintains that 'some are chosen and some are not'. Check out the push-out rates in our public schools and colleges and universities. Check out the percentages of colored faculties. Some are treated better and some are rejected, neglected and truncated, to use Professor Lonergan's terms. Whoever rules, we must adjust to. That is what assimilation is and that is what domination is also. There is no second. Nothing else 'must-be' is the philosophy and theology behind this discriminatory practice system. Power is its first name and its last name is 'by any means necessary'. Two doctrines support this theological and political practice in the USA. One is even called a doctrine, the *Monroe Doctrine*, and the other is called *Manifest Destiny*, which states that God has given some Americans the Divine Right to manifest our Destiny, which is to acquire land (power) by any means necessary. *God* has given us this Divine Right? God does not give anyone or any nation or country to be a divine bully. That would be a mad God in any theology. God is a God of unconditional love and not an unconditional bully. God does not hate Him/Herself: 'Be ye perfect as your heavenly Mother/Father is perfect (Mt 5:48). Thus, love yourself unconditionally like God the Father/Mother loves Him/Herself unconditionally.

We are perfect in so far as our love is perfect. There is no such thing as imperfect love. Imperfect love is another word for hate. There is love and there is hate. There is no third. How many times have we heard a person say, 'I love you, but on one condition'. I have never heard this one, 'I love myself, but on one condition'. It does sound foolish because it is foolish. You do not put conditions on loving yourself.

We use a double standard when we apply love to our neighbor. In true love there are no double standards.

So how did we learn to hate others and consequently hate ourselves. I propose that we learned it from our educational institutions. From kindergarten to PhD, we learn it. It is written all over our curriculums dominated by the masters of self-hate, the ruling classes. The oppressors rule at the expense of the oppressed. First divide the oppressed, then take their land, next exploit them and finally get rich. We have mastered this institutional procedural imperialistic method for 1,600 years. Globalization continues this madness.

In order for injustice and war to prevail we must teach it. It does not drop from thin air. It does not grow on trees. So where does hate of self come from? It comes from our methodology of repression. A method is always a way to do something. In our schools we teach methods of how to hate ourselves so that we can hate others. If you possess hate by means of education, then you can practice it and teach it, too. Fear of neighbor plays an integral part in the method. Education in Latin comes from *educo* – to lead out of ignorance. We turned it around to mean to lead into ignorance. Hate is ignorance and war because love is enlightenment and peace.

Our Western military colleges are experts at teaching hate overtly. The rest of Western schools teach it covertly. To maintain institutionalized violent institutions such as imperialism and capitalism and globalism, you have to teach self-hate. There is no second way. True love of self implies true love of neighbor. True hate of self implies true hate of neighbor. There is no third. If there is a third I would like someone to show me. Can one give what one does not possess? No. Can one give what one possesses? Yes. So teach self-love so we can possess it. Jesus put it pretty plainly to us. You can't say, 'Lord, Lord, and then turn around and hate your neighbor. That is not love. True love is saying, 'Lord, Lord, and then turning around and loving your neighbor. Now you truly understand God's love of self and your love of yourself. You cannot give what you do not have. So you must challenge every institution, both secular and profane, that is teaching self-hate to teach self-love without any conditions. Once conditions set in, the process is tainted. The process cannot be tainted. It must be pure like God's love is pure for us, only then you will be perfect as your heavenly Father/Mother is perfect. There is no other way, but through true love. With the latter statement, I will now delineate a few of the elements of a Chicano Theology of Liberation.

The Concept of God

The concept of God is maternal and in the New World as exemplified by the great miraculous apparition de *Nuestra Señora de Guadalupe* and *La Morenita* – the Dark Virgin. It is not paternalistic European Catholic, Protestant and Calvinistic like in the Old World. You cannot put new wine into old wineskins. For the Chicano and Chicana Catholic, Guadalupe is not a male. She is Woman, she is Mother, and she is Destiny. Will she abandon the poor and downtrodden like the paternal European concept of God? No, she will not. She is our dearly beloved Mother. Fathers abandon their children, but mothers rarely do. Women suffer greatly, like death, at childbirth and perhaps that is why God allows such extreme pain. Mothers love their children above all things. And Guadalupe loves us above all things. Our concept of God is maternal. It could not be otherwise.

The Concept of Justice

The concept is this; '*Todos hijos de Dios o Todos hijos del Diablo*' (We are all children of God or children of the Devil). God can not allow favoritism among Her/His children. Thus, we are all children of God or of the Devil. We cannot serve two masters, we can only serve one. When we play favorites, we are playing the game of the Devil and not doing the will of God, unless your concept of God is a double standard. With God there are no double standards for His/Her children. We are all equal under God. True, we all have different gifts, but that does not make us unequal. That makes us unique because of our gifts, but not better. No person is better. We are all the same. We have one body and one soul. I do not know of any one that has either/or. We are the same. When God created us, He/She created us equally. This concept is very profound, even though those in power would have us believe otherwise. Otherwise does not exist because it creates division, and God did not create us so that we could be divided. What divides us is not who we are, but who we want to be. Sadly, some of us want to be better, that is, chosen. Remember Jesus told us that he/she who loses his/her life will win it ? What appears negative will be positive. Egotism is at the root of self-hate, and we must love ourselves before we can understand what it means to love our neighbor, 'the Other'. Again, I do not know of a third option. The criterion for self-loving is our love for our neighbor. Unconditional love is a circle. It is not a straight line. Conditions on love create divisions and double standards. Under the Law of Christ, that is unacceptable. We are all children of God, and we should love one another as God so has loved us. To put conditions on love is to put conditions on God. God's love for us is without condition. We have to love ourselves and our neighbor as God loves Her/Himself and us.

The Concept of being Bilingual and Bicultural

For Chicanas and Chicanos this phenomenon is probably the most misunderstood concept by non-natives. Mexicans of North America are a mixture of Spanish and Native American, but if you look very closely you will see that we are much more Native American or African, than Spanish. Yet, if you look in any government form we are considered white. Because of our oppressive condition we are probably more black than white. Many of our children do not speak Spanish any more because the process of assimilation or rather the process of Calvinization has taken a toll on our Spanish language, but not on our culture, our biculturalness. Whereas many European and Asians have capitulated to Calvinism because they are not returning to their homelands, this, however, is our homeland. It has always been our homeland and it will always be our homeland. We did not come here. We started here. Even though we share it with many races, many, especially those in economic and political power, find it very difficult to understand. Our biculturalness is rooted in our religion and in our customs and traditions. We share a cosmicity with the world that few people can see much less understand. We will not die to that cosmic reality.

José Vasconcelos mentioned in his book, *Indología*, 1927, that our sociology was that of G.F. Nicolai. Nicolai wanted Germany to be the 'cosmic race'. The cosmic race is the opposite of the Aryan race. The sociology of Nicolai and his cosmic race was a sociology of equals. Nicolai wanted Germany to incorporate this ethos into its being. Instead, Germany imprisoned Nicolai and started World Wars I and II because they thought they were better than and not equal to others. Individualwise and nationwise the USA is acting like Germany was acting before World Wars I and II. In the last 200 years we have been a bully nation to the Native Americans North and South and to the poor nations of the world. Europe has also been, and now Japan and China are following in their footsteps.

Imperialistic nations preach brotherhood and sisterhood, but practice enemyhood. They do not understand cosmicity. Cosmicity is the incorporation of two or more cultures into one. Hence, the word 'cosmic'. It is difficult for a mono-cultural nation to understand this phenomenon. It does not possess the experiential knowledge to digest this reality intellectually nor will it listen. What it will do is be afraid of it and be violent towards it. Look at how the USA is reacting to the present immigration issue. Even a Berlin-type wall is being built to keep out the Mexicans. They forget that we have been here before the USA and will always be here forever. We have always been treated badly by the Euro-Americans. Now, they are afraid of us because of our numbers, and because they think that we are going to treat them exactly like they have been treating us. They know exactly what they have been doing, and they are afraid to the point of initiating a national social psychosis (national hysteria) because of immigration from Mexico. Little do they know that we love them much more than they have ever loved us. To hate them would mean that we hate ourselves. We do not hate ourselves, even though we have been taught to do so.

Cosmicity implies equals and not betters. Our purpose is not to emulate their actions towards us but to liberate that kind of attitude towards others. A wise person/nation would try to make friends and not enemies. In the last two to three hundred years has the USA made friends with the Native, African or Mexican Americans? No. Currently the USA is preaching diversity, but practicing adversity. Unless the USA loves itself, it will never understand diversity. That is why it practices adversity. All imperialistic nations suffer from the same disease. We can find solutions to polio, cancer, diabetes, etc., but we can not find solutions to hate. Give me a break.

We will never find a solution, if we do not learn how to love, how to find non-violent ways to solve the problems the ruling classes themselves in their ignorant powerful nation states create. Those with power have always been behind the reason for the problems of injustice. Let us not kid ourselves by believing that those without power are the cause for the injustices in the world. Read the signs and sins of the times. Global warming and pollution of soils, lakes, streams, rivers and oceans are caused by those with power. Our Native Americans always and forever have told us to not desecrate Mother Earth, and those with power have abused and raped her in the past centuries for money. Power and greed must stop raping Mother Earth: Ya basta tanta injusticia trájica para hacer dinero. Mother Earth is already retaliating with perfect diseases, droughts, floods and storms. Read the signs and sins of the times.

We are the water, the rivers, the lakes, the streams, the land, the grass, the flowers, the trees, the skies and every thing that is, we are. This biculturalness is what most fail to understand, except our Native American brothers and sisters. We have always been one with them. In many ways our struggles are ones of culture with the European. Our lands are sacred, and we are one in harmony with our Mother Earth. One must die to their culture to understand another culture. Poor people are always dying to their culture. They have no choice. They want to survive. Powerful people need to die to their culture of violence so that there can be peace on earth.

Powerful people all over the world are behind all the poverty and genocide in the world. Rumor has it intellectuals in these powerful groups are the ones really responsible for so much injustice and inhumanity. My experience moving files at the American Academy of Arts and Sciences would confirm that rumor. When I challenged the director on a known issue on racial matters, he threw a fit. In another issue in another state, I at least was told, 'We know about the injustice, but please do not tell anyone'.

The Concept of Family

It would be obvious that if our concept of God is maternal, then our mothers and sisters would be the nuclei of our families. Mothers and sisters ensure that the center of the universe is the family. Family, and not the individual, is the key to everything. In Anglo culture, the individual is the center of the family. In the USA we preach 'rugged individualism' as the center of our philosophy and of the universe. The world revolves around me. This again stems from our religious beliefs. North American Protestant (Calvinistic) religion emphasizes salvation of the individual, not the family. A modern term is privatized religion or private religion. Even Anglo or German or Irish or Polish Catholics have been sucked into this phenomenon because of assimilation. They assimilated out of Catholicism (universal) into Calvinism (the chosen ones). I will add the Jews into this assimilated phenomenon also. Look at how American Jews in Israel get along or rather do not get along with the Palestinians. I cannot help but to come back to the central message to all white clergy of Martin Luther King's *Letter from the Birmingham Jail*. This letter would confirm my point of the teaching of self-hate in our churches and schools. Hate never happens by accident, just as unconditional love does not either. We teach unconditional love from the pulpit, but practice conditional love. We have done it for 1,600 plus years.

The churches and schools want to be prophetic against Caesar, but they both get big tax-breaks from 'Caesar'. Dante stated it best in *The Inferno* that because the Church did not 'render unto Caesar what is Caesar's and unto God what is God's' (Mt 22:21), the Church brought corruption upon itself and destruction upon the state. The prophetic mission of the people of God cannot be compromised. If to be prophetic you have to pay taxes, let us not waste any time. Pay them! Drop those hand-outs and let us follow Christ. Perhaps the more riches we possess as the people of God, the least prophetic we become. Remember we cannot serve two masters. Martin Luther and Martin Luther King were on the right track. We are either going to serve God or Mammon. To not know the difference creates madness in the believer and chaos in the non-believer. At some point we have to stop this folly and start loving ourselves so that we can start loving our neighbor.

We know who we as capitalists, imperialists and globalists serve. We preach good will and practice self will or is it self hate? Where is our unconditional love, our non-violence? Let's show ourselves; let's show the world. We want to see. If we cannot show ourselves or the world, then what in God's name are we doing? Time is running out. Like the Chicano/a family, the world is a family. The family is the center of the universe. The world as family is also the center of the universe: 'Todos somos uno'. In the Chicana/o family, the individual is one with the family and not apart from the family. Salvation and liberation is within the family and not without the family. The world is a human family, and the glue to keep it together is unconditional love. This is applied to individuals and to nations. Educational institutions and their intellectual leaders cannot compromise unconditional love. We are only one family: 'Todos somos uno'.

Perhaps this concept of the family in a Chicano/a Theology is the last hope for the USA and for the world because the world is a family and not an individual. Perhaps instead of nation states we should be global communities in the service of love with one another. The world is getting smaller and time is running out.

What are some of the elements of a Chicano family?

You know about wife or husband and their children.
The family is public information. You make it a point that all know your family.
Family is not a secret. You do not exist outside the nuclear family.
Person always talks about spouse and family.
Person is highly communal.
Person is an extension of family.
Person does not exist outside of family.
Person is an integral part of family.
Person marries spouse and spouse's family.
Couple's interests take second place to children's interests.
Grandmothers maintain cosmicity of family at all costs. No exceptions.

Applied on a global scale, these elements are essential for the family of nations to survive the twenty-first century.

La identidad de la piel entre el mundo con poder y el mundo sin poder (The Identity of the membrane between the World with Power and the World without)

It was José Ángel Gutierrez who stated that Chicanos and Chicanas were *la piel* (the membrane) between the North and the South. I would also add the East and the West. As a Chicano and a Chicana in the USA you are born to live with one foot in the world of affluence and one foot in the world of poverty, with one foot deeper in poverty than in affluence. Chicanos and Chicanas are at the crossroads and everything passes through us. The North needs the South so they go through us, and the South needs the North so they go through us. The East needs the West so they go through us, and the West needs the East, so they go through us. Who gets crucified in the middle of all this mad phenomena which is mostly bad? We do, together with other poor people, born and raised here in the USA in the cultures of poverty. We, in cultures of poverty experientially and not theoretically, know what it means to be crucified. Yet, this globalization goes on day and night every day without anyone stopping to think how such injustice in the name of God and progress is created among the masses of humankind, and we dare to call ourselves civilized? There is no civility in so much inhumanity. We are heading toward the *last* world war because after this one, there will not be enough of us left to fight again. At which point, the trickle left in the North will ask the trickle left in the South and the trickle left in the East will ask the trickle left in the West, 'My God, my God, what did we do? Why could not we love each other unconditionally? We put so many conditions on our love that it was not love anymore, but rather hate. Now, what are we going to do with a poisoned earth and its poisoned waters, and so much fire all around us?' And Jesus will return once again and appear on the horizon and once again exclaim to us: 'Oh ye of little faith, you could not love yourselves as the Father/Mother and I love you. The Kingdom of the God of love was always within you. Now look what you have done to the Earth and yourselves for not loving one another. At the center and heart of all creation is love, and I will forever love you.'

El derecho al respeto a lo ajeno es la paz (Benito Juarez)

To my knowledge Benito Juarez was the first Native American president in the New World. The above saying means that if you want peace you must respect what belongs to others. I believe he was referring to the French Empire and its plan to take over Mexico. You cannot take over a country because you have the power. Look at the USA in the Middle East right now and how well it gets along with its own people of color. Especially the Native American and their half brothers the Mexicans, not to mention our African-American brothers and sisters who helped built the USA. Our track record is not very good. We want to force democracy in the Middle East while here at home we practice demoncracy through racial profiling and racism against people of color. That is not what I consider respect of others. Our prisons are overflowing with people of color and our prisoners are treated so badly. There are many immigrants in these prisons whose only crime was to cross the Rio Grande to look for work because the poverty caused in Mexico by the 'superpowers' is so wanton. What are poor people supposed to do? Stay in their countries and starve to death? First World countries have always and forever been responsible for the poverty of the countries in the Third World. All the genocide in the poor countries of the world can be tied to the superpowers. Now, not forever can they claim to be innocent. They can lie to themselves and to their people, but they cannot lie to the poor people of the world or to God their avenger. We have an old saying in Spanish: '*Con Dios no se juega*' (Don't mock God). I would interpret it this way: Don't mock God by exploiting the poor. God does not take lightly to exploitation of any kind, especially human beings. Another saying: '*Nadie se va de este mundo hasta que las paga*'. My interpretation is: God will see to it that all will pay for the wrong they did to others. All cultures have their innate warning signs of how God works to promote justice. No culture is exempt. So if we want peace, we must respect the rights of others as if they were our own.

The Concept of Education

A Chicano Theology would agree that since 1971 we were talking about the 'push-out' rate in Houston, Texas. Thirty-six years later, not much has changed in the percentage rate. In 1971, there were less than 15,000,000 Latinos in the USA. Today we are over 45,000,000 (actually, no one knows how many Latinos/as there are in the USA today). When *A Chicano Theology* was written in 1987, all the Chicana/o leaders agreed that the educational system had failed Chicanos/as. It is still failing them. If we adhere to the Calvinistic assimilative curriculum, I am sure it will not change unless Latinos/as organize and put a stop to this method of education that is so exclusive to people of color. In Costa Rica, a tiny country in Central America, the average school achievement is at least two years of college. Rumor has it that Cuba has a better education rate than we do. I know that they know how to educate Latino/a doctors, but we do not know how. We have to assimilate them to be good Calvinists before we can do anything with them. Instead of being part of the solution of healthcare for all, the American Medical Association in the USA is really a big part of the problem. The same goes for the training of native Chicana/o clergy and religious leaders. Unless you assimilate to a euro-centric formation process, you will not be professed or ordained. There has not been any change for Chicanos/as ever since Bishop Lamy of Santa Fe excommunicated Fr. Antonio José Martinez of Taos. The Chicanos/as have been in the Southwest since the late 1600s and still the Magisterium of the Catholic Church sees us as immigrants even though we were here together with our Native American brothers and sisters long before anyone else. Immigrants are those who do not understand what is going on in the USA.

People of color in the USA know exactly what is going on spiritually, economically and politically. All one has to do is look and listen or ask them. They will not lie to you. Those who manipulate the power structures also know exactly what is going on, but they do not care. Educational, economic and religious institutions of power know what is happening. The more power they have in the system, the less they want to change it. Power without a conscience creates inequality and misery for many. Power with a conscience could level the mountains of injustice. With the modern developments in technology and science, there should not be so much poverty and wanton misery in the world today. Injustice and inequality do not grow on trees, it is taught in our secular and religious schools. We reap what we teach. When it comes to injustice and misery, nothing happens by accident. Instead of our schools being instruments of liberation, they have become instruments of *'pansa llena, corazón contento'*. Nothing will change because as 'long as our stomachs are full, our hearts will be content'. Food stamps and food banks are not a liberating process, but rather a controlling process. What really authentic revolution worth its grain of salt since the beginning of time was started by people on a full stomach? I cannot think of one. We already have the tools for education as a process of liberation, instead of a process of assimilation. What we do not have is the courage, because we are afraid. Fear is a poor excuse for anything. Pontius Pilate washed his hands of Jesus, and we wash our hands of the poor and oppressed. Oppressors love to play the Pontius Pilate game. I would swear, if it was not wrong to swear, that Pontius is their patron saint. I have seen this scenario so many times in our secular and religious schools. If we would adjust the curriculums of the schools to the needs of the poor people, instead of adjusting the poor people to the needs of the curriculum, then education would truly be an educational experience. Lupe Angiano mentioned that for Chicano/a and Native American children, the educational experience for them was a process of mental retardation. With so many 'Pontius Pilates' on secular and religious schoolboards, it should come as no surprise to anyone. We reap what we teach.

The Concept of Chicano/a Leadership

I left this until the end because it is the central problem in North America today. It could be the central problem in the world also. Leadership today like yesterday leaves much to be desired. These lands are still inhabited by Native and Mexican Americans. We never left our lands like most other latecomers to America did. We trusted leadership that it would live up to its treaties. In neither the Native nor Mexican American treaties were the treaties honored. These actions were a direct premeditated attack on the American Constitution by White Americans. After that wanton attack, those leaders in power acted cowardly and not bravely. There were many White Americans who were honorable but most were not. These Americans were the exception, but not the rule. The grave inhumanity and grave injustice against the Native Americans, the African-Americans, the Mexican Americans and Asian Americans has never stopped. The objective is to control and the method is by any means necessary. I already mentioned this but now I want to put it in the form of a leadership issue. I mentioned before that injustice does not happen by accident. The leadership is not chosen by accident either. The problem with a democracy is that it is the will of the majority and not necessarily the will of those oppressed by that majority. Plus, if the majority is wrong then what are minorities to do? People of color cannot capitulate to the injustices against them. With five Amendments to the Constitution on voting rights, it is obvious that injustices happened and continue to happen. But I ask, why five amendments for the 'democratic' right to vote?

After the 9/11 retaliatory action by *Al Qaeda,* how many minorities consulted were Chicanos/as and Native Americans? Ward Churchill, in 2006, was finally crucified by the administration and the *alcahuetes* on the faculty senate of his school for his views on 9/11. Where is the backbone of the intellectual community when an academic Native American is being crucified? I knew right away that he would be done for because he dared to tell the truth. The truth is something powerful people in my country are afraid of because it is like the Devil fearing to see the face of God. You do not mock God and expect a reward. God does not work that way. I was hoping that the academic community would be reasonable, but I was wrong. My first instinct was and is still correct today. I remember writing a letter for Mary Daly against Boston College. I showed it to James Luther Adams who encouraged me to send it in. James Luther Adams was a great mind and a great friend. In his essay, 'The Theological Basis for Social Action' I saw the basis for the elements found in *A Theology of Liberation.* Two quotes I remember from him were: 'Pope John Paul II should stay at home' and the second one was, 'I believe Heidegger was with the Nazis'. He was right on both counts. He was the one who told me to always join a group and to read Antonio Gramsci, the great Italian intellectual. I am always hoping that at one point or another, intellectuals will see the light, but they refuse to see it. There are things hidden from the wise that God allows the humble to see very clearly. Poor people are poor because of political economics and not because of intelligence. My mother is a reader, but she cannot write in any language, yet her family is a highly intelligent group of people who go back to the Cherokees in East Texas. My father's family are first generation immigrants from Mexico. All my people have phenomenal talents, faith and a phenomenal intelligence. You have to be very intelligent to survive so many generations of neglect and oppression by so many negative forces around. I am sure other poor people, especially of color, can say the same about their families. You have to know the world of the oppressed and the oppressor in order to survive. You are constantly dealing with two intelligences and two spiritualities at the same time just to survive. Most oppressors are only playing one game, but the poor have to play two, the world of the oppressor and the world of the oppressed. Why were and are the oppressed people of color not consulted about 9/11? Because they know why we were attacked! It is no secret what the world powers do to the poor nations of the world, and mockingly they do it to them in the name of God. God will never be fooled and neither are Her/His poor. Both our President and our Congress's response was retaliation with the force of the mightiest army in the world. Afghanistan and Iraq are still defending themselves and they have already won. The World Powers do not know how to accept failure. They should consult their poor whom they oppress within their own boundaries, but their pride will not allow them. '*El que nacio pa papa pa papa*'. The poor just sit back and suffer and watch 'leaders' make fools of themselves. What can one do when those in power do not listen to the wisdom and cries of the oppressed?

What is a true leader in a Chicano/a theology? First and foremost, a true leader is she/he who defends the oppressed, like Biko, Cabral, King, Romero, Sánchez, Malcolm X, Day, Jones, Che, Chavez, Brown, Mao, Castro, Jesus, Huerta, etc. and the list could go on of the millions who have died for justice during the twentieth-century, possibly the bloodiest century in the history of wo/mankind. With all the advances of the technology and scientific discoveries of the last century, we are still at war using this technology and science for violence instead of for peace. Why? Dr Ricardo Sánchez, a Chicano husband, father, poet, prisoner and genius stated it this way:

Yes, it's more than let us (Chicanos/Chicanas) go. Perhaps it is White America, those who rule – I'm not talking about the average white person, even though they may have a $75,000 mortgage on their house and a $4,000 to $10,000 mortgage on their car. They are enslaved; they're in park. They can't do anything but continue in the same rut, going round and round in a circle, getting no where. Not those, those are not the ones who are the enemies. Those are also frustrated human beings, middle class, but hurting.

No, the enemies are the people with the real power, who dictate policies that are serving their own needs. I'm talking about those who influence the world. Those people should be the ones to become more humanizing, more ultimately human beings in concern and caring love.

Yes, they do have programs against us. There is genocide. Chicanos suffer the same kind of genocide that Jews have through our Indian reality, through our mestizo reality, through the destruction of our language, through the destruction of our culture, and through the imposition that tells us if we want to survive here we must assimilate! The only model we have is that stuffy linear model that says nothing to us about our spirituality. Our churches condone it. They haven't done any better. They work hand in hand with the growers; they work hand in hand with the industrialists; they work hand in hand with the prison wardens to destroy us, to pillory us in every way they can. Yes, we see it in many ways. We are abused, misused; we are killed.

It's not just let my people go; it is also stop murdering our people, stop murdering our ideas, our hopes, our needs. Stop murdering the need that all human beings have to respect themselves, existentially, philosophically, spiritually.

The cry, the plea of our people in this continent has been: 'Yes, let us be free. Once, someday, let us taste of it.' Not the freedom to go and kill in Vietnam or any other uprising. Not the new crusade against the new infidels, wherever they may be, for social, economic, and political aggrandizement, but the cries for peace, serenity, and a means to luxuriate in thinking, in creativity, in realizing that your children will eat food that will nurture their bodies, and that they will have access to material that will nurture their minds and their souls. Their reflection will be manifested throughout the social fabric, not as furtive, isolated, alienated beings who can put tattoos on their hands, arms, backs, and who will put graffiti on the wall to say, 'I too exist: I think; therefore I am.' The reason I think I am is because I can indicate it. I can write it somewhere, if only on my body or on a wall in a decaying tenement building in a barrio in El Paso, in Los Angeles, in San Antonio, and in Albuquerque. I have no other means of expressing my humanity because I have been kept voiceless.

Or perhaps it is a new Exodus, a new intellectual spiritual Exodus wherein people begin to reaffirm and manifest their humanity by being able to create. To create is to have the means to create, not the mind, because we all have the mind. We are capable of writing fine poetry, of creating beautiful music and painting fantastic pictures and becoming tremendous architects, but lack the access to do it. We need to be able to get into the process where the resources reside so that we can have the means of owning and of truly developing our talents and our minds.

That is the Exodus, the coming-out of these enclaves of poverty, destitution, and denigration into that world where our minds have value, where our spirituality can manifest itself, where we can walk beautifully and proudly. Then we won't have to just survive: we can thrive, all human beings can thrive. That kind of an Exodus, an Exodus out of poverty, horror, (torture) and fear, and pestilence, and ignorance and lack of education, medical treatment and so many different things. And realizing that medical treatment, a good education, good food, and all those things are human rights – human rights! – because the world belongs to all the people of the world, and not to the few who can manipulate, but to all the people of the world.

No, it is more than let my people go. Let us go into that world that is also ours, this land. Let us go into it in every way we can to create something we must create. It is not a question only of the master allowing. It's a question of doing it, in spite of the fact that some people stand there to be masters. It's a question of our no longer being slaves, or remaining cool, no longer being followers but creators because we have it within us as human beings to create a new way of life. It's a question of our saying that we truly love ourselves, that we truly love our children who are given examples of courage, not acquiescence. No more '*sí patrón*'. No one was born with an inherent right to be a *patrón*! No one was born with an inherent responsibility to be a willing slave. Those who are in master positions enforce the system by being despoilers of human life, desecrators in the finest sense of the word. They desecrate all that is humane and plausible. That's how I see it.' (Dr. Ricardo Sánchez in *A Chicano Theology*, 91–3).

I have no more to add than what this genius of a man has said for all Chicanos/Chicanas, dead, living, coming and to resurrect again. Amen.

Chapter 8

The Gospel is the Power of God for the Salvation of Everyone who Believes

Hwa Yung[1]

My father was born just before the turn of the twentieth-century in a village in Guangdong, China. Those were difficult days for a once proud nation that was in a state of serious cultural and socio-political decline, the result of a tired and moribund Confucianism, coupled with a blind traditionalism which refused to come to terms with the modern world. Eighteen years after his birth, the corrupted Qing dynasty was overthrown in the revolution of 1911 which gave birth to modern China. From then until 1949, when Mao and the Communist Party finally took complete control, China was in a continuous state of war, both with itself as well as with imperialistic powers, particularly Japan.

Father followed a military career through all these years, fighting both in the incessant civil wars and also against Japan, and eventually rose to a senior position under the Kuomintang. Yet, when Mao finally triumphed against the Kuomintang, he refused to join Chiang Kai-Shek, who fled to Taiwan. The reason was simple: as he saw it, the key reason for the Communist victory was the widespread corruption within the Kuomintang.[2] Indeed, he must have been one of the very few senior officers who left China penniless in 1949, because he refused to be sucked into the systemic corruption of the Kuomintang government. Father was not perfect by any means and, in particular, not without failings in private. Nevertheless, in his public life, he diligently sought to live out the Confucian ideal of the *qing guan*, the government official of impeccable integrity, who serves selflessly to bring about national salvation and advancement for one's country. But like many such officials in Chinese history, he saw the state self-destruct through cynical power abuse and financial corruption of the highest order. Thus he left China broken-hearted.

The family subsequently moved to Malaysia (then Malaya) at the height of the Communist rebellion in the country, when the British colonial government invited my father to help in counter-insurgency intelligence work. We grew up poor, but deeply proud of both our cultural and family heritages. Father also took pains to instill into our lives, through study of the Confucian classics, the same principles he had lived

---

[1]   Dr. Hwa has asked that the Chinese tradition of surname first, forename last be respected in his essay. In the Western convention he would write Yung Hwa.

[2]   The full story of the corruption of Chiang and the Kuomintang can be found in Sterling Seagrave, *The Soong Dynasty* (Harper & Row, 1985).

by. I can still remember the years when, as a restless and playful primary school kid, I was repeatedly punished for failing to memorize the ancient classics by heart!

Some time in my early teens, partly through the influence of the Methodist mission schools, I came gradually through a conversion experience to faith in Christ. That experience deepened through my high school years. But I never saw my conversion as a complete break from my past, except for the decision to stop participating in ancestor worship, an integral part of Confucianism. Perhaps even then I had begun to sense, what for me is now a settled conviction, that the Gospel of Christ brings to fulfillment in a most unexpected manner some of the deepest and highest longings of the Chinese tradition! Later I came to realize that this, together with the multi-religious and multi-cultural milieu of Malaysia in which I grew up, helped shape my reading of the Bible profoundly.

The Methodism into which I was baptized was strongly influenced by the prevailing Liberalism of much of contemporary Methodism in America. But gradually I found myself moving in my university years in Australia towards a more biblically-centered faith, shaped largely by mainstream Western Evangelicalism of the 1950s and 1960s. It was also in those years that my conscious theological pilgrimage started, and when my problems with Western theology began!

To begin with, I had rejected the futility of the Social Gospel which permeated so much of the Methodism I had been initiated into in my teens. I felt that it could only be sustained if we rejected some of the explicit claims of classical Christianity. Moreover, precisely because it lacked the full-orbedness of the Bible's message, it was insipid because it had little or no answers for our human inner spiritual quest. But the dominant strain of Western Evangelicalism to which I had gravitated appeared to be just as problematic, by talking primarily, if not exclusively, about evangelism and our need for conversion, whilst denying that the Church had any social responsibility in a broken and suffering world.[3] Like the Social Gospel, this too was clearly against any plain reading of the Bible and equally guilty of distorting its message. Moreover, the apparent dichotomy upon which Liberals and Evangelicals operated was inconsonant with the holistic worldview of my own Chinese tradition. This holism is clearly seen in the following passage from the early Confucian classic, *Da Xue*, or *The Great Learning*:

> The ancients who wished clearly to exemplify illustrious virtue throughout the world would first set up good government in their states. Wishing to govern well their states, they would first regulate their families. Wishing to regulate their families, they would first cultivate their persons. Wishing to cultivate their persons, they would first rectify their minds. Wishing to rectify their minds, they would first seek sincerity in their thoughts. Wishing for sincerity in their thoughts, they would first extend their knowledge. The extension of knowledge lay in the investigation of things. For only when things are investigated is knowledge extended; only when knowledge is extended are thoughts sincere; only when thoughts are sincere are minds rectified; only when minds are rectified are our persons cultivated; only when our

---

[3]   Although when all their good works among the poor, undereducated, orphans, drug addicts, marginalized and generally underprivileged are taken into account, pre-Lausanne evangelicals were often much sounder in their practice of Christian compassion than in their theology.

persons are cultivated are our families regulated; only when families are regulated are states well governed; and only when states are well governed is there peace in the world.[4]

With such a manner of thought, no dichotomy exists between the inner cultivation of the individual and the external transformation of the world.

The denial of Christian social responsibility emerged out of Protestant Fundamentalism's overreaction to modernity's Social Gospel in the early twentieth-century. As the heir of Fundamentalism, much of pre-Lausanne Evangelicalism held a similarly distorted theology. Fortunately, at this stage of my life, I began reading Evangelical writers who had a much clearer and firmer grasp of the biblical message. For example, in his exposition of Paul's statement, 'I am not ashamed of the Gospel, for it is the power of God for the salvation of everyone who believes' (Rom 1:16), Francis Schaeffer pointedly noted that 'Christianity is not Platonic ... Platonism says that the body is bad and is to be despised. The only thing that matters is the soul. But the Bible says God made the whole man, the whole man is to know salvation, and the whole man is to know the Lordship of Christ ... Salvation has something to say not only to the individual man but also to the culture.'[5] Thus in the context of our need for healing from all human alienations, be they spiritual, psychological, sociological and environmental, Paul could say, 'I'm not ashamed of the gospel intellectually because it is going to have the answers that people need ... because it is the power of God unto salvation in every single area; it has answers for both eternity and now.'[6] Any lingering uncertainty over this was fully laid to rest with the Lausanne Covenant of 1974. Its robust affirmation 'that evangelism and socio-political involvement are both part of our Christian duty'[7] came as a breath of fresh air in the midst of the confused evangelization-humanization debates of the 1970s.

In time I came to grasp more fully how the early incorporation of the Platonic body-soul distinction into Christian theology had laid the foundation for a pervasive dualism in western theology since the time of Augustine.[8] Indeed, Carver Yu, a Chinese theologian, has asserted that the roots of this dualism can be traced even further back to the pre-Socratic Greeks. The adoption of their understanding of reality as 'reality-in-itself,' uncontaminated by anything other than itself, led to the view that reality is made up of discrete self-subsistent things, with dynamic interaction and interpenetration of being categorically excluded in principle. This perception of the un-relatedness of the world gave rise to a dualistic model of reality

---

[4]   *Da Xue* (*The Great Learning*), 'The Text of Confucius,' Para. 4 & 5, in W. Theodore de Bary, Wing-Tsit Chan & Burton Watson (eds. and trans.), *Sources of Chinese Tradition*, Vol.1 (Columbia University Press, 1960), p.115.

[5]   Francis Schaeffer, *Death in the City* (Inter-Varsity Fellowship, 1969), pp. 74f.

[6]   Schaeffer, *Death in the City*, p. 76.

[7]   See, for example, Para. 5, 'Christian Social Responsibility,' in 'The Lausanne Covenant' (Lausanne Committee on World Evangelization, 1974), in http://community. gospelcom.net/lcwe/assets/Lausanne_Covenant.pdf, accessed 8 Jan 2007.

[8]   David J. Bosch, *Transforming Mission. Paradigm Shifts in Theology of Missions* (Orbis Books, 1991), pp. 215–7.

in the Western mind, in contrast to a holistic biblical one.[9] The overall result is that the universe is dichotomized into dualistic categories at every point: the individual and the external world, soul and body, spirit and matter, the religious as against the secular, and evangelism versus socio-political concerns. Thus, when it comes to mission theology, we ask: Is the soul more important or the body? Is salvation primarily spiritual (saving the soul) or physical and socio-political (saving the body and society)? Generally speaking, if Liberals have been guilty of 'horizontalizing' mission, conservative Christians have been equally guilty of spiritualizing it. In other words, both have been domesticated by the same dualism – only that they opted for opposite sides of the divide.[10]

With the increasing rejection of a dualistic worldview view because it is unjustifiable on biblical grounds, many are opting for a much more wholesome understanding of mission. Biblical revelation informs us that at the heart of the human predicament lies our alienation from God. Thus, logically and theologically, salvation has to begin with our reconciliation with God. But in practice we cannot always insist on starting with evangelism, irrespective of the immediate needs of the person or community concerned. Rather, the model that Jesus gives us in the New Testament is that he meets all at their respective points of need, before pointing them to their deepest need. Or, as Vinay Samuel and Chris Sugden assert, 'Any discussion of priority in the focus of the Church's mission will depend not on the concept of mission, but on the context . . . . The Jericho road sets its own agenda.'[11] Such an approach enables us to take the distinctive message of the Bible seriously and empowers us to address the various dimensions of the human seriously, without getting stuck in silly debates about which Christian duty has priority over others.

However, even before the above was fully resolved in my mind, I stumbled upon my second major problem with Western theology, which concerned the realm of the supernatural. I had grown up with the consciousness of the supernatural all around. Admittedly, the worldviews of many Asians are in truth rather confused, incorporating ideas taken from a variety of beliefs stretching from animism to theism and non-theism. Superstitions clearly abound. But there can be no denial that the supernatural is real and is there! Despite the fact that I had gone on to study science at an Australian university and published papers in that field, I could see New Testament miracles repeated before my eyes. Yet again, I found that I appeared out of sync with the Christianity into which I had been initiated. Here at least the Liberals were consistent but not the Evangelicals. The Liberals denied the supernatural both in the Bible and the present; but the Evangelicals fought tooth and nail to defend the miraculous in the Bible but rarely could cope with it in real life.

---

[9]   Carver T. Yu, *Being and Relation: A Theological Critique of Western Dualism and Individualism* (Scottish Academic Press, 1987), pp. 63–114 and 147–235.

[10]   Hwa Yung, *Mangoes or Bananas? The Quest for an Authentic Asian Christian Theology* (Regnum, 1997), pp. 49–55.

[11]   Vinay Samuel and Chris Sugden, 'God's Intention for the World,' in Vinay Samuel and Christopher Sugden (eds.), *The Church in Response to Human Need* (Regnum, 1987), pp. 128–160, and here p. 211f.

The crunch came while I was studying theology in England. One day a lecturer, a stout defender of the miraculous in the Bible, expressed in class some skepticism towards the story of Daniel's three friends surviving Nebuchadnezzar's furnace (Dan 3). He suggested that some natural event might have been embellished into a miracle story. Leaving the issue of the historicity of the book of Daniel aside, I could not resist a cheeky question. I asked, 'But in my part of the world, you will see regularly worshippers in Chinese and Indian temples walking on fire without being burnt?' His reply was matter-of-fact: 'I have never seen that so I cannot comment.' End of discussion! I concluded from that encounter that I could learn a lot of good Western theology from my theological teachers in England, but I will probably not learn much to help me minister in my culture. And what good would theology do if it cannot empower us for the latter?

This set me on another quest which eventually led me to realize how much the Western mind had become domesticated by modernity, with its roots in Enlightenment thought. The autonomous rationalism initiated by Descartes and the narrow empiricism pioneered by Hume had so emasculated the worldview of modernity that it had left us with a merely mechanistic universe. There is no place for the supernatural and, increasingly, there is no place even for God. Coming from my background, I could appreciate the blessings that the Enlightenment had brought to the world, such as modern science, technology and medicine, as well as the importance of rational thought. But I found it unnecessary to take seriously the skepticism that came with it, especially in the realm of faith and ethics. Increasingly it became clear that the lack of appreciation for the supernatural in Western theology had seriously crippled its reading of the Bible, leading to at least two serious consequences.

The first is that much of Western systematic and pastoral theology fails to address the whole area of demonic powers, both at the personal and the cosmic levels. I still remember the paucity of books in this whole area when I tried to read up on the subject during my years at theological college in the late 1970s (although the situation has improved very much since). I also found it almost unbelievable that serious scholars could simply reduce Paul's teaching on 'principalities and powers' to mere sociological structures. Meanwhile, I was trying to find tools and a theological framework to minister to people who were genuinely demon possessed or oppressed, or in some form of spiritual bondage or another. The fact is that unless we can handle the problems in this area, people in the non-Western world are not going to listen very hard to any proclamation of the Gospel.

The other consequence is that the Western church does not quite know how to fit the 'signs and wonders' of the Holy Spirit, as manifested in classical Pentecostalism and in indigenous non-Western Christianity, properly into its theological framework. Until recently, classical Pentecostalism which originated in Azusa Street (1906) has tended to be treated as some form of aberrant religion. The same attitude was taken towards the various versions of non-western indigenous Christianity which also took the New Testament teaching on the gifts of the Spirit and 'signs and wonders' seriously. But towards the end of the last century, with Pentecostalism and the charismatic movement becoming increasingly accepted in the West, together with the recognition that many of the most dynamic churches in the non-Western world take healing, exorcisms, prophecy, and other expressions of the miraculous seriously,[12] it increasingly looked as if, by New Testament standards, the real aberration is 'mainline' Western Christianity! With almost two-thirds of the Church now existing in the non-Western world, it is almost certain that Christian theology in the twenty-first century will have to take the supernatural far more seriously than it has in the past two hundred years.

After four years of theological studies in England, I started pastoring and teaching systematic theology back in Malaysia. Almost immediately, I ran smack into my third problem. Quite apart from the preceding two issues of dualism and the supernatural, I found many of the concepts and formulations in Western theology quite alien to the Asian mind. Of course, there is a basic core of Christian truths that is supra-cultural. But many of the theological ideas I had learnt were formulated in response to questions shaped by Western culture and modernity. And many of these just do not seem to make sense in Asia, except among the Westernized elite!

For example, we spent much time discussing the proofs for the existence of God in our Philosophy of Religion classes. Yet I found that, with rare exceptions, hardly anyone asks such questions in Asia. The existence of God or 'gods' is presupposed by almost everyone, and the question asked instead is, given the multiplicity of claims, how does one know who is the true God? Or, again, how does one explain Christian concepts in cultures in which these are quite foreign? For example, how are we to teach the idea of sin and guilt in Asian cultures where often the primary concern with wrong-doing is shame? We should never forget that what Hendrik Kraemer once said of African Christianity applies equally in Asia. He noted that it was not the consciousness of the sin that brought the African to Christ, but rather the continued contact with Christ that brought the awareness of the sin![13] Another example is seen in the use by Western evangelists of John 3:16 as a starting point for presenting the message of Jesus. But it would be folly to assume that 'For God so loved the world that he gave his only Son that whosoever believes in him will not perish but have eternal life' makes the same sense in, say, a Buddhist culture, where there is no belief in a personal creator God. Further, what do we communicate when we attribute 'love' to 'God' in the Buddhist thought world where it is passion that holds us in bondage to *samsara*? And who wants 'eternal' life anyway, when our primary concern should be to escape from the endless (read 'eternal') cycle of birth and rebirth?

Many other examples like those above can be easily given. Yet, there was hardly any serious systematic theology text in existence that I could draw on that even began to wrestle seriously with the subject from Asia's multi-cultural and multi-religious perspective. All the major systematic texts available were written out of the West from

---

[12]   Cf. Philip Jenkins' comment: 'The churches that have made most dramatic progress in the global South … retain a very strong supernatural orientation.…They preach messages that, to a Westerner, appear simplistically charismatic, visionary, and apocalyptic. In this thought-world, prophecy is an everyday reality, while faith-healing, exorcism, and dream-visions are all basic components of religious sensibility.' *The Next Christendom* (Oxford University Press, 2002), pp. 7f. See further my discussion in 'Pentecostalism and the Asian Church,' in *Asian & Pentecostal – the Changing Face of Christianity in Asia* (Regnum Books, 2005), pp. 37–57.

[13]   This observation may appear somewhat oversimplified, but is nonetheless broadly correct.

certain confessional traditions and/or responding to certain philosophical questions posed by modernity. Turning to the writings of many Asian Protestant theologians in my search for answers, I came across helpful pieces here and there. For example, Kosuke Koyama's *Waterbuffalo Theology*[14] was in some ways a masterpiece of how one formulates theology in a rural Buddhist environment, even if his subsequent embrace of an implicit religious pluralism has made his contribution somewhat less valuable than what it could have been. Similarly, some compendiums published by the Asia Theological Associations also provided help in wrestling with some of these questions.[15] But generally speaking there were two disappointments.

The first disappointment was that, despite initial helpful explorations with many ideas, few writers went further to discuss the subject matter in an in-depth or systematic manner. But there was a greater disappointment. Most Asian scholars, myself included, were trained in the West. And consciously, or unconsciously, most ended up domesticated by Western paradigms, especially that of modernity. Many of those in the ecumenical tradition have much to say about the Gospel and socio-political change, but their approaches differed little from that of the Social Gospel or the later liberation theologies of various shades. At the same time, they had embraced the Enlightenment denial of objective truth in religious beliefs, and adopted salvific universalism and, often as well, religious pluralism as their starting points. On closer examination, their theologies read like Asian versions of Western theologies of the more Liberal kind. On the other hand, conservative writers were hardly doing better, with their writings largely locked within a Western Evangelical framework. In other words, the tendency for Asian scholars, whether ecumenical or conservative, is to borrow heavily from their Western teachers and counterparts. Asian elements abound in their writings, but usually only superficially and not as core elements in theological formulation. It is like, as I suggested in my book, *Mangoes or Bananas?*,[16] 'yellow' on the outside but 'white' on the inside!

With these three issues troubling me (their resolution came only later) I almost lost confidence in my theological pilgrimage. Some of my good western friends urged me to go back to work on a PhD in the west. But I told them that I could not bring myself to go back to do a doctorate in systematics, even to the most illustrious of institutions, because I would die emotionally. For then I would have to spend the bulk of my energy and time justifying my presuppositions to Western teachers and examiners, whose Enlightenment mind-set would probably mean that they and I live in different thought-worlds.

Happily two things happened at this stage. First, I came into contact with the work of a network of scholars through the International Fellowship of Evangelical Mission Theologians (INFEMIT) and the Oxford Centre for Mission Studies. Through them I came to know people like Archbishop David Gitari and Kwame Bediako of the Africa Theological Fraternity, René Padilla and Tito Parades of the Latin American

---

[14]   Kosuke Koyama, *Waterbuffalo Theology* (SCM, 1974).

[15]   See for example, Bong Rin Ro and Ruth Eshenaur (eds.), *The Bible and Theology in Asian Contexts* (ATA, 1984) and Bong Rin Ro and Mark C. Albrecht (eds.), *God in Asian Contexts* (ATA, 1988).

[16]   I have argued this in detail in *Mangoes or Bananas?*, esp. pp. 147–219.

Theological Fellowship, and Vinay Samuel of Partnership-in-Mission Asia, all of whom were dedicated to developing a truly indigenous Evangelical scholarship in the non-Western world. The other happy thing that happened was that I decided to spend my sabbatical in the early 1990s working towards a doctorate in missiology at Asbury Theological Seminary. It was through these that I came to resolve fully in my mind the problems I had with Greek dualism and the biases of the Enlightenment, as well as the manner in which theology must be indigenized or contextualized for it to speak with power to a culture.

The result of this process gave birth to two clear convictions in my mind. First, I became increasingly convinced that Martin Kähler was right when he said that 'mission is the mother of theology.' One just has to look at the writings of the New Testament, the Patristic Fathers, the Reformers or John Wesley, to see that the best theology has often emerged out of missiological and pastoral concerns. Second, I came to realize that the success of the Western world and the dominance of its culture in the last two hundred years have been so overwhelming that non-Western Christians in general, and Asian Christians in particular, lost confidence in their own cultures and histories. However, for us to articulate a theology that can effectively address our part of the world, Asian Christians must recover a proper sense of confidence in the highest and best in their own cultures.

Over the past ten years or so, I have been working largely around the issues I have raised above (although my present responsibilities have afforded me little space and time for the task). For example, some years ago, I began work on a systematic theology that is set within the broad Asian religio-cultural context. Malaysia, my present home, provides an ideal setting for this task with its very mixed population of Malays and other indigenous peoples, Chinese, Indians and Eurasians, and wherein all the major religious traditions of the world interact. Hopefully it will be a theology that escapes both the dichotomy of Greek dualism, which has plagued so much of Western theology, and the debilitations of Enlightenment thought, with its denial of objective religious truth. It will also seek to take the supernatural seriously. This would include a fuller exploration of the work of the Holy Spirit, which does not merely reduce him to some benign inner influence in human life, but rather draws out the full implications of what Paul means by proclaiming the gospel 'through the power of signs and miracles' (Rom 15:19). It will further seek to examine the whole realm of the demonic, and its relation to sin and evil in the world, but without sensationalizing the subject as some Western writers like Peter Wagner do.[17] Where possible, it will also seek to respond contextually to the specific questions posed by Asia's religions and cultures.

Increasingly, I have found myself pushed back to raise fundamental questions concerning the task of apologetics in the Asian church. Admittedly this is not a very popular word today, a reflection perhaps of the loss of confidence in the Gospel in certain quarters. The politically correct word today, of course, is dialogue. But apologetics and dialogue go together, as Robert Wilken's comment on the Patristic

---

[17]   See my article 'A Systematic Theology That Recognizes the Demonic,' in A. Scott Moreau, *et al.*(eds.), *Deliver Us from Evil: An Uneasy Frontier in the Christian Mission* (MARC, 2002), pp. 3-27.

writings makes clear: 'In their works in defense of Christianity the apologists met Greek and Roman thinkers argument for argument, a dialogue that was carried on without interruption for three centuries and resumed in the high Middle-Ages.'[18] The product was Patristic theology which not only helped advance the work of the Church through centuries of persecution, but also remains the Christian Church's most important theological resource down the ages, apart from the Bible itself!

Given the obvious rise of the Asian cultures in the twenty-first century, it would be utter folly for the Church to ignore this matter if it is going to be taken seriously in the coming days. Like the Patristic Fathers, we must enter into a serious apologetic-dialogue with the deep structural questions of Asia's religio-cultural and intellectual traditions. For example, given Vedantic Hinduism's rejection of a personal God in preference for an impersonal *Brahman*, is ultimate reality personal or impersonal? And what would the intellectual and human consequences of our choice of answers be? With Buddhism, we will need to pursue the question of what is the 'self' and whether it is permanent or impermanent? If it is impermanent, then what is the point of pursuing enlightenment, since the person who attains it is not the same as the one who pursued it! But if it is permanent, what becomes of the fundamental postulate of *Theravada* Buddhism, *anatta* or no-self? And with Islam, given the present sense of being politically oppressed by the so-called Christian West and prominent debates over the rights of Muslim minorities in America and Europe, the question that must be pursued is how much does Islam itself respect and provide for the human rights of minorities? For both in history and the present, wherever Islam has been dominant, the full provision of human rights for minorities, including Muslim minorities and women, has always been ambiguous. Only through such an apologetic can the Church demonstrate with confidence, yet humility and respect for the other, that the Gospel of Christ does have answers for the deepest spiritual questions and highest longings of Asia's religious and cultural traditions.

This dialogue with Asian traditions of course brings us to the question of the relation between Christianity and other faiths and, in particular, the interaction between special and general revelation. Those who embrace religious pluralism, which asserts that all religions are effectively different paths to the same reality, have of course given up on the distinction between the two. But what needs pointing out is that pluralism is largely a product of Western Liberal religious thought, rooted in Enlightenment skepticism. This cannot be more clearly stated than by Tom Driver, himself a pluralist. He notes that pluralism is certainly not a 'universal' point of view, but one through which Western Liberal Christianity is now trying to make sense of the fact that the First World does not represent the totality of humanity. He goes on to state that, 'The agenda ... is certainly Western ... couched in Western terms, addressed to Western audiences, and aimed at the Western conscience.'[19] Indeed,

---

[18]   Robert L. Wilken, *The Spirit of Early Christian Thought: Seeking the Face of God* (Yale University Press, 2003), p. 14.

[19]   Tom Driver, 'The Case for Pluralism,' in John Hick and Paul F. Knitter (eds.), *The Myth of Christian Uniqueness: Towards a Pluralistic Theology of Religions* (Orbis Books, 1987), pp. 203–18; here p. 206.

despite its advocacy by some writers like Koyama and C.S. Song, few Christians in Asia at the ground level actually take it seriously.

But having said this, it has to be noted that the tendency among many Asian Christians is to think like Karl Barth that much of general revelation is pretty useless. I have elsewhere suggested that this too is an inadequate approach and untrue to the biblical tradition.[20] For the interrelationship between special and general revelation to be adequately addressed, we need to hold together in proper tension our respect for the highest and best in others' religio-cultural traditions, as well as our firm commitment to Christianity as a missionary faith. This brings me back to my father and his stand against corruption at a crucial period in China's emergence into the modern world. This story will not easily fit into traditional Evangelical categories. For here we have juxtaposed in history a corrupt 'Christian' President[21] on the one hand, and a Confucian scholar and soldier who diligently sought to stay true in his commitment to integrity in public life on the other. That would certainly be a good text to write a systematic theological essay on the relative merits of general revelation versus special revelation, which does not at the same time compromise the unique claims of the latter. But much homework needs to be done by the Asian Church before we will be able see an adequate essay on this.

My path to this point has been through childhood poverty, conversion out of a non-Christian background to faith in Christ, years of trying to find my identity as a Chinese Christian living as a citizen in Malaysia, a predominantly Islamic country, and asking through all these what relevance has Christ to Asia. It has brought me to the point where I have come to believe, in the footsteps of the Apostle Paul, that 'the Gospel is the power of God for the salvation of everyone who believes.' Like Paul, I too am not ashamed because it has the answers to the deepest spiritual longings and the toughest intellectual questions of human existence. This brings me to my last point. As Asia emerges into the world of this century, it is still a continent mired in poverty, corruption, totalitarianism, watered-down democracies, and denial of human rights and freedoms. Thus, despite the economic successes of some countries, one key question that continues to confront Asia is how can we succeed in nation-building that incorporates all the blessings of modernization and economic growth, together with social justice, democracy, civil society, political stability and peace? Does the Christian message have any relevance in twenty-first century Asia at this point?

I began the essay with the story of my father, of how he and his contemporaries sought to bring national salvation and modernization to China. Those familiar with the China scene today tell us that there are many in China, amongst them numerous intellectuals and cultural leaders, who are raising the same questions all over again. Interestingly, many call themselves 'cultural Christians,' in the sense that they believe Christian values have the power to transform both culture and nation, and are thereby

---

[20]   Hwa Yung, 'Towards an Evangelical Approach to Religions and Cultures,' *Transformation: An International Evangelical Dialogue on Mission and Ethics*, 17/3 (2000), pp. 86–91.

[21]   However, it should be noted that there are fairly reliable reports of genuine moral change in Chiang Kai-Shek's life after his move to Taiwan following the 1949 debacle.

attracted to it, even though they themselves are not professing Christians. Many of them are looking now to the Christian faith as the answer to the future of China. In one case, a scholar from the Chinese Academy of Social Science, the top think-tank of the Beijing government, is said to have expressed the following opinion:

> One of things we were asked to look into was what accounted for the success, in fact, the pre-eminence of the West all over the world. We studied everything we could from the historical, political, economic, and cultural perspective. At first, we thought it was because you had more powerful guns than we had. Then we thought it was because you had the best political system. Next we focused on your economic system. But in the past twenty years, we realized that the heart of your culture is your religion: Christianity. That is why the West has been so powerful. The Christian moral foundation of social and cultural life was what made possible the emergence of capitalism and then the successful transition to democratic politics. We don't have any doubts about this.[22]

This is an amazing statement by any measure and would be unbelievable, if not for the fact that many others, including myself, have heard similar sentiments expressed.

But should this surprise us? After all, even a secular paper like *The Economist* can say that, 'Democracy is the child of the Reformation .... The Reformation declared that every individual was responsible before God for the way he lived his life .... It took almost three centuries for that proposition to work its way through into the realm of politics, but when it did the result was, literally, revolutionary .... Each man and woman would have an equal voice in making the people's decision. That is democracy.'[23] Other scholars have said similar things. For example, Harold Berman, the doyen of American scholars on religion and law, argues that the concept of human rights, the legal framework by which they were sustained, and the psychological basis by which they were upheld in Western civilization were 'historical achievements created mainly out of the experience of the Christian Church in the various stages of its life.'[24]

A similar view has been expressed by M.M. Thomas, sometime President of the WCC Central Committee and well-known advocate of 'humanization' in the debates of the 1960s and 1970s, though in a different way. Speaking in the context of the 1950s, he expressed his conviction that the Gospel of Christ is 'the foundation of a true secular humanism'[25] by which we can build a better world for all humanity, and that in revolutionary Asia, socialism, rationalism and democracy denote forces that speak of liberation. He urged Christians not to play shy of humanist ideologies and movements, rather to enter into dialogue with these and other renascent religions, and to present 'the Gospel of Christ as the power which can redeem them from their "most terrible perversions" and reestablish them in such a way that they do not

---

[22] Quoted in David Aikman, *Jesus in Beijing: How Christianity is Transforming China and Changing the Global Balance of Power* (Regnery Publishing, 2003), p. 5.

[23] 'Islam and the West: A Survey,' *The Economist* (9.06.94), pp. 1–18; here p. 13.

[24] Harold Berman, *The Interaction of Law and Religion* (SCM, 1974), p. 72.

[25] M.M. Thomas, *Towards a Theology of Contemporary Ecumenism: A Collection of Addresses to Ecumenical Gatherings (1947–1975)*, (WCC, 1978), p. 29.

betray, but realize, their true human ends.'[26] One does not have to agree fully with Thomas to see his point.

Clearly, this aspect of the Gospel of Christ is not being discussed adequately in the Church today. But if Christianity is to make a serious contribution to nation-building and cultural rejuvenation in the present and future Asia, the Church must seriously engage with this issue, both theologically and existentially. Western Christians often appear reluctant to articulate this thesis too strongly, either out of fear of being charged with cultural imperialism, or because they have forgotten that the Gospel actually has given so much to their civilization! Then there are those who have bought into the secularization agenda, suggesting that democracy, human rights, civil society, economic growth, the end of corruption, political stability and so forth, will eventually emerge willy-nilly with modernization. But is that so? When newer nations today look at the West, what they desire most are the prosperity and the freedoms, set within and undergirded by institutional and legal frameworks that protect the weakest and the least. They are definitely not attracted by its gross secularity and increasing disinterest in spiritual things. They have looked at the grand twentieth-century Enlightenment experiment called Marxism, perhaps the most secular of secular ideologies, and found it utterly wanting – for it has produced neither the prosperity nor the freedoms they seek.

There is little doubt that over the course of this present century, the Christian Churches in the non-Western world have and will come into their own. The Asian church will grow numerically and missions will expand rapidly – though hopefully not in a triumphant manner, but rather through humble service, acts of reconciliation, self-sacrifice and love. It will pursue these in the confidence that the Gospel has the power to transform human life in its various dimensions for the better. It is precisely here that churches, both East and West, and North and South, should come together to articulate a fresh vision of what Paul's conviction, that 'the Gospel is the power of God for the salvation of everyone who believes,' can mean for the whole Church and the whole world. Certainly we do not have to be ashamed, because the Gospel of Christ does have the answers, both for now and eternity.

---

[26]   Thomas, *Towards a Theology of Contemporary Ecumenism*, p. 37.

Chapter 9

Mujerista Theology:
A Praxis of Liberation – My Story

Ada María Isasi-Díaz

Time and time again I hear myself saying that I am a daughter of the 1960s. Undoubtedly, the social movements of the 1960s marked me for life. By then I was living in the USA and was greatly influenced by the struggles of the Civil Rights Movement and the Peace Movement, then focused on ending the war in Vietnam. In January of 1967 I went to live in Lima, Perú. Being a member of the Order of St. Ursula, I had requested to work as a missionary. I was assigned to teach in a school for girls established by the nuns in a poor area of Lima. Shortly after my arrival I was told I would also work in the parish where the school was located, implementing the 'Council Mission,' a program designed to bring the teachings of the 2nd Vatican Council to every church in Lima.

The people who lived in that area were poor working class people, many of whom did not have regular jobs. Most lived in houses that had no electricity, so I had to be very realistic about the amount of homework I could assign since the students had to work by the light of kerosene lamps. They had no running water and usually the children were assigned the task of walking to one of the common faucets placed throughout the neighborhood to gather in plastic buckets the dribbles of water, which frequently dried up. Most of the streets had houses on only one side since the other side contained an open ditch in which the people dumped human waste as well as garbage. It was not unusual for the tubes placed under the intersection of the streets to get plugged with garbage and filth would spew onto the dirt streets, often flowing into the people's shacks.

Food was very scarce in these homes, as I soon learned. The school added a class each year and I was assigned to teach the oldest class, the founding class of the school. The second year I was there, when many of the girls reached puberty, some would simply faint in class, weak from menstruating. We soon realized that the vast majority were coming to school in the morning without eating anything. We were able to add breakfast for the students to the lunch we provided for them and also for all the other neighborhood children.

Lima was a wonderful place to be during the 1960s. The church was led by a young cardinal, a Franciscan friar, committed to the understandings of church that emerged from the 2nd Vatican Council. Both the Catholic Workers Movement and the Catholic Youth Movement were very active, led by priests, whom I got to know and admired, pledged to enable the poor and the oppressed to become self-defining and to change the structures that kept many in poverty. Extremely important for me was the influence of Sister Rose Dominic Trapasso, then director of Catholic Charities, a woman of great simplicity and indomitable commitment to the poor. It was during this time that Gustavo Gutiérrez, who developed Latin American liberation theology, began to write and circulate his first theological schemas. And it was also at this time that I got acquainted with the work of Paulo Freire, the Brazilian pedagogue who coined the term '*conscientization*' to emphasize that knowledge involves a consciousness of reality that goes beyond understanding to transformation. Praxis, dialogue, enablement, lived-experience – all of these concepts so central to my theological work I first learned from Freire.

One of the priests involved in the struggle for liberation and whom I went to for spiritual guidance recommended that I spend the first year in Lima listening and observing. Though this was not easy for me to do (for I am a great talker) I embraced this discipline wholeheartedly and observed intensely, absorbing all I could about what was happening in the lives of the girls in the school and the people of the parish. The theological and pedagogical understandings being developed at the time provided me with the theoretical framework I needed to begin to think from a theological perspective in a systematic way. Above all, however, it was the faith of the people that impacted me for life, personally and theologically.

One particular event marked me for life, the yearly procession of the patron of Perú, The Lord of Miracles.[1] Since I was working in the parish with both the men's and women's groups that organized the procession, I was invited to walk in the position of honor in the procession, right in front of the image carried on high on a bier decorated with lights and flowers. In order not to turn my back to the image out of respect, I walked backwards. The procession stopped often at altars prepared in front of different homes. At each stop prayers were offered together with more flowers and candles. Then one of the men, assigned for this very special task, would climb the bier and he would be handed the children to be blessed. He would lift them up close to the image and make the sign of the cross with them. It took us seven long hours to walk to the next parish where we left the procession for the night. The next day, early in the morning, we gathered for Mass at the neighboring parish to begin our return procession.

During those two long tiring days I struggled with myself, trying to be open to the experience I was having. But no matter how hard I tried I found myself time and again being judgmental, thinking that the people's religion was simplistic and bordering on superstition. Around mid-morning on the second day I had one of those experiences that are so difficult to describe. All of a sudden I felt as if something had cracked inside me. I started seeing what I was involved in and feeling about it differently. The faith of the people trumped my attitude of 'superiority.' Where before, I had seen ignorance; now I began to see a rich faith that supported the people in their daily struggle to survive. I began to understand how their relationship with God was not simplistic but rather an uncomplicated belief that God loved them and cared for them. I did not have the words back then but that day I realized why at all

---

[1]   Tradition has it that there was a great earthquake and that only the wall of this church with a fresco of the scene of the Crucifixion remained standing. This became the main object of devotion of the people.

times I must have an unequivocal option for the poor and why I must privilege their way of seeing and understanding reality.

I stayed in Perú for three years, then returned to the USA after leaving the convent. By then I had a thorough understanding of classism and economic exploitation, of the marginalization of the poor, of the systemic oppression suffered by two-thirds of the world.

It took me six years to find a path to follow in the USA. I eventually began to work as a Religious Education Coordinator in an inner city parish in Rochester, New York. Then, I had another life-changing experience. One of my friends made it possible for me to participate in the first Women's Ordination Conference (WOC), which took place Thanksgiving weekend, 1975, in the outskirts of Detroit, Michigan. It was an excellent conference that provided the opportunity to reflect on the sexism prevalent in the Roman Catholic Church and guided us to find ways of becoming involved in changing the oppression we suffer as women. I was born a feminist at that conference.

For the next seven years I worked diligently at making the ordination of women to a renewed priestly ministry in the Catholic Church a reality. I was part of a small group that established an on-going organization to work on this issue. I served on its governing body, called the Core Commission, and then I served as staff to the organization for three years.

Besides the activism on behalf of women of organizations like WOC, the late 1970s and early 1980s saw the development of a feminist theology in the USA. Just as Latin American liberation theology had provided me with a framework for understanding classism and economic oppression and for thinking about how it relates to religion and theology, feminist theology gave me the structure to study and understand sexism in Church and society. Little by little, I began to think more and more theologically; that is to say, I began to see how sexism influences religious thoughts, teachings and practices to the detriment of women. Just as in Lima I had been in the right place at the right time, where and when liberation theology began to be elaborated, now I was in the midst of one of the main movements that fed and interacted with feminist theology.

One day in the office of Women's Ordination Conference, a classroom in an old parochial school that had been closed, my colleague at the office and sister in the struggle, Rosalie Muschal-Reinhardt, read me a letter that had just come in from one of the women who had been part of WOC since the beginning. In the letter this wonderfully committed woman told us that she had to step back, that she was burned-out from being so involved in WOC. For weeks I thought about this and tried to articulate my expectations regarding the ordination of women and what role my involvement in WOC played in my life. Little by little I began to elaborate *la lucha* – the struggle – as a lens and as a theological category.

First, I started to wonder whether I also needed to step back. I wondered whether I was losing perspective, whether my life had no meaning beyond the organization and the movement for the ordination of women. Early in my involvement, with the effervescence that a new insight always gives me, I had indeed thought that in five or ten years at the most we could bring about change in the Roman Catholic Church. The sad fact was, however, that we were going backwards. Although the Vatican

Biblical Commission in April of 1976 had concluded that Christ's plan would not be transgressed by permitting the ordination of women,[2] later that year the Sacred Congregation for the Doctrine of the Faith, ignoring the conclusion of the Biblical Commission, issued the *Declaration on the Question of the Admission of Women to the Ministerial Priesthood*, which said, 'the Church, in fidelity to the example of the Lord, does not consider herself authorized to admit women to priestly ordination.'[3] Since we were making no progress, what was I to do?

For years my mother had signed off her letters to me by talking about *la lucha* – the struggle. She always has insisted we needed to thank God for the struggle and ask for strength to persevere rather than asking to be spared from it. My mother, even today at age 94, still sees life as a struggle. That same thought was also what I had heard repeatedly from the poor in Lima. They did not concentrate on suffering but rather on struggling against suffering, struggling to move ahead in life. This gave me a new insight into my commitment to the issue of women's ordination. My larger commitment was to justice, which I had come to see as struggling against economic oppression and which now I also saw as a struggle against sexism. The ordination of women for me has been a banner issue, an important specific issue that helps us to focus on what needs to be done to bring about radical change in the Roman Catholic Church. But I also knew that were we to convince the Church authorities to ordain women, in no way would we be finished with the struggle against sexism. Little by little, I began to understand what my mother had been telling me. Life is not a matter of this or that struggle but *all* of life is a struggle. If I saw my life as a struggle for the ordination of women, then I could indeed burn out, be discouraged, and lose hope. But if I saw all of life as a struggle, then no matter what face the struggle has, the struggle is a blessing.

It was also at the WOC Conference in 1975 that I met Sister Marjorie Tuite. A woman of great energy, an activist brought up in the Civil Rights Movement, and a brilliant tactician when it came to challenging societal structures. Margie became my mentor. One of the many, many lessons I learned from her was to 'make the connections.' At the WOC office we came up with a graphic of the interconnection between various forms of oppression – classism/economic exploitation, sexism, racism/ethnic prejudice, and many other 'isms.' The interconnection among different forms of oppression gave me an added understanding of the wholeness of the struggle, of how the work for justice for women contributed to working for justice for the poor. Just as the different 'isms' form structures of oppression that reinforce each other, so concentrating on the ordination for women could reinforce the struggle for justice in other areas such as economic justice.

But I was not yet done learning about *la lucha*. One of the women in the Core Commission of WOC was Sister Jamie Phelps. As a black woman Jamie was keenly aware of racial prejudice. Knowing that I had not been raised in the USA and that I had lived here for only a decade, Jamie warned me time and again about racism in the

---

2   'Biblical Commission Report. Can Women Be Priests?' *Origins* VI(6) (1976), pp. 92–6.

3   Sacred Congregation for the Doctrine of the Faith, *INTER INSIGNIORES* – Declaration on the Admission of Women to the Ministerial Priesthood (15 October 1976). http://www. ewtn.com/library/CURIA/CDFINSIG.HTM. Accessed Jan. 21, 2007.

women's movement. It was true that there were white women in WOC committed to struggle not only against sexism but also against racism. And it was also true that I had been sought after and welcomed by WOC. But Jamie was right. After the first few years in WOC, I began to notice a certain prejudice against me as a Latina.

During my years in WOC I had become a member of LAS HERMANAS, a national organization of Latina Catholics. Guided by my friend Yolanda Tarango, a Chicana nun, I began to understand the ins and outs of racial/ethnic prejudice in the USA. Having grown up as part of the privileged race in Cuba, even today I fail repeatedly to recognize the workings of racial/ethnic prejudice and continue to be devastated when I experience it personally. Through painful personal experiences, as had happened with sexism, racial/ethnic oppression became the third lens I use in analyzing injustice and struggling for liberation. As I became more and more immersed in USA society, I learned how historically the matrix of oppression in the USA emerges from the sad and pitiful chattel slavery system that prevailed in this country as a legal structure from the time of the colonies until the end of the Civil War in 1865. Despite legal advances made during the Civil Rights Movement in the 1960s, racism continues to be deeply entrenched in societal and personal patterns of behavior. Latinos, considered non-whites and often called 'brown,' are regarded by the dominant group in the USA as part of the racial minority, minority not in numbers but in rights and opportunities. And I belong to this so-called racial minority.

Also during the time I was working for WOC, Yolanda and I had teamed to do several workshops with Latinas in different parts of the country and I was moved, as had happened to me in Lima, by the faith of grassroot people, and by how admirably capable Latinas are of explaining their beliefs and the role of their faith in their daily lives. Listening to Latinas at these workshops and the work with LAS HERMANAS to give voice to Latinas in Church and society convinced me that it was time to write a theology book from Latinas' perspective. Yolanda agreed to work with me. In the book we wanted to present the religious understandings and practices of Latinas and we wanted, as much as possible, to allow the voices of different Latina women to be heard. We were able to raise a very modest amount of money, mostly from women's religious congregations, to gather groups of Latinas in different parts of the country simply to hear from them about God and how they related to God. For us the gatherings were a way of doing research, but they meant much more for the women. The very first group we met with referred to the weekend gathering as a 'retreat,' a time of reflection and prayer, and so did every group thereafter. For most of them it was the first time anyone had asked them about their beliefs, much less respected them.

We used the material gathered at these 'retreats' for the first elaborations of *mujerista* theology. This first round of intentionally speaking with Latinas about their religious beliefs and practices planted the seed for several theological understandings that I have been developing ever since. First, I began to see that *mujerista* theology was not only an advocacy theology, as is Latin American liberation theology, but that it was theology being done by those who are marginalized and oppressed because we are women and because we are Latinas. This led me to see that, differently from Gutiérrez's liberation theology, *mujerista* theology is not a second moment that follows liberative praxis, but rather that doing theology itself constitutes for Latinas a liberative praxis. This is what the women we interviewed then and continue to interview today say. Many of them have repeatedly told us how those weekends of theological reflection changed their lives. The simple fact that they were taken seriously and that their input was valued, affirmed them as persons or, in ethical terms, enhanced their moral agency. Doing *mujerista* theology refers not just to the articles and books that have been written but also to the reflection on their lives that influences the future actions of the Latinas women who reflect on the meaning and implications of their religious beliefs. And, for my part as a Latina woman, to claim the right to do theology, to write books, give lectures, and attempt to influence the academy and the churches, it is indeed a liberative praxis.

Second, the Latinas with whom I have worked for so many years have taught me the importance of *lo cotidiano* – the everyday.[4] *Lo cotidiano* is in *mujerista* theology a praxical, hermeneutical, and epistemological category. For Latinas, the struggle to deal with and survive *lo cotidiano* is very real. Their lives are enmeshed in *lo cotidiano*. They are preoccupied about today; they struggle to make it through today. To survive today they have to use their wits and every ounce of energy they have. They indeed engage continuously in reflective action – praxis – to make it to tomorrow. *Lo cotidiano* is the lens through which they look at life and it is also what they know, what they need to know, what they have to know. This is why I have come to believe that the greatest virtue of marginalized and oppressed people is that of trust. They trust that if they make it through today, tomorrow they will be able to face what comes and they will be able to move ahead. I believe that trust, the daily bread of Latinas, is part of the joy they have. Trust is what makes joy possible.

Third, the first round of 'retreats' with Latinas to gather information about their religious understandings and practices convinced me that we had to look for a name of our own. In the very first article I published about Latinas' theology I used the term *Feminismo Hispano*.[5] However, by the time I began to work consistently on elaborating a theology from a Latina perspective, I knew that the feminist understandings being used by women theologians were not adequate for the work I needed to do. In the book I co-authored with Yolanda, we talked about a 'Hispanic Women Liberation Theology.' After we finished work on that book, I realized the distance that exists between the kind of theology I am doing and Latin American Liberation theology, which remains the point of reference for all liberation theologies. In what became *mujerista* theology, because we take seriously that theology is 'faith seeking understanding,'[6] and because we claim that Latinas who reflect on their religious beliefs and practices are 'organic intellectuals,'[7] *mujerista* theology is done

---

    [4] For a fuller elaboration of *lo cotidiano* see, Ada María Isasi-Díaz, *La Lucha Continues – Mujerista Theology* (Orbis Books, 2004), pp. 92–106.

    [5] See, Ada María Isasi-Díaz, 'Toward an Understanding of Feminismo Hispano in the USA,' in B. Hilkert-Andolsen et al. (eds.), *Women's Consciousness, Women's Conscience* (Winston Press, 1985).

    [6] Anselm of Canterbury, *Cur Deus Homo*, 1.1, cited in Justo González, *A History of Christian Thought: From Augustine to the Eve of Reformation*, vol. II, 2nd ed. (Abingdon Press, 1987), p. 159.

    [7] Antonio Gramsci, *Prison Notebook,* eds. and trans. Q. Hoare and G.N. Smith (International Publishers, 1975), pp. 6 and 330.

not just by academics but also by grassroot Latinas. Besides, this new theological discourse takes into consideration gender and culture, a consideration almost non-existent in Latin American liberation theology, particularly at the beginning.

Two other elements played a big role in creating the term *mujerista*. First, African-American women theologians began to use the word 'womanist.' My work has been influenced by the first generation of womanist theologians, many of whom I know personally. I have always respected and tried to learn from their struggle against racism, which is indeed part of their daily bread. There was also the fact that several of us Latinas believed it was necessary for us to take power and name ourselves. We were tired of being a mere 'adjective,' a certain kind of feminism. We wanted to have a name of our own. *Mujerista* is an invented term. Later we learned it has been a term used previously in the women's movement in certain parts of Latin America, but our adopting it had nothing to do with the previous use of the term. I have tried to stay away from defining a *mujerista*. I have suggested only the broadest of descriptions by talking about *mujeristas* as persons who opt for Latinas, who have our liberation/ fullness of life as their goal because they see it as an important element of who they themselves are. Yes, this means that men can be *mujeristas*. Yes, this means that non-Latinas or non-Latinos can be *mujeristas*.

In the prologue to *Hispanic Women – Prophetic Voice in the Church* (1988) I gathered the main strands that initially influenced the production of *mujerista* theology and presented it as a cultural,[8] feminist, and liberation theology. The attempt here was to identify the main forms of oppression Latinas suffer in the USA and to associate *mujerista* theology with the struggles against those forms of oppression. Under cultural theology I included the struggle against ethnic prejudice. Calling it feminist was meant to highlight the struggle against sexism that *mujerista* theology seeks to serve. Finally, the liberation aspect of *mujerista* theology points to the economic exploitation the vast majority of Latinas suffer. *Mujerista* theology, by gathering these strands and weaving them together, highlights the culture of our ancestors and the one we are creating here at present as we come together from many Caribbean and Latin American countries and as we intermingle with other cultures present in the USA.

In September of 1983 I moved to New York City. I had left WOC but not the movement to change the Roman Catholic Church. I saw no better way to contribute to such change than by becoming a theologian. It was almost by chance that I decided to study at Union Theological Seminary (UTS) and I could not have chosen a better place. I went to UTS during a period when women professors and women students were at the forefront of the institution. UTS had been home to Reinhold Niebuhr, Paul Tillich, James Muilenburg, and other noted male scholars. But when I arrived at UTS, it was the women scholars who influenced me significantly. My advisor for seven years was Beverley Harrison. Her socio-economic critique of society and her contributions to feminist ethics helped bring clarity and focus to my own insights. Nothing influenced me more, however, than her generous spirit

---

[8]   I call it a cultural theology to make clear how seriously I take the cultural context of Latinas in the doing of *mujerista* theology. I explain that we have no choice about being Latinas but we indeed have a choice of what we do about the fact that we are Latinas.

with all of the students. I studied with Phyllis Trible, who instilled in me a love for the Bible and taught me to handle texts in ways that have proved very important in my use of Latinas' narratives in *mujerista* theology. Mary Pellauer taught me to be bold in my thinking and to break loose and venture into uncharted territory. Victoria Erickson helped me develop the theoretical framework for the ethnographic work that characterizes *mujerista* theology. Janet Walton was a wonderfully rigorous intellectual companion willing to embark with me in areas of study new for both of us. I also must acknowledge four male professors: Cornell West, whose critical philosophical thinking opened avenues of thought I continue to mine twenty years later; Will Kennedy, who had worked with Paulo Freire in Geneva and helped me to reinforce learnings I had started to grasp fifteen years earlier; Tom Driver, who challenged me to elaborate the intersection of theology and culture; and James Cone whose example in elaborating new theological perspectives was inspiring.

However, the richness I received from my professors pales when compared to the influence and wealth of learning I imbued from the community of women students who gathered at UTS in the 1980s. Angela Bauer, Pamela Brubaker, Katie Geneva Cannon, Hyun Kyung Chung, Marilyn Legge, Margie Mayman – all of them sister-scholars whose work and friendship have remained my mainstay ever since.

It was during the time I worked at two different parishes in Rochester, New York, and the time I was a member of the Office Ministerial Team at Women's Ordination Conference that I started to work ecumenically. In Rochester I met women ministers of other denominations. Since I was given the opportunity to preach in the Catholic parish where I was working, I became part of a group of women ministers that met every week with a woman professor of Old Testament at the local Catholic Seminary to study the texts to be read the following Sunday and to share ideas we could use in elaborating our sermons. In 1974, just as I was arriving in Rochester, eleven women deacons were illegally but validly ordained priests in the Episcopal Church. For two years I followed closely and supported Episcopal women who anxiously waited until 1976 for their church to pass legislation making the ordination of women legal.

Attending UTS, a non-denominational seminary with mostly Protestant students and Protestant professors, made it possible for me to grow in appreciation of the importance of ecumenical dialogue and relations. Then in 1987, while a PhD student at UTS, I was hired as Director of Program and Associate General Director by Church Women United (CWU). This ecumenical association with a long-standing commitment to social justice provided me with a unique opportunity to imbibe a true ecumenical spirit. Also, working for CWU gave me great exposure and I began to be invited as a speaker throughout the USA.

Public speaking has been important to the development of my theological thought. Speaking has always come easily to me, and I have the sense that I can think better knowing I will have an audience. The many meals and discussions I have shared with organizers of events where I have been invited to speak have been a rich source for my theological work. I have also relished the 'question and answer' time that follows my presentations. People's questions, their disagreements and agreements with what I have said, all of them have helped me to be clearer, making me take into consideration lived experiences very different from mine, pushing me to see implications I had not considered. My favorite way of writing an article or a book starts with meeting with Latinas and discussing with them the subject matter I am focusing on. After doing whatever library research I need to do on the topic, I present my ideas in public lectures. I keep working with the material, taking into consideration what different audiences say and new insights that come to me as I share my thinking with others. Only after having enriched the material by taking into consideration all that I have learned from others do I proceed to write the article. Then, if it fits into the subject matter I am teaching, I give the article to students for their input before writing the final draft.

It is a fact, at least it has been for me, that my teaching career has been my most prolonged and fruitful time of learning. I was hired a year after I received my PhD by Drew University to teach both in the Theological School and the Graduate School, which had been without a full-time professor of ethics for a couple of years. I was welcomed warmly and was hired with the understanding that I would re-establish the Christian Ethics program. I proceeded to do so, emphasizing that the focus of the program first and foremost was to be on Christian *Social* Ethics. I wanted the program to provide for students an opportunity to grapple with the philosophical basis of ethics and also to focus on moral development and moral agency. As I started to teach, I was keenly aware that I knew at best fifty percent of what I was to teach. Even if most of the material I assigned I had studied when I was at UTS, every week meant re-reading all of it and writing three new lectures, one for each of the classes I was teaching. Over the years I found out that only after I teach a class for the third time do I really have a good grasp of the material and can present it with certain ease. By then I am also aware of what needs to be changed in the course, of new material that has to be integrated, of new perspectives on what I have been teaching that someone has written about. The work of a professor is indeed never done! I find myself doing research constantly.

Important to my work as an ethicist and a theologian have been the international contacts and relationships that I have developed. The two main organizations I have worked with in this regard have been the Ecumenical Association of Third World Theologians (EATWOT), and the World Council of Churches. My life and work has been greatly enriched by knowing and working with, among others, Mercy Amba Oduyoye of Ghana, Hellen Wangusa of Uganda, Denise Ackerman of South Africa; Sister Mary John Mananzan, Sister Leonila Bermisa, and Archie Lego of Philippines, Elsa Tamez of Costa Rica, Tania Mara Sampaio and Sister Ivone Gebara of Brazil, and many, many others. Knowing them and their work has opened vistas I could not have even imagined on my own. Coming into contact with such different realities from my own has challenged me to see interconnections that I would have never guessed.

From 1997 until 2003 I was able to travel every year to my native Cuba. I had left in 1960 as a refugee when my father and mother decided they did not want to bring up their family in a communist country. I have always thought of myself as being in exile, and though I am grateful to the USA for the opportunities it has offered me and I participate fully as a citizen of this country, at heart I have never been anything but a Cuban. For each of the six years I traveled to Cuba I was able to teach at the Protestant Seminary in Matanzas. It was the President of the 'Seminario Evangélico', Miriam Ofelia Ortega, who welcomed me and made my travel to Cuba and teaching at the seminary possible. The last two years I was allowed to travel to Cuba I also worked in a Catholic parish in Santiago de Cuba, on the eastern end of the island. It was a blessing for me to work with Father José Conrado Rodríiguez on those occasions and to realize that I could contribute something to my own people, that in Cuba I could also be a theologian, teacher, and pastoral minister. Since 2003 I have not been allowed by the government of the USA to travel to Cuba but that has not diminished my desire to look for ways to contribute to my own county, to my own people.

I love to read; I love to teach; I love to give conferences; I love to write. But what I love most is to talk with Latinas, to learn how they understand life, how they handle the many problems and difficulties they face every day, how they continue to push ahead, facing life with a certain freshness and joy that makes it all worthwhile, and how their religious beliefs and practices play a role in all of this. This was what captured my imagination and my heart early in my life, walking in that procession in Lima. This is what continues to be at the heart of all that I do, of *mujerista* theology. I have tried to capture Latinas' understandings and ways of dealing with life in all the work I have published. The first book, the one I co-authored with Yolanda Tarango, *Hispanic Women – Prophetic Voice in the Church*, was published before I received my PhD. When we finished the book, we could not get it published. It was only thanks to the sisterly support of Rosemary Radford Ruether that the book became available in print in 1988 with a revised edition published in 2006. My second book, *En La Lucha - A Hispanic Women's Liberation Theology*, a revised version of my PhD dissertation, was first published in 1993. A second edition appeared in 2003. *En La Lucha* remains the best book to read by anyone interested in the method I use in *mujerista* theology.

In 1996 I collected a group of articles I had published in various collections, revised them, and published them in *Mujerista Theologv: A Theology for the 21st Century.* Some of the chapters in this book are old favorites of mine. The book opens with the article I published in *Inheriting Our Mothers' Gardens,* a book that Letty Russell invited me to edit with her, Kwok Pui-Lan and Katie Geneva Cannon. Also included is, 'By the Rivers of Babylon': Exile as a Way of Life,' the first article I wrote from the perspective of living in exile from my country, Cuba.

Mujerista Theology also includes one of my PhD comprehensive examinations turned into an article, 'Solidarity: Love of Neighbor in the Twenty-First Century.' This is the article I have written that has been most widely read. I have seen it used extensively in PhD dissertations. It is assigned in undergraduate courses as well as in seminary and doctoral programs. One day I received a call from a graduate of Drew Theological School asking me if I would be willing to send a greeting to the men in a prison in upper state New York where he was working. A group of prisoners were taking some theology courses (a program of New York Theological Seminary) and they had read my article on solidarity. I finished by going to the prison to teach a class, and the men wrote their own piece about what solidarity meant for them. This article is the basis for one of the chapters in the book that I am writing at present, *JUSTICIA: A Reconciliatory Praxis of Care and Tenderness*.

In 2004, Orbis Books issued a second book with articles I had published previously, *La Lucha Continues – Mujerista Theology.* The first part of the book, 'The Personal is Political,' includes three autobiographical articles in an attempt not only to identify my subjectivity but also to indicate the role my subjectivity plays in my theology. The second part, 'In God's Image: Hispanas/Latinas and Our Struggles,' includes articles in the four areas that I have been working on lately: reconceptualizing differences as richness, not divisive factors; a philosophical-theological elaboration of *lo cotidiano* – the everyday; the role of emotions in ethics; and reconciliation as an intrinsic element of justice.

My mother taught me by word and example that we have to embrace *la lucha* – the struggle. My friend Nina in Puerto Rico talks about *bregar* – the word used there to talk about dealing with life, about facing whatever comes and moving ahead. Cubans in the island talk incessantly about *resolver* – about 'solving' the situation, meeting the need whatever it might be. For me, doing *mujerista* theology is all of this: it is *la lucha;* it is my way of *bregar* and of *resolver.* I see doing *mujerista* theology as a praxis of liberation, as a way of making a contribution to the struggle for fullness of life for Latinas in the USA, convinced that no one can be fully liberated unless we all are liberated. I do *mujerista* theology in the hope of contributing to my church and to all the churches theological understandings that can enrich what they teach about the divine and about our relationship with the divine. I do *mujerista* theology to influence society, to call us all to be concerned about others and for others, particularly those who are oppressed – who are poor, marginalized, exploited, abused, suffering discrimination. I do *mujerista* theology simply because I love to take the insights I gain from Latinas, myself included, and fashion them into narratives that can bring joy to others, that can contribute to their fullness of life. I do *mujerista* theology simply because it is life-giving to me, because I believe it is life-giving to Latinas.

Chapter 10

A Tale of Many Stories

Emmanuel Katongole

How does a Catholic priest from Africa, one moreover trained as a philosopher for the National Seminaries in Uganda, end up teaching theology at a Methodist Divinity School in the United States, people often ask of me. Their question is often a mixture of curiosity and in some cases, disappointment. It is easy to understand the curiosity, for 'Methodist' Duke seems to be a long way from 'Catholic' Katigondo. The disappointment is often more difficult to discern, but it seems to be connected to a feeling that for an African-Catholic priest to teach and live in the United States involves a significant shift in and indeed betrayal of loyalties. This might indeed be the case, but it is not for me, rather it is for others, especially those who know me well, to make that judgment. On my part, however, I do not think that the intellectual, emotional and spiritual focus of work has changed much, even as the location has shifted from Katigondo to Duke. I still see my work as an attempt to understand Africa's complex history and performances and Christianity's role within that history. In this way, I hope not only to depict ways in which the church can shape a more hopeful future on the continent, but to generate a fresh conversation about Africa, one that is able to reinsert Africa within a re-imagined vision of catholic Christianity.

Trying to generate a fresh theological conversation around Africa, however, is not some abstract theological pursuit; it is deeply connected to the strange situation in which I find myself as a 'Resident Alien' at one of the leading schools of theology in the United States. Among other things, being at Duke has allowed me to see that even though there is much talk about a Southern shift in World Christianity, and more specifically about the growth of the church in Africa, Africa has not become the subject of serious theological inquiry in the United States, or generally in the West. On the contrary, by and large, African issues and concerns remain peripheral to the theological project in the West. In theology, just like in other disciplines, no serious attempts are made to engage Africa's history, traditions and the historical challenges facing African Christians. In the absence of serious inquiry, engagement with Africa comes to be reduced to Christian activism grounded in some form of sentimental humanitarianism. This is particularly disastrous for the future of World Christianity; for in the absence of serious intellectual/theological engagement, talk about the growing significance of Africa within World Christianity sounds hollow, or at best it is a hope based on the usual misleading generalizations and outdated clichés. Moreover, I have come to realize that without critical and sustained engagement with, as well as fresh theological scholarship on Africa, Western Christianity in general and western theological reflection in particular degenerates into a kind of solipsistic self-importance or trivial preoccupation. Accordingly, I view my theological task as one of providing a helpful interruption to the theological discourse in the West by pointing to the gifts and challenges from Africa. In order to provide such interrupting dialogue, I find that my speech has to constantly shift between the technical, purely intellectual verbiage of the western academic theology and the very mundane concerns for water, food and survival of African theological preoccupation.

That is why it is not only the content and urgency of the theological task that has been heightened by my particular context, but also the very style and methodology of my theology continues to be shaped by this intersection. Another way to put it is to note how this intersection has led to the emergence of the notion of journey as a central methodological and epistemological category around which my work revolves. For my unique situation as a Catholic within a Methodist setting, as a philosopher teaching theology, and as an African living in the United States requires (involves) me to be constantly on the move, both literally and figuratively, constantly crossing borders and boundaries between countries, disciplines and spheres of influence. If such 'traveling' has heightened a sense of nomadic or pilgrim existence – belonging to more than one 'home' but never really fully assuming any as the 'real' home – it offers new possibilities for the creation of new forms of 'knowledge' about Africa, about the world, and about the Church as the sign and sacrament of God's new future in the world. Attending to three of these intersections of my work: as an African living in America; as a philosopher teaching theology; and as a Catholic among Methodists, helps me highlight the sense in which notion of journey continues to shape the epistemological and methodological priorities of my work. This may not only offer an example of how global theological thinking is ever being shaped (and re-shaped) at the nexus of multiple stories, it might give voice to others – and I assume that is every one who does theology from a self-conscious position as a resident Alien of Global Christianity.

Journeys in and out of Africa

Even though over the last five years, I have come to regard Duke as my 'home', there is a sense in which I have never left Africa and Africa has never left me. Emotionally and intellectually Africa is not only my home, it is the focal point of my research, scholarship and indeed my work. In fact, when I accepted the invitation to join Duke Divinity School faculty in 2001, it was with the explicit understanding that Duke would fund at least one trip every year to enable me to return to Africa not only to visit family and friends, but to establish contacts between Uganda and Duke. Over the last five years, I have frequently traveled back to Uganda, sometimes for shorter periods and other times for extended periods of teaching in Uganda. My most recent trip to Africa was for a meeting with 36 key Christian leaders in the East African Great Lakes Region. The meeting, co-hosted by the Duke Divinity Center for Reconciliation, which I co-direct, was to explore ways in which the search for peace in this part of the world, so marred by conflict and violence, can be deepened. As with other previous trips, I was able to get a fresh and deeper appreciation of the gifts and challenges of Christianity in Africa. It is these gifts and challenges, stories of pain *and* hope that I bring back to my Western audiences, both in the classroom and at the parish where I serve. This means that my theological convictions and insights derive not simply from textbook learning, but are shaped through an ongoing engagement with Africa that these journeys make possible.

Over the years, I have learnt that important as communicating fresh insights about Africa is, cultivating a fresh conversation about Africa in the West requires and involves the transformation in the lives of the audience, which happens through journeys. I have accordingly invited and led various groups of students, colleagues and parishioners on journeys throughout Africa. The aim of these journeys is not simply to provide experiential contact with Africa, but also a reflective and transformative space through which specific forms of 'knowledge' connected with the imagination of new ways of being in the world are fostered. Accordingly, the African journeys are framed as a two week 'Pilgrimage of Pain and Hope' during which students, colleagues and parishioners learn from, reflect and interact with host African audiences and congregations. Another similar program allows Duke Divinity school students to spend ten weeks of field education at a parish in Uganda. Through these and similar journeys, new forms of knowledge about Africa are fostered, which not only offer a deeper understanding and connection with Africa, but also ways of interrupting the usual detached epistemologies that tend to distance the world of Africa from the West even as they purport to offer 'expert knowledge' about Africa. It is these new spaces, therefore, that are capable of creating new communities of fellowship between Africa and the West, between Christians in the so-called 'Mac-world' and Christians in the so-called 'Third World', in ways that both provide alternative spaces of identification and loyalties that transcend national, racial, and economic boundaries. In other words, the journeys both foster and become one way to live into that new future that the church is invited to be a witness thereof.

Crossing Disciplines

I was lucky, during my graduate years at Leuven, to come across the work of Stanley Hauerwas, now my colleague at Duke. I must admit, however, that it was only reluctantly that I began to read Hauerwas – for I had gone to Leuven to study philosophy, and Hauerwas was a theologian! Moreover, my pursuit of philosophy was very pragmatically driven. I wanted philosophy to help me understand the complex challenges and forces that shaped life on the African continent. Since my seminary/theological education had significantly lowered my expectations of theology as a discipline, I did not think there was a lot to be gained by reading the work of a theologian.[1] However, as I read Hauerwas, his focus on narrative within theological ethics not only struck me as true, but I was also able to see more clearly how human understanding is largely a matter of assembling narratives that help locate one's life in a particular history. As I read more of his writings (as well as the other theologians he was in dialogue with), I began to appreciate theology as a serious intellectual discipline that could contribute to historical understanding,

---

[1] See my 'Hauerwasian Hooks and the Christian Social Imagination,' in L. Gregory Jones, R. Hutter et al. (eds.), *God, Truth and Witness: Engaging Stanley Hauerwas* (Brazos, 2005), pp. 131–152.

and even more importantly, offer possibilities for re-imagining the future. With this discovery, I registered for a part-time MA in Religious Studies while I worked on my PhD research in philosophy. Working at the intersection between theology and philosophy proved extremely productive. While philosophy offered me the skills with which to understand the past and think differently about the present, theology helped shape my imagination about future possibilities. My PhD dissertation in philosophy on the work of Stanley Hauerwas offered me the possibility of working at the intersection of philosophy and theology without feeling the need to choose one over the other.

It is this intersection between philosophical analysis and theological imagination which is, in many ways, the main hermeneutical framework and methodological impetus behind much of my scholarship. Thus, whether the topic is poverty in Africa, African culture, the Rwanda Genocide, the legacy of Idi Amin or AIDS/HIV in Africa, I approach it in a way that assumes the need for historical and philosophical analysis is as integral to the theological task as the display of how a re-imagined future in Africa might look like. Without doubt working at the intersection *might* mean that my work is disappointing to theologians and philosophers alike. Theologians who are not used to viewing critical analysis and the foray into archeological perspectives – that seek to get to the underlying stories – might find my work too philosophical; on the other hand, philosophers simply wouldn't know what to make of the explicitly theological interest that drives my work. Nevertheless, it is now obvious to me that the intersection of philosophy and theology is not only necessary to understand the challenges facing Africa, but that it offers fresh opportunities to imagine a new future for Africa. Moreover, this opportunity to work between disciplines confirms my conviction that the theological task in our time must proceed not only with a keen awareness of what is going on in other fields of knowledge, but also in deep conversation with the cognate human disciplines of history, economics, anthropology and political theory. This task is made even more urgent in our time in which the multiple and complex interaction of globalized forces and ideologies isolate, marginalize and shape life and identities in Africa and in the Global South generally. Understanding these forces and ideologies requires of the theologian not only critical skills of social analysis, the ability to engage multiple disciplines.

The Church: A Different World Right Here

The intersection between philosophy and theology means that my work moves between critical analysis and imaginative re-description, or between understanding the present and imagining a more hopeful future. I find that these two tasks must always go hand in hand. An understanding of present challenges without imaginative possibilities for the future can be paralyzing; while an imagination of future possibilities that is not grounded on an understanding of the present challenges can be fantastic utopia. In the end, however, the task of theology I have come to acknowledge is not so much about offering ways of managing the present as it is about describing a new future that is made possible by the story of God.

This has implications for the way I understand the primary challenge of reconciliation. So many times 'reconciliation' refers to the difficult task of managing, mediating and mending broken lives and estranged communities in ways that help them to 'reconcile'. A more primary understanding of the mission of reconciliation, however, has to do with describing a world that is made possible by the story of God's love through Jesus Christ. This world is what Saint Paul describes as 'New Creation' in 2 Corinthians 5: 17: 'If anyone is in Christ, there is a new creation.' It is within this story – God's love in Christ – that Saint Paul talks about reconciliation and not primarily as a task, but as a gift, which God has given to anyone who is in Christ (2 Cor 5: 17-20). That is why reconciliation is, in the first place, a journey towards a new future or a 'New Creation'. Where the Church becomes both important and crucial to this journey is in its being a sign and sacrament of that gift – a demonstration plot of the 'New Creation', in which the new life that the story of God makes possible does become 'already-concretely' made or visible.

This is one reason why the notion of Church is central to my work, as a concrete form of political imagination, as one way of imaging a 'different world right here', a world 'gestated in the deeds of everyday life' as Jean Marc Ela taught me (see my *A Future for Africa: Critical Essay in Social Imagination*, 2005). Being a Catholic teaching at a Methodist seminary, I am constantly reminded of this vision of the Church as God's new future as I live and work within denominational boundaries. For the Church that is the point of reference for my work, is not the 'church' of the current denominations – but the Church as it can and will be – as the bride of Christ, drawn from nations, tongues, tribes and denominations.

The commitment to a new future, to a 'different world right here' has led me to privilege 'interruption' as a determinative theological category connected to the task of social imagination. The Church as new future is 'gestated in the deeds of everyday', and in very concrete signs and gestures that so often emerge as Sallie McFague's 'wild spaces' within the stubborn persistence of the present world. That is why, what excites me about the language of global Christianity is not simply its statistical shift southward, or the conservative or neo-conservative appeal of its expression in the Global South, but whether such a Christianity is able to interrupt in fresh and renewing ways the performance of our present Western-dominated world marked by inequality, poverty, violence and consumerism. What excites me is whether such a Christianity is able to shape 'wild spaces' through which a new future begins to take shape; and whether in the ambiguous performance of our time, we can discern something of genuine 'demonstration plots' of God's 'New Creation'.

It is the quest and fostering of such that energizes and drives my work and keeps me going in the strange place called Duke and in a strange country called America. It is because I have been set on a journey towards that 'New Creation' and have come to realize that being set on that journey involves living and working at different locations, using whatever gifts are at hand; constantly on a journey, grounded in the present, but ever straining to see and live in a new future, a different world right here.

Chapter 11

Indigenous Peoples in Asia:
Theological Trends and Challenges

Wati Longchar

The development of contextual theologies is part of the larger movement of liberation and self-hood occurring in the two-thirds world. Though contextualization has been a way of doing theology throughout the history of Christian thought, the recent emerging contextual theologies in the two-third world, such as dalit theology, minjung theology, feminist theology, etc., significantly differ in their methodology, approach, focus and content from the dominant traditional theological discourses. However, although liberation is the primary focus and goal of present contextual theologies, they also differ considerably in their approach to liberation. For example, feminist/womanist theology reflects on the struggle of women in male-dominated structures and its primary commitment is women's liberation. Black theology reflects on the 'Black experience' and the struggle of the Black people from various forms of racial prejudices and discrimination. The Minjung Theology is a product of the struggle of the Korean people against the dictatorial regime particularly in the 70s. The Dalit theology's main focus is to dismantle the oppressive caste structure and liberate the dalits from various forms of caste discrimination, etc. Similarly, indigenous people's theology, my own experience and theology, also differs from other contextual or dominant theologies. Therefore, this paper will attempt to highlight major trends, methodology and distinctiveness of indigenous people's theology.

Indigenous People and their Context

There is no universally accepted definition of 'indigenous people'. They are identified as tribals, *adivasi*, ethnic minorities, native, aborigines or 'Indians'. In many countries they are the 'first peoples' in the land, but always a minority group. A working definition used by the United Nations Sub-Commission on the Prevention of Discrimination and Protection of Minorities is useful:

> Indigenous communities, people and nations, are those which having an historical continuity with pre-invasion and pre-colonial societies that developed on their territories, consider themselves distinct from other sectors of the societies now prevailing in those territories, or parts of them. They form at present non-dominant sectors of society and are determined to preserve, develop and transmit to future generations their ancestral territories, and their ethnic identity, as the basis of their continued existence as peoples in accordance with their own cultural patterns, social institution and legal system.

Socially, indigenous people are the most exploited and divided people in the world. Their history is a history of defeat, suffering, and oppression. They have suffered discrimination, genocide, exploitation and alienation in different stages of their history. As a result of many years of slavery and subjugation, the indigenous people have lost their self-esteem and confidence, which has developed into a feeling of inferiority that prevails even today. In the eyes of the dominant communities, indigenous people are looked down upon as backward, primitive and uncivilized people living in the hills and forests. The term 'tribal', 'indigenous', etc., then itself carries a very strong pejorative, negative and derogatory meaning. Further, in a caste-dominated society, such as India, the indigenous people such as myself suffer the stigma of being untouchables.

Politically, they are the most powerless people. Within nation-states, indigenous people are not only economically marginalized, but also politically disenfranchised. Political oppression, militarization and all forms of ethnocidal attack take place every day. Violence, conflict and killing become every-day affairs and realities. Inter- and intra-communities clashes are on the increase. Everywhere we hear indigenous peoples reclaiming and reasserting their right to self-determination, including: (1) the right to the ownership of their lands as the territorial base for the existence of their populations; (2) the right to use, manage and dispose of all natural resources found within their ancestral lands; (3) the right to control their own economies, and the right to economic prosperity; (4) the right to restore, manage, develop and practise their culture, language, traditions and way of life in accordance with their worldview, and to educate their children in them; (5) the right to determine the form of self-government, and to uphold indigenous political systems; (6) the right to engage in foreign relations and trade if they so desire; (7) the right to form alliances and federations with other indigenous peoples for the attainment of common goals; and (8) the right to a life of peace and security.[1]

In recent years, a peculiar form of alienation, injustice and humiliation is being enforced with fast-emerging globalization. With the accelerating deterioration of the global economic and political situation, the indigenous people face further marginalization and graver threats of continuity and sustainability. Indigenous people all over the world suffer many forms of injustice. Two examples may be cited here in displacement and suppression. In different parts of the world, indigenous people have become the victims of big reservoirs, mega projects, wildlife sanctuaries, mines, industries, etc. They are forcefully evicted from their ancestral land and the abode of the various spirits they worship, using repressive measures and often without proper compensation. They are simply ignored, silenced and despised, all in the name of development, so that the indigenous people's rights and their existence are completely ignored and the indigenous people who are already powerless and exploited are further reduced to powerlessness and bondage. Being thus improvised and disposed, people flee in large numbers to the cities to eke out their existence around slums and shanties in abject poverty and misery.

---

[1]   Colin Nicholas, 'A Common Struggle: Regaining Control', in C. Nicholas and R. Singh (eds.), *Indigenous Peoples of Asia – Many People, One Struggle* (Asia Indigenous Peoples Pact, 1996), p. 9.

Since the dominant societies do not listen to their cries and do not recognize them with human rights and dignity, some indigenous people have taken up armed struggle. Governments, instead of recognizing this movement as a justice issue, try to suppress the movement by military power. In the process, many villages were burnt to ashes, not only once, but three or four times and many innocent people have been killed. Churches were used sacrilegiously as concentration camps. Worshippers were beaten up or tortured to death and, to add to this, women were raped even on the pulpit of worship. Such human rights violations go on and on in many places in Asia and elsewhere. Many people continue to live in tears, pain, fear and suffering. All that people can do is to weep silently within their hearts. Indigenous people continue to experience such misery, pain and humiliation all over the world. We hear cries of indigenous people in Aotearoa New Zealand, Australia, Bangladesh, India, Sri Lanka, Indonesia, Japan, Myanmar, Philippines, Taiwan, Thailand, Fiji and many other places.

Theological Development: An Historical Overview

The history of Christianity among indigenous communities in many parts of Asia is between 150 and 200 years old. The Christian missionaries were the first people to come and work for the liberation of the people. They transformed the society by abolishing some of evil practices, such as slavery, headhunting, lavish feasting, etc. Many modern institutions were first introduced by the church – the first school, the first hospital, the first translation work and the first printing press among many others. These all changed traditional societies. However, Christian missions, no matter which denomination or society, all considered themselves 'superior' and consistently maintained an exclusive attitude towards the traditional religion and cultures. They came with a strong view to conquer 'other worlds' by Christian faith. Conversion was understood in terms of replacement of the old ways of life, including rejection of traditional cultures and value systems. Today, many people have forgotten their traditional value system. The church in Asia is predominantly poor and the majority of Christian communities in India, Myanmar, Thailand, Indonesia, Bangladesh, Malaysia and Nepal are from indigenous communities.

Roughly, we may divide the history of the development of Christian theology among indigenous people into three stages:

Receiving Stage (1800–1950s)

During this period, the churches in most Asian countries were under Western missionaries. All the decision-making, material and human resources for mission work were controlled and came from the 'mother churches'. Churches were required to implement the policies or decisions that were made thousands of miles away. In their effort to contextualize theology, the missionaries pursued the 'Translation Method' of doing theology. Perceiving that the Western culture is superior and the only valid expression of Christian faith, they attempted to translate the theological formulations of the 'mother' churches abroad in appropriate native languages by means of adopting and adapting local terminologies, idioms and categories.[2] It was thought that Christian faith developed in the west is *the unchanging truth for all ages and for all contexts*, and should be accepted without any question. Therefore, native culture and traditions were never considered valuable resources for doing theology. Christians who participated in traditional festivals were excommunicated from the church. Drums, traditional songs, dances and value systems were condemned as evils and prohibited among the believers. There was very little or no awareness of the religio-cultural experience of the people. Theology was alien to the people; it spoke an alien language and ideas. Theology was outside of the people's reality. God's revelation was accepted in a very narrow way reducing indigenous people's religion and culture as mere *preparatio evangelii*. It was a period of receiving without any question. Theology was formulated elsewhere, imported from outside and taught by outsiders. The church and its theology was a stranger in the society.

Learning Stage (1950s–1980)

During the 1950s and 1960s, the national movement, post-independence reconstruction, nation-state secular democracy, fight to end poverty, and development of infrastructures were some of the major concerns in Asia. The struggle for self-identity of the church, unity of the church and mission and indigenization or enculturation of theology became a priority for the churches in Asia. During this period many Western missionaries left or could not continue their mission work because of political reasons. This caused painful experiences of leadership transition within the church. The churches who were still struggling to stand on their own were left without trained leaders. However, the absence of Western missionaries created more space for local people to exercise their rights, responsibilities and leadership in the church. The legacies such as education and health care services were continued under the leadership of local leaders. The propagation of the Gospel among different communities or groups by their own initiative, the importance of promoting wellbeing and social justice and safeguarding human rights are noteworthy, as are three other theological developments or models of theology.

The *philosophical model* was borne in the wake of nationalism, particularly during the 1940s, when many Asian theologians became critical of missionary theology. They began to use freely the concepts, doctrines and symbols of other religions, especially Hinduism, Buddhism, Taoism, etc. in doing theology. They tried to work out theological hermeneutics in terms of Hindu/Buddhist/Taoist philosophical thought patterns and thus, theological language became highly abstract and rational. Unfortunately, like the other dominant theological reflections in the West, such a theological approach became abstract and intellectual exercises unrelated to the real life situation of the people. It gave a notion among Asian Christian thinkers that the indigenous people's spirituality is not philosophically deep enough to articulate

---

[2]   O.V. Jathana, 'Indian Christian Theology: Methodological Reflection', *Bangalore Theological Forum,* XVIII(2–3), (1986): 71.

theology. The indigenous peoples' view of life and spirituality were undermined and discarded in doing theology. People studied indigenous culture and beliefs simply from the traditional missiological perspective as a dark world to be conquered. People did not think or could not imagine that the cultural values and spirituality of indigenous people can also enrich and help in understanding and contextualizing Christian faith in the cultural setting of the people. Such a one-sided theological paradigm again alienated indigenous people from their own religion and cultures.

In the 1970s and 1980s theologians such as Paul Devanandan, Rymond Panikkar, S. Samartha, and S.C. Song, to name a few, made significant contributions with the employment of the *dialogical model* to do theology. A central theological claim of this model is that without taking into account the unacknowledged riches of God's work with the whole of humanity and other segments of God's creation, Christian theology cannot become authentic and liberative. Theology is seen as a product of creative and active engagement in dialogue with people of other living faiths and ideologies. Dialogical theology is to be celebrated for liberating God's revelation from the monopoly of Christians. Although the advocates of dialogical method were not always sympathetic and sensitive to indigenous people's spirituality, culture and religion, the affirmation of God's revelation and lordship over the world, in all cultures and religions widened the understanding of the mystery of God. In spite of the ambiguous nature of culture, God works in and through all religions and cultures. This understanding has created awareness to appreciate and respect the differences of others and also one's own spirituality, religion and cultures. Though some of the evangelicals are very critical of the dialogical method, arguing that it sacrifices the uniqueness of Christian faith, there is a growing awareness among younger scholars that we should go back to the roots to make Gospel rooted and meaningful.

Initially, liberation theology in Asia was greatly influenced and shaped by the Latin American liberation methodology. The indigenous communities, women and the other marginalized movements have widened the horizon of liberation theology from its Latin American impetus. Along with economic and political issues, the cultural and religious dimensions of discrimination are taken seriously in liberation theologies in India. It has influenced people to reread the Scripture from the perspective of the poor and oppressed in their struggle for justice and freedom. Commitment to the victims, the oppressed and struggling poor as the basis and the starting point of theology has inspired the alienated indigenous people to discover their identity, right and dignity. It has motivated people to engage themselves in new ways of doing theology by relating the Gospel to the socio-politico-cultural realities.

Self-theologizing Stage (1990s–present)

After the departure (even during the missionary era in some churches) of missionaries, the three self-movement (self-government, self-supporting, and self-propagation) in the church was launched by many churches in Asia. The contribution of Chinese churches is significant in this movement. Today we can proudly say that many churches are able to stand on their own feet in terms of support and mission. However, one important aspect was left out, e.g. 'self-theologizing'. *Self-theologizing* was never considered as an important component for the self identity of the church until recently. This period of self-theologizing is now a dominant model of theological undertaking. In it scholars from the other regions can help to widen the theological perspective of a people. However, there is a difference between the *sympathetic* and *emphatic* theology. The indigenous people themselves must do their own theology relevant to their context. *We* must work for *our* own liberation and transformation. It was only in the 1990s that many churches in Asia recognized the importance of 'self-theologizing' to make the church and its mission rooted in the actual life of the people.

Theology and Indigenous People's Spirituality

Indigenous people's theology is a newcomer and this emerging theology among the alienated minorities may be called 'Indigenous theology'. It is a people's theology born out of the experiences of various forms of injustice and exploitation in the context of their assertion for right and identity. It is a theology that attempts to express Christian faith in socio-cultural, religious, traditional and liturgical thought patterns of the people. Indigenous theology is a resistance theology – resistance to affirm justice, identity, dignity and wholeness of land and all its inhabitants. The experiences of oppressions and hardships, and their traditional stories, myths, symbols, dances, songs, and their connectedness to land and environment become the vital resources for doing theology. It reflects on the issue of ethnic, cultural and political identities of people from the subject of people, land and Sacred Power to give them hope.

The indigenous people's theology is a contextual theology, a theology from 'below' and 'underside of history'. It aims to liberate them from their inferiority complex, from oppression and discrimination by attempting to rediscover the liberative motifs in their cultures and religion, and by reinterpreting the Bible and Christian traditions from the perspective of people. Hence, the focus and goal of the indigenous theology is liberation and transformation. It aims to restore their self-identity and dignity by creatively engaging with the Gospel and culture in their struggle for social, economic, religious, cultural, political and ecological justice. In the process of working for their own liberation and transformation, and creative participation in wider society, the indigenous people work for the liberation of both the oppressors and the oppressed. It is, therefore, a theology that includes liberation of the whole of humanity and of the entire God's creation.

Methodologically speaking, the point of departure of the indigenous theology from the other contextual theologies such as dalit and minjung theologies is that, the indigenous theology seeks liberation from the perspective of 'land' because it is the land that sustains and nourishes people and give them an identity. Among the indigenous people, their history, culture, religion, spirituality and even the Sacred Power cannot be conceived without 'creation/land' or 'space'. The land and its inhabitants are two aspects of one reality. Human liberation will be void and empty without affirming the integrity of the goodness of land and its resources. Liberation without land is not liberation. It will lead to slavery and destruction. Therefore, the land and its resources that sustain and nourish all beings and give them an identity and selfhood is not merely a justice issue to be set alongside other justice concerns. It is the foundation of history, existence and identity.[3] Poverty, war, oppression, ethnic conflict and identity problems cannot be understood or solved without relating to integrity of creation/land. Justice to creation/land becomes very central to liberation and human dignity and fullness of life. That is why doing justice to 'land' is the starting point of the indigenous people's theology and their search for liberation. Commitment and dedication to the harmony of creation/land springs forth in love, nurture, care and acceptance. This methodological priority of justice to land is essential not only because of their 'earth-centred' worldview and tradition, but because of our contemporary ecological crisis, misuse of resources, market culture, war for oil and survival crisis of many people. This methodological priority of doing justice to land is the primary departure from the other contextual theologies.

Christian theology as an ongoing reflective activity of the faith experience of the people in a given context, and one cannot do theology without reflecting on the cries, stories, desires and longings of the struggling people. The history of human life has many dimensions and they are all resources for doing theology. I would like to elaborate just one dimension – *Culture*. While the Gospel frees people from their bondage, it is culture that sustains and nourishes people's identity. It is the worldview of the people. In spite of its ambiguous nature, the work of God is immanent in all culture. God's presence is manifested in land and in every culture, albeit differently and imperfectly. There are no people and culture without God and every culture possesses some forms of divine manifestations. Therefore, culture is one of the most important resources for doing theology. There is no authentic theology without culture.

As other communities, the indigenous people also uphold a very distinctive cultural value system. Culture has both liberative and oppressive elements. The task of theology is to challenge and transform the oppressive elements, recover and affirm, and integrate the life-affirming values into our life. The indigenous worldviews differ from one community to another; however, it may be relevant to point out a few common elements of traditional culture to show the importance of culture in doing theology. To make our focus clear, I would like to make a random comparison between the indigenous and the dominant Christian views of reality:

---

[3]   For this insight, I owe a deep gratitude to Prof. George Tinker's article on 'American Indian & the Art of the Land' which appeared in *Voices From the Third World,* Vol. XIV/2 (1981) and 'Spirituality and Native American Personhood: Sovereignty & Solidarity', in K. Abraham and B. Mbuy (eds.), *Spirituality of the Third World* (Orbis Books, 1994), pp. 127–8.

Traditional Western 'Christian' View	Traditional Indigenous View
Humanity is the ontological basis of all realities. Perceives everything from anthropocentric perspectives	The land is the basis of all realities – human selfhood and identity. Perceives all realities from creation perspectives.
Realities are perceived dualistically. A sharp distinction is maintained in understanding life. Dichotomic in thinking.	No sharp dualism. There is no clear-cut distinction between sacred and secular, religion and non-religion, etc. Holistic in thinking.
God's self is seen in history, especially in human history.	The self of the Supreme Being is seen in creation and an inseparable relationship is maintained.
Jesus Christ is the focal point of reference of all religious activities.	No historical person in which their religion is centered. The earth is the focal point of reference and all religious activities are centered on the soil.
There are written creeds, scripture, etc. Scripture is sacred and central for faith.	Though oldest religion, there is no scripture or creed. The earth is sacred and central for life.
Nature is something detached or outside of God.	We cannot perceive the Supreme Being apart from creation. God is in creation.
Task orientation. A person is measured by what he or she performs. The task is the focal point. Very much achievement focus and competition oriented. Saving over giving.	Person orientation. Relationship between individuals in society is more important than the simple performance of tasks. Cooperation is valued more. Giving over saving.
Manipulation of environment. There is no sacred in God's world. Exploit as much as possible to extract profit.	Adaptation to environment. The world is sacred. It is our mother. How can we sell and exploit our mother!
Highly individualistic.	Highly group-oriented.

Such view of life is not primitive and uncivilized. It is just a difference of emphasis and priority. The indigenous people give more priority to community and preservation of land/space. These values are also not mere abstract concepts, but part of people's life and existence. In spite of the process of Christianization and modernization, such value systems continue to liberate, sustain and nourish life. Those cultural resources by creatively co-relating with Gospel can empower, transform people in their historical struggle for social, political, economic justice and identity. Honestly speaking, the indigenous scholars have not given sufficient attention to cultural values in doing contextual theologies. This neglect has been one of the most serious obstacles for the churches in their attempt to be truly rooted in land and people. Theology will still remain a stranger among the indigenous people without integrating those liberative traditions. The challenge is great for us.

The Challenges for Indigenous Theologians

Indigenous communities are now in a new context. The most outstanding sign of our times is the suffering and cries of human persons and other living beings throughout the world, as their victimization proceeds in a systematic and unprecedented manner under the global market regime. The global empire and the greed of global capital are making a tremendous impact on the geo-politics of the world, and destroying and threatening all life, especially the poor and marginalized such as the indigenous communities. In today's world, 'growth' is considered as the only principle for liberation in the capitalist economy of globalization. The concepts of 'care for one another', 'just economy' and '(sabbath) rest for creation', etc. are considered as non-productivity and the root of all human problems from poverty to sickness to political instability. Any attempt to slow down economic growth is labeled as immorality. The global market turns human beings and their cultural activities and earth's resources into commodities for profit. The weak, namely the migrant workers, farmers, consumers, small entrepreneurs and the whole eco-system are the victims of globalization. The countries from the South have become suppliers of raw materials, cheap labor, and food needs. The unjust financial system, ever-increasing ideology of consumerism, materialism, individualism, competition and greed erode life-affirming values, fragment communities and increase poverty, and its value system is driven by powerful financial corporations. The value of life is determined in the speculative market. Those who failed to participate in the capital market remain marginalized. The vast majority of people remain poor, albeit their active participation in production, due to their inability to enter in the market of finance capital. While capital is an asset, or a cause for celebration, labor is viewed as a curse, a source for distress.

One may argue that everything that touches the life of all living beings, from spirituality to sexuality, ethnic politics, the oppressed communities' resistance movement, ecological movement, human rights movement are inter-related to capital control. They intensify more conflict among various religious and ethnic groups, nations, and gender oppression. It would be appropriate to give some examples how hegemonic power and mammon intensify conflicts by reducing people and nature to mere commodities.

Growing Religious Fundamentalism and Conflicts

The escalation of tensions between the Muslim world and the West, as well as terrorist activities sponsored by religious sectarian groups in Asia and elsewhere, and the revival of many sects with a fundamentalist tendency within the living religions and cultures, stand witness to rising religious fundamentalism. Some political leaders consider indigenous people's resistance movements in Asia as Christian instigated movements by Western Christians. Prohibition of religious freedom and the state sponsored religious terrorism testify to this reality. They all continue to challenge us in the way we think and act as Christians.

Gender Justice Issues

Militarization and globalization intensify marginalization of women. In some places, rape is a part of war-games. The expanding international tourism, accompanied by the increase of sex tours of men of many countries,[4] with many young boys and girls sexually abused and cruelly treated. Globalization has opened the door for many women to leave their home countries to work as domestic workers, factory workers or entertainers. There are many stories of violence, and even killing of those migrant workers.

Environment Degradation

The greed for capital leads to control and manipulation of strategic economic locations like Iraq, Palestine and so on. The uncontrolled and one-sided exploitative economic development projects have brought with them various ecological crises. The rape of Mother Earth manifests in uncontrolled logging, indiscriminate use of chemicals in agriculture, inconsiderate disposal of non-biodegradable waste; and human beings' many other 'ecocidal' acts due to negligence, ignorance or greed destroy the ecosystem. The indigenous communities who depend on earth's resources are the most affected people.

Loss of Spirituality

With the increasing influence and impact of materialism, secularism, and liberalism in the postcolonial era, the indigenous people continue to experience challenges and stagnation in spirituality. These include loss of focus in discipleship and spiritual formation, loss of indigenous wisdom, character and values, and infiltration of western culture and ideology through the influence of neo-Pentecostal and new religious movements. Information technology and military power contribute to the decline of the indigenous cultures and discrimination against minorities.

Identity and Power Struggle

Most communities in Asian countries have experienced and continue to experience identity crises through history. In the process, some develop a 'meeting-place' identity in which post-colonial nation-state and economic policies have denied justice for many indigenous communities leading them to armed resistance. Ethical problems such as corruption, abuse of power, and prostitution, communal problems such as

---

4   It exposes not only the issue of gender discrimination but also that of North-South inequality. Recently, the demand for younger women and girls as targets for prostitution tourism is remarkably increasing, due to the fear of AIDS.

ethnic conflicts, racial tensions and breakdown of family structures and continued marginalization of tribal people continue to rise in such a 'meeting place' identity.

All of this is our reality. The future of contextual theologies such as indigenous people's theology will be determined in its ability to create counter movements and theology against hegemonic power and life-threatening free market system.

A Call for Life-centered Theology

Indigenous people's theology calls for a life-centered theology in contrast to the old and dominant theological discourse which supported imperialism. From the time of Constantine, the theological metaphors developed supported the male rulers and oppressors. In other words, the theological concepts developed under the imperial regime not only legitimized a religion for the one who is the master and the ruler, but also to sanction, to exploit and manipulate all segments of God's creation for extraction of maximum profit. There is no place for the people who have been ruled and oppressed for centuries and protection of Mother Earth. This dominant theology includes its *concept of God*. The dominant images of God that developed during the imperial power were images such as Ruler, Lord, Master and Warrior. All patriarchal, political and military images made Christianity a religion of, and for, the ruler, elite and the upper-class. They are not capable of liberating the poor and marginalized people from unjust systems and practice. Such ruler's theology supported colonial governments, war, invasion and unprecedented exploitation of earth's resources. The imperial construct of the concept of God will not be able to liberate the people and earth who have become the victims of power.

Likewise the *understanding of mission* fails as the discourse on God as ruler and master reinforced a success-oriented or triumphalistic mission. Language like 'Mission Crusade', 'Mission Campaign', 'Home Penetration', 'Mass Evangelization' etc. are all military language and concepts. Christians, by and large, engaged in denominational expansion rather than God's mission. Success was measured by how many churches have been planted, converted and baptized. Mission became very exclusive and never recognized God's revelation in other religious traditions. But, mission is God's mission. God is the owner of the mission, but not the churches. The churches are sent to be missionaries to witness compassion and justice with the poor and the victims. We are called to witness compassion and justice with the poor. But Christians have manipulated and acted as if we are the owner of mission.

Finally, in the *understanding of creation* is another seed of imperialism. Western Christian interpretation of creation is anthropocentric – humanity is the reference point of all realities. Nature exists for humans. Apart from rational beings, the other segments of God's creation cannot come under the scheme of salvation. There is no sacred and mystery in nature, but it can be manipulated and controlled for the benefit of human beings. To exploit nature is divine will. This one-sided theological interpretation justifies expansion of colonial power and exploitation of nature. The ideology of globalization and the expansion of a global capital market are deeply rooted in this interpretation. The unprecedented exploitation of nature and present ecological crisis testify to the failure of the Christian understanding of creation.[5]

Therefore, we need a new theological paradigm in which God is perceived as fellow sufferer, a great comforter, divine power and not as a dominating or controlling power. This must not be understood as a dialectical power in weakness but as liberating and transforming power that is effective in compassionate love, care and service. Mission is also to be understood as 'servant-hood' in God's liberating act.

Indigenous people's theology then is an attempt to reconstruct a life-centered theology based on the Jesus movement in Galilee. The Jesus movement was movement against *Pax Romana*. He was crucified by the power of the Roman Empire, his disciples became martyrs, and his community of faith was persecuted under the Roman Imperial Regime. Jesus' movement was against the power of destruction and death. His movement was anchored in the hope of resurrection of all living beings. In the struggle against the powers and principalities of the Roman Empire, Jesus stood with the people who were suffering and struggling under the regime of *Pax Romana*.

Discipleship involves following Jesus in his efforts to bring an end to all hegemonic powers that challenge the sovereignty of God over people and earth. The story of epiphany is the model for indigenous people's theology in the age of power and greed of market. The Magi from the East who went to meet the child Jesus in the manger were obliged to go back to the empire and report to him the whereabouts of the baby whose presence alarmed the Emperor of an imminent threat to his power. But instead of meeting the imperial obligation the Magi left through a different route, not a route that lead to the power and Empire, but a route that protects the life and hope of the marginalized. Meeting and encounter of the Divine signify a change of route. Old routes towards power are not the way to establish divine love and righteousness.

Discourse on indigenous people's theology can make a difference in our times by turning and rerouting to the Jesus of Galilee movement. In the Jesus movement, we see a decisive reversal from power and money to people in pain, from ruler to ruled, from oppressor to the oppressed. Jesus' movement was a life-centered movement against the power of destruction and death. He stood for a different value system – peace, love, service and liberation of poor and earth were the message of Jesus, but not of power in the sword and in mammon. Jesus became the voice of the oppressed and voiceless. Jesus' paradigm was life-centered theology. This option, for protection of life as the locus of indigenous people's theology, requires sacrifice and a radical departure from power, institution and mammon.

Indigenous people hold a very high life-nature-centered spirituality, an ethics of responsibility and respect for all God's creation. This understanding, when interpreted with sound biblical exegesis and theological implication, can provide a powerful antidote to the exploitative dominance that has characterized many Western attitudes to the surrounding world. Further, the strong sense of community and life-rooted

---

[5]   For more details refer to my work on *Tribal Worldview and Ecology,* and *Traditional Tribal Worldview and Modernity* (Jorhat: Tribal Study Centre, 1997).

worldview is a wonderful asset to be shared with postmodern in a Westernized, individualized world of people who have lost a sense of corporate identity and life. In the world of rationalization, mechanization, objectification, and fragmentation, the vision of interrelatedness of all realities in indigenous traditions would help us to do theology in a new way, that is, to remodel theology from the perspective of 'space' and 'interdependences'. Indigenous people's theology is uniquely placed to provide ideals and models to help counter these trends.

Chapter 12

Global Warming:
A Theological Problem and Paradigm

Sallie McFague

The Time is Now: An Analysis of the Problem

In the late 1980s I attended a meeting of the World Council of Churches on 'climate change.' I did not know much about it, but the term sounded relatively benign. I was in for a big surprise. I recall feeling a knot in my stomach when I heard about glacier melt. I wasn't thinking of the global consequences for submerged islands and coastal cities. Rather, I was thinking about myself. As a regular hiker in the Canadian Rockies, I saw the melting of glaciers as a personal loss: I loved those towering ice-covered mountains circling turquoise lakes. I felt anger and resentment – not unlike one feels at the unnecessary death of a good friend. How could this awful thing be happening to one of the most beautiful places on earth? I felt even worse when I was told that *we*, people like myself, were to blame.

Almost twenty years have passed since my introduction to global warming. It has grown, both in my mind and within our culture – after two decades of denial – to epitomize the fragility of the human experiment on earth. We know 'the time is now': there is no time left for either further denial or delay. Acceptance of the reality of global warming is finally widespread, including even such reluctant players as the Bush administration and most of the oil companies. Denial has been unmasked, although large segments of Western culture have not yet accepted it, and governments and the fuel industry are not eager to take action. Nonetheless, we are now in a different place than I was twenty years ago: we know that something must be done, and done soon.

Yes, but here's the rub: effective action on global warming is probably the most discouraging task that human beings have ever undertaken. By comparison, mobilizing the Allies in World War II was relatively straightforward. The enemy was clearly identified and we were the 'good guys.' Such a war is an in-your-face-danger to which people react immediately – and feel good doing so (studies during the war showed that psychological health was up). On the contrary, climate change (global warming) is slow, insidious, partly invisible – and *we* are the enemy. Moreover, *we* are a (largely) innocent enemy: *we* high-level consumers of energy are merely living ordinary Western lives, doing what everyone else in our society is doing. Even as we gradually learn how deeply our actions are affecting the planet's health, the problem still seems amorphous, abstract and remote. A Katrina hurricane or a torrid summer such as 2003 may jolt us to attention for a while, but the impact fades.

However, let us imagine that a number, a large number of people, do become centrally and more or less continually concerned – and *want* to act. The two main avenues for action are personal and/or political. Many people are attempting to live simpler, more environmentally-friendly, low-energy lives by changing behavior at the personal level. However, what these folks soon realize is that the corporate and political institutions of our society pose enormous barriers to such personal changes: the lack of low-energy transportation and buildings; a constant barrage of advertisement for SUV's, high-energy electronics and appliances; a global food market that transports produce half-way around the world at an enormous expenditure of energy. Discouragement sets in: Does it make any real difference what individuals do in their personal lives if the culture and political structures are against them?

Let us now imagine that these people decide they must change the systemic structures that are literally 'fuelling' the energy explosion that is producing global warming. How do they do this? In a democracy, there is only one way: by changing the government and *that* is only possible by changing people's hearts and minds so that they vote differently. In other words, the 'political' rests on the 'personal', on substantial shifts within voting bodies on what they want governments to do. Prior to 9/11, a grass-root movement of NGO's, church groups, and many others was beginning to surface, united by the slogan 'a different world is possible.' Many things were meant by that slogan, but one important thread was certainly an embrace of a communitarian rather than individualistic view of humanity. At the heart of any revolution bent on changing human behavior lies an anthropology – an understanding of who we human beings are and where we fit into the scheme of things. This communitarian turn is critically important, for it is hard to see how we can tackle our impending climate crisis without it. Sadly, at least for the time being, it is largely dormant, silenced by the 'War on Terror.'

We are, then, in a very difficult place. The kind of thinking we need about ourselves and our place on the planet – our interrelationship and interdependence with all other human beings and other life-forms – has been deadened by the hand of a consumerist/militarist paradigm that exalts the comfort and superiority of elite individual human beings. We *need* to elect representatives to our governments who will create laws to limit human energy use at all levels – from emission caps on oil refineries to regulations on emissions from the family car. The 'personal' and the 'political' need to join to legislate the kind of human action in the world that will create a just and sustainable planet. Individuals *cannot* do this simply by trying to live 'environmentally' within an energy-mad society. The system must be changed – the major forces within society that regulate and control our use of fossil fuels.

I would venture that many of us *want* such regulation. Those who do have a communitarian view of life are asking for HELP. We cannot live differently – at least with any effectiveness – within a society that allows individuals to use any amount of energy they can afford. We want systemic changes that will help all of us (and all of us like the comforts of a high-energy, consumer culture) to live as we ought and want to live.

'The time is now': there is no more time for either denial or delay. We must change our view of ourselves – our anthropology – so that we will elect different representatives who can help structure our society in ways that are good not just for some privileged human beings, but for all human beings, and all other life-forms. This is what global warming is telling us: we cannot continue to live as selfish individuals, heedless of the consequences of our profligate, adolescent behavior. The ominous 'tipping point' of the global temperature may be less than fifty years away – that point at which gradual global warming tips over into out-of-control exponential heating. Fear is not the reason to change, however, for apocalyptic scenes often come back to haunt us with escapist solutions. Nonetheless, the tipping-point stands as a cautionary tale that global warming is not simply 'another problem' facing us; in many ways, it epitomizes *the* problem – the problem that starts with our false view of ourselves, the view that we are separate individuals who enter into relationships when we feel like it and have the right to get all the worldly goods we can legally garner. Increasingly, from all sides – ecology, cosmology, feminist thought, First Nations' views, the NGO's, process theology, and many religions – a common anthropology is emerging: we are not our own: *we* belong to the earth.

Theology and Anthropology: What Can Religion Tell Us About Ourselves?

Deep down, beneath all our concepts and ideas about ourselves, is a sense, a feeling, an assumption about 'who we are.' This is not a question people commonly ask of each other – or of themselves – any more than they ask 'Who is God?' These questions are seen as too personal or too abstract or too intimidating for civil conversation. Nonetheless, they are the deepest questions of human existence and lie uneasily beneath any glib answers we might give, were we to be asked. However, we act all the time on the basis of these deep assumptions of who we are and who God is, even while not acknowledging that we even have such assumptions. When we respond with approval to an ad for an expensive car telling us that 'we deserve the very best,' we are implicitly acknowledging that privileged individualism is our assumption about human nature. When we say that God is interested in spiritual not secular matters (and therefore not in cars), we are implicitly confessing that we believe in a distant, uninvolved God.

Who I am and who God is are taken for granted in a culture: the answer lies with the unacknowledged and accepted conventions of what is meant by 'I' (a human person) and 'God.' But it is precisely the false conventional views of God and ourselves that permit the continuing destruction of our planet and its inhabitants. The environmental crisis is a theological problem, a problem coming from views of God and ourselves which encourage and/or permit our destructive, unjust actions. For example, if I see myself (deep down) as superior to other animals and life-forms – a privileged individual (Western, white, educated, etc.) – then of course I will act in ways that support my continuation in this position. If, as a human being, I am basically 'on my own,' then it is also 'up to me' to maintain my superiority. This sense or feeling of separate and responsible individualism need not be conscious; in fact, it usually is not. Rather, it is considered by most privileged Western human beings to simply be the way things are. It is seen as 'natural' rather than as a personal belief.

Likewise, if I imagine God (deep down) to be a super-being, residing somewhere above and apart from the world and who created and judges the world but otherwise is absent from it, then I will conduct my affairs largely without day-to-day concern about God. If the God I believe in is supernatural, transcendent and only intermittently interested in the world, then this God is not a factor in my daily actions. Whether or not I treat myself to that expensive car is certainly not of relevance to such a God.

So, we are suggesting that *who* God is and *who* we are must be central questions if we hope to change our actions in the direction of just, sustainable planetary living. It is useless to censure people for their actions when the roots of those actions lie in deep, unexamined assumptions. The problem lies in our theologies and our anthropologies. The problem, as many have pointed out, is a 'spiritual' one, having to do with our *will* to change. We already know more than enough about the disaster ahead of us – having more knowledge (or technology) will not solve the problem. Only changing human wills can do so.

But is this not impossible? It is not sufficient 'to know the good' in order 'to do the good.' While the Greeks believed this, Saint Paul knew better, and most of us think Paul is the better realist. So why bother with new theologies and anthropologies? Aren't they just more 'knowledge'? Yes and No. Yes, because obviously they fall into the category of knowledge, but No, because it is a peculiar kind of knowledge, the deepest possible kind – who we are and who God is. If we change these basic assumptions, our behavior may change as well. To be sure, it will not happen necessarily, easily, or universally, but it can and might happen. Or to put it negatively, unless *another* option becomes available to us, we have nothing to choose but the conventional view of God and ourselves, a view that is destructive of ourselves and our planet.

If theologians, who are one of the keepers and interpreters of this deep knowledge, allow false, inappropriate, unhelpful, and dangerous notions of God and ourselves to continue as our society's assumptions, we are not doing our job. The primary task of theologians (and perhaps the only task) is to guard and encourage right thinking about God and ourselves. This, of course, is but one small task needed for the planetary agenda to change. Others – doctors, car manufacturers, teachers, parents, corporate leaders, lawyers, agriculturalists, etc. – have other very important offerings to make to living better on earth. The particular task of theologians is prior to our action, at its roots. It is a limited task and mainly a linguistic one: suggesting different language for talking about God and ourselves – with the hope that different action may follow. The limitations of this task and its possibilities are perhaps seen best in the negative: if we do not change our basic assumptions about God and ourselves from an individualistic to a communitarian view, can we expect or hope people to change their behavior? If we know nothing else, do we have a choice?

Chapter 13

Beyond Suffering and Lament:
Theology of Hope and Life

Nyambura J. Njoroge

The Foundation of My Theological Journey

My childhood dream was to become a science high school teacher in rural Kenya. But God had a different agenda. In my second year of teaching, I resigned and enrolled in a theological college to become a parish minister.[1] Not surprisingly, my idea of parish ministry was in the rural setting where I had witnessed my parents' dedication in church ministry and community service of close to forty years.[2] Even though after college, I had made my home in the outcasts of Nairobi City, the Kenyan capital, I never imagined myself working in the city. Upon graduation I was posted to the low-income area of Nairobi with a high rate of unemployment and poor housing.[3] However, another resignation letter was about to go to the post after two years in the parish. Moreover, I was prepared to quit the church all together. I felt totally inadequate to serve in the midst of extreme poverty, indignity and suffering. At the time, I was living on the 'well-to-do' other side of the city once owned by European settlers, and in which was set the *Out of Africa* movie featuring the life of Karen Blixen from Denmark.

I felt the church was totally irrelevant to the daily needs of the parishioners. Women, in particular, faithfully attended worship services and other church functions in large numbers but suffered from many gender-based injustices. Further, I found that even though the majority of the parishioners were children and young people, the whole ministry was adult-centred. The male-dominated church leadership made

---

[1]   Some of my friends were dismayed because ordination of women ministers (in missionary-founded churches) was unheard off in the 1970s in Kenya. Also because I was leaving a good paying job compared to poorly paid pastors. Furthermore, I was in my early 20s and ministry was generally associated with older men with less education.

[2]   My father was first a teacher and later a pastor in the Presbyterian Church of East Africa (PCEA). My mother was a church elder and a midwife. Because there was no hospital nearby, my mother was the village 'doctor' and 'pharmacist' to the extent that our home was known by her name, which was very unusual in a patriarchal setting.

[3]   In PCEA when one declares interest in the ordained ministry, one goes through a process of interviews and evaluation at different levels. When all involved are convinced one has the 'call to the ministry', the church trains the candidate and upon graduation, the appointment committee of the church decides the presbytery and the parish that prepare one for ordination.

little effort to listen and attend to the needs of children, the youth and women. The parish had dynamic women leaders but they were confined to women's organization and teaching Sunday School. They, for example, were totally excluded from the parish council.[4]

Young and the only woman in the highest decision-making court in the parish (kirk session), I was increasingly becoming impatient and frustrated. I started a spiritual battle: a battle far from being won as I write this piece. I am a believer in Christ, but I struggle to keep my faith and hope in God alive. So far, the way I keep going is to lament in prayer and in writing as I wrestle with the Scriptures and other sources of my faith. I must admit, however, that the faithfulness and fruitfulness of the leadership provided by my parents and their contemporaries continue to inspire me. They were women and men of limited means and education but they valued education for the community.[5] I felt secure, cared for and loved. They provided a firm foundation for my theological journey.

In Search of Empowering and Liberating Ministry

Providentially, and with encouragement from my family, I was convinced that I should consider further education in theology. I craved to be equipped for empowering and liberating ministry. After four years in the parish, I ventured into a new world of critical social analysis. After seven years, I earned MA in religion and a PhD in African Christian Social Ethics, focusing on African Christian women's moral agency.[6] But the dream of returning to Kenya took a different route. I made a detour into global ministry focusing on partnership between women and men.[7] At the best of times, I feel that this detour was in God's plans but many are the moments I wonder if I did not board the wrong flight after my studies. At times, biblical Jonah becomes a good companion and I join him in his depressed moments in the belly of the proverbial whale. Simply put, I endeavored into academic theology in search of life-transforming and life-giving theologies and ethics to prepare myself for empowering and liberating ministry.

---

[4]   PCEA had ordained women elders in other parishes since 1965.

[5]   My village has two public primary schools, and two community-built high schools. One is girls' boarding school and the other a co-ed day school and the PCEA congregation started both. In addition to the Presbyterian Church there is a Roman Catholic Church about three miles apart.

[6]   In my works such as: *Kiama Kia Ngo An African Feminist Ethic of Resistance of Transformation* (Accra, 2000); 'Woman, Why are You Weeping?', *The Ecumenical Review,* 49/4 (1997): 427–38; 'Groaning and Languishing in Labour Pains', in Musimbi R.A. Kanyoro & Nyambura J. Njoroge (eds.) *Groaning in Faith: African Women in the Household of God* (Acton Publishers, 1996), pp. 3–15; 'Hannah, Why Do You Weep?', in Grace Wamue & Mary Getui (eds.) *Violence Against Women: Reflections by Kenyan Women Theologians* (Acton Publisher, 1996) pp. 21–6; 1990; and 'Confessing Christ in Africa Today', in John Pobee (ed.) *Exploring Afro-Christology* (Peter Lang, 1990), pp. 131–6.

[7]   I joined World Alliance of Reformed Churches (WARC), Geneva, Switzerland and later the World Council of Churches (WCC), Geneva, Switzerland to co-ordinate the global program on ecumenical theological education and ministerial formation.

My flight to academic theology in the United States of America (USA) exposed me to a totally different context from my village and city. Yet issues of injustice, stigma and discrimination became more illuminated. One of my most memorable classes was ethics in the New Testament with George Edwards at Louisville Presbyterian Seminary in Kentucky. Two of the topics we explored were economic justice and liberation of gay and lesbian people,[8] topics that deserve urgent and critical study in the churches in Africa today.

However, what put me completely off balance during my studies was how to reconcile the abundant (chronic) poverty and injustices I had witnessed in Nairobi and the great affluence I saw in this predominately European-American environment. Things got more complicated when later I moved to Princeton Theological Seminary for doctoral studies and then finally to Geneva, one of the most expensive and globalized cities in the world. Nonetheless, living in the USA and Europe has provided me with many opportunities to travel to different parts of the world. I have witnessed the extensive diversity of God's abundant gifts as well as unspeakable destruction of God's creation and suffering beyond Africa. This experience has increased my desire and passion to wrestle with theological and ethical issues as well as my faith. To say the least, the kind of affluence and 'conflict free' context I live in today make me raise issues with God about the enormous suffering in Africa. Why all this madness and destruction? For how long do we have to endure such indignity and misery? Do we indeed belong to the human race? Why this disproportionate suffering in one particular continent? It only gets worse when I read well-researched documents on the impact of sexual and gender-based violence, wars, genocide and abuse of the environment in many African countries. The reality has become intricate due to the havoc caused by the global HIV and AIDS pandemic and other diseases in the continent.

A Decolonizing and Transforming Experience

When I was filling application forms for a visa for the United States in 1984, it read: 'first name ... middle initial ... and last name' rather than asking for the surname first as I was used to following the British style. This simple exercise may sound trivial but it has made a big difference in my sense of being and theologizing. It was decolonizing and transforming. It gave me a sense of pride and confidence of who I am and it sustained me in the months ahead of culture shock in Louisville, Kentucky – but also much more. Having grown up in a context where being Christian and using so-called Christian (European) baptismal names as the first name was the norm, this moment was very revealing and liberating. After all, the British system of naming insists on surnames which do not exist among the Gikuyu[9] people in Kenya. The Gikuyu naming system is different from the British or even other tribes in Kenya. Women, for example, did not change their names upon marriage as the British established in colonial Kenya during its colonial rule. Indeed, for once, I could use

---

8   At the time, George Edwards, a well-known peace activist, with his wife Jean, had published *Gay Liberation: A Biblical Perspective* (Pilgrim Press, 1984).

9   Gikuyu is the largest tribe in Kenya among 42 groups. It is sometimes spelt as Kikuyu.

my African name as my first name without feeling that I am not Christian enough. Of course, naming was just one of the things missionaries had interfered with, many African cultural aspects had been demonized, creating a crisis of identity.

Later, I could follow the long debate that transpired when pioneering African theologians coined the name African theology. But hardly had it occurred to me how deep was the psychological damage meted on African identity by depicting Africa in negative ways, e.g. the 'dark continent' and 'underdeveloped'. Probably no other image has caused greater harm than the 'dark continent'. Therefore, any time the question 'What is in a name?' is raised I pay critical attention and seek to understand the context because behind the question there is a long and often very painful story.[10] I have discovered that to theologize from such a point of weakness (colonized and exploited people) means an uphill battle. This initial step of reclaiming my Gikuyu name (and indeed my God-given identity as an African) marked the beginning of critical awareness of the ethics and spirituality of resistance, transformation and not giving up. Some of the ongoing processes of rapid globalization, nevertheless, sometimes hinder the task of decolonization and transformation. We must restore our God-given identity and take our rightful place in God's household. That said, when I critically reflect on these years as a theological student and now theologian, I have come to realize how my theological and ecumenical journey has been shaped and influenced by my triple identity of an African Christian woman in a globalized world. Fighting patriarchy, gender discrimination, racism, and my capability devalued rather than affirmed is an ongoing battle.[11] But we shall overcome.

Ending the Suffering of the African People

In the course of writing this paper, I stumbled over the words of John Pobee, a Ghanaian Anglican priest and ecumenical theologian:

> At the heart of the Christian message stands the cross, the symbol of torture and human inhumanity. Suffering has been the reality of humanity, Africans and Christians included. Indeed, Matthew 16:24 exhorts the followers of Christ to take up that cross and follow him. *In this sequence of thinking, the cross symbolizes the reality of Africans. Such suffering unites all humanity in Africa across religious, cultural, ethnic and tribal lines.*[12]

---

[10]   See my 'Let's Celebrate the Power of Naming', in I. Phiri and S. Nadar (eds.) *African Women, religion and Health: Essays in honor of Prof. Mercy Amba Oduyoye* (Orbis Books, 2006) and 'Reclaiming Our Heritage of Power: Discovering Our Theological Voices', in I. Phiri, D.B. Govinden and Nadar (eds.) *Her-stories: Hidden Histories of Women of Faith in Africa* (Cluster Publishers, 2002). pp. 39–57

[11]   See my works: 'A Spirituality of Resistance and Transformation', in Nyambura J. Njoroge and Musa W. Dube (eds.) *Talitha Cum! Theologies of African Women* (Cluster Publishers, 2001) pp. 66–82 and 'Honoring Courageous Women: Troublemakers in the Face of Injustice', in Elizabeth C Miescher and Maria Jose Arana (eds.) *Networking for Reconciliation* (Basel, 1999), pp. 191–201.

[12]   John Pobee, 'Let Ethiopia Hasten to Stretch Out Its Hands to God', in *The Ecumenical Review*, 49/4 (1997): 425, emphasis mine.

As I have already observed, it is the extreme suffering of the Kenyan people that led me to academic theology, which is clear in most of my published works since 1988. Both individual and collective suffering has pushed me to struggle to see how I can be part of the solution. As the saying goes, 'the struggle continues'. The causes of suffering in Africa are multidimensional. So are the solutions. The spiritual footstool is just one among many other solutions and therefore we must cultivate holistic interdisciplinary ways of looking for solutions. Theologians must build partnerships with other professionals in our search for solutions.

In my journey of faith, however, I have realized there is great danger in focusing too much on the cross and suffering. There is a tendency of depicting Africa as the 'suffering and hopeless continent' adding to other negative images already mentioned above. Fortunately, there are people who are able to go beyond the cross as a symbol of suffering to a liberating message. For instance, the Lutheran World Federation[13] (LWF) Department of World Service facilitated the creation of crosses of various sizes from spent bullets or shells after the civil war in Liberia. A post card with the picture of these crosses reads:

> A symbol of suffering, resistance and peace from Liberia – The biblical vision of changing swords into plowshares (Isaiah 2, Micah 4) is an inspiration for peace efforts. In Liberia, this vision has found new meaning. . . . 'In a dream I had the idea of turning spent bullets and rocket shells into symbols of peace', says George Togba, who was a car mechanic before the civil war. The marketing of thousands of these peace symbols to Europe and America has turned the project into a source of moderate income. Togba (and 30 compatriots), who joined rebel forces during the conflict to protect his family, is now a Christian peace activist and supports his family by peaceful means.

Liberian crosses and George Togba's vision tell me that it is therefore important to focus on individuals and local communities who work to stop the suffering and even prevent more crosses from being erected. From our *lived* experiences we can explore the Scriptures to motivate creative imagination, new dreams, ideas and visions. I am particularly interested in biblical texts that give the most marginalized (such as women) voice and courage to act and to declare that violence, suffering and death do not have the last word. Yes, we may not bring the dead back to life but our actions like that of George Togba and his 30 compatriots can create peacemakers and life-giving activities. Even in the midst of fierce storms of injustice and madness of violence, there are those who choose to stop the suffering. They do not give up the struggle despite or because of evil structures and systems that hinder their efforts.

Recently, some of these individuals and communities that support them are being documented in autobiographies. I have in mind people such as Nelson Mandela, Wangari Maathai, Desmond Tutu and Pauline Webb and many unsung heroines and heroes well known in our local communities. Today we know that the caring and healing hand of God is hidden in grandmothers who shoulder most of the responsibility of rearing millions of orphans (about 43 million due to wars and diseases including HIV and AIDS), who otherwise are left to fend for themselves. Theologians stand to gain if we pay more attention to the lived experience of those individuals and

---

[13]   Also with headquarters in Geneva together with WCC and WARC.

communities who have made significant difference in ending suffering and restoring dignity in seemingly hopeless situations.[14]

Many of us wonder how Nelson Mandela managed to overcome bitterness over his oppressors. My conclusion after reading *Long Walk to Freedom* (1994) is that he remained focused on the mission of ending injustices and suffering. He also strongly believed in the human capacity to do good, no matter how long it took to achieve freedom. On the other hand, he believed that freedom comes with responsibilities and he owed it to his people to keep hope and faith alive. Over the years, Mandela understood that patient endurance bears lasting fruits, something Jesus affirms in the parable of the sower (Luke 8: 15). Likewise, Wangari Maathai in *Unbowed: A Memoir* (2006) demonstrates that lasting change is a slow and painful process. Therefore, change requires dedication, determination, persistence and patient endurance to arrive at desired fruitfulness.

Transforming Theological Education and Leadership

Certainly, the other aspect that has shaped and influenced the way I do theology is my professional responsibilities. One of my tasks is to work with theological educators and students at the global level. This means critically examining the way churches prepare church and community leaders for a broad range of ministries both ordained and unordained. Therefore, theological curricula, pedagogical processes and contextualization of theology and theological education are some of the issues we focus on. We spend quality time assessing what is best in a given context and the extensive diversity of cultures, religions and geopolitics. We are particularly aware that churches must help Christians to discern their individual vocation irrespective of their professional preoccupation. Facilitating Christian education and character formation which attest to the Gospel of Christ in our daily lives is a daunting task. It means parish and teaching ministries need to be structured in ways that create spaces for followers of Christ to acquire basic truths about Christian faith irrespective of the level of their education. In many parts of Africa, Christians are semi-literate or non-literate. Listening to the Scriptures read to them is fundamental in their faith formation. This is why symbols, images and rituals are important because they provide other ways of communicating the Gospel. On the other hand, theologians must consistently scrutinize church theology, doctrines, rituals, symbols and practices to safeguard misuse and misinterpretation of the Scriptures, as the case has been throughout history.[15]

For instance, in this era of global HIV and AIDS pandemic, churches have been forced to re-examine fundamental concepts like sin, punishment, stigma, and discrimination. Even though HIV and AIDS are diseases there is much more to

---

[14]   See, for example, my 'A New Way of Facilitation Leadership: Lessons from African Women Theologians', in Ogbu Kalu (ed.), *African Christianity: An African Story* (Pretoria, 2005) pp. 446–467.

[15]   See, for example, my 'The Bible and African Christianity: A Curse or Blessings?', in Musa Dube (ed.) *Other Ways of Reading: African Women and the Bible* (WCC Publications, 2001), pp. 207–236.

them than medical aspects. Since 2000, I have been part of a small community of theological educators in Africa attempting to develop theological literature and theological curricula that speak to the multidimensional reality of HIV and AIDS.[16] As I have written elsewhere, HIV and AIDS speak multiple languages and thrive in multiple pandemics and crises. This reality has forced some African theologians to make a 'U-turn' in their teaching and theologizing. HIV and AIDS have taught us to theologize on sexuality, sexual violence, gender justice, some of the issues we did not dare study in seminaries a few years ago. When I was in seminary in Kenya the word homosexuality was unknown to most of us. Today church leaders, especially in the Anglican Communion, have championed the debate where some blatantly condemn gay and lesbian people. Seminaries are being forced to study the issue rather than simply justify the condemnation because the Bible or the archbishop says so! Although stigma and discrimination have been with us since the days of slave trade, colonialism and apartheid, HIV and AIDS have forced us to re-examine their devastating impact on individuals and communities more than ever before.

Another example of theologizing education is creating theological literature that takes seriously people with disabilities who for a long time have been neglected and excluded in the life and mission of the Church, including theological institutions. Together with Ecumenical Disability Advocates Network (EDAN), a program of WCC, we are critically examining church theologies and practices to ensure that people with disabilities, their families and caregivers are included. This process includes transforming theological curricula to meet their needs and concerns. Many of these changes demand new ways of reading and interpreting the Scriptures even though one may not be a trained biblical scholar. In this case, I have found myself seeking help from biblical scholars to facilitate contextual bible study methodologies for theological educators and pastors to empower them to help ordinary Christians in reading and interpreting Scripture. Contextual bible study methodologies in Africa are becoming popular, especially in dealing with sexual violence, gender inequality and HIV and AIDS in the church and society. Teaching ministry is fundamental. The words of Bell Hooks, an African American activist and prolific cultural critic sum up my approach as a teacher:

> My hope emerges from those places of struggle where I witness individuals positively transforming their lives and the world around them. Educating is always a vocation rooted in hopefulness. As teachers we believe that learning is possible, that nothing can keep an open mind from seeking after knowledge and finding a way to know.[17]

---

[16]   This work is featured in a WCC CD-ROM on the statements and publications on HIV and AIDS made since 1986 to date. Also see my 'The Disease that Speaks Multiple Languages and Thrives on Other Pandemics', *Journal of Constructive Theology*, Volume 10/2 (2004).

[17]   Bell Hooks, *Teaching Community: A Pedagogy of Hope* (New York: 2003), p. xiv.

Embracing the Divine Within Us

As indicated earlier, causes of suffering in Africa are multidimensional and the context has become very complex with the onslaught of the HIV and AIDS pandemic. Therefore we need an holistic interdisciplinary approach in our endeavor to make a difference. These causes are both local and global, so are the solutions. Christians in Africa and elsewhere express our spirituality in great diversity to the extent that some theologians prefer to talk about Christianities. The same is true with other religions that make their home in Africa. Therefore, diversity even of other religions and cultures must be taken seriously. This calls for a global theological mind. More importantly, we need to establish a common ground that will lift us beyond our differences in order to achieve the common good for all humanity and creation. Such an entry point might focus on sharing and reflecting on our individual and/or collective experience with the divine within us as we discern God's will for us on how to nurture life in its fullness. In other words, we must strive to embrace the divinity in us as people who believe that we are all created in God's image. This way we will not limit ourselves to our local contexts and social-cultural constructs. Rather, we will be able to see ourselves as beloved children of God and of the universe so that together we work to resist evil and its destructive forces. It is not a simple process. Undoubtedly, it requires unparalleled faithful and fruitful leadership, full of passion and humility. We need engaged critical theology and faithful actions beyond our given contexts.

Chapter 14

Method and Context:
How and Where Theology Works in Africa

Agbonkhianmeghe E. Orobator, S.J.

My first encounter with theology as an academic discipline dates back almost a decade and a half. That encounter triggered a series of questions, summed up in the one question: *Why study theology?* The practical use of this discipline did not appear obvious beyond the immediate concern of proximate preparation for ordained ministry. Since then, these questions have not ceased to stimulate my theological imagination. Presently, with the benefit of teaching theology to an inquisitive, intelligent, and oftentimes unconvinced audience of seminarians, religious, and lay people, the questions have shifted to one of method and, more critically, of context: *How* to do theology *in Africa*? In a unique way, these 'how?' and 'where?' questions define, challenge, and orient theological activity in contemporary Africa. While the former relates to method, the latter focuses on context; and both fix the boundaries of a wider theological synthesis that shapes today's African theological mind.

Older generations of African theologians inherited a theological method that was recognisably Western, inherently scholastic, and characteristically steeped in metaphysical categories of thought. Their theological activity unfolded within a tightly regulated denominational and ecclesiastical framework. This was true of theologians in mainline churches and their Protestant and Evangelical partners. That period was before the advent of Pentecostalism in Africa. Understandably, the principal preoccupation of these older generations of theologians revolved around how to fit African religious beliefs into constructed Western theological syntheses and categories. Understood in this way, their task was relatively simple: design appropriate, local receptacles for the universal truths of Western Christianity. They might, for example, inquire into the compatibility of the Catholic Christian notion of 'Communion of Saints' and the African experience of 'Ancestor Veneration'. This was quite apart from the more widespread concern with the adaptation and indigenisation of liturgical rubrics and forms of worship. This approach continues to dominate a certain strand of theological activity in Africa christened 'Inculturation Theology'. There are many examples of how this approach has been taken to the extreme and then used as a substitute for critical theological investigation of received notions of faith, beliefs, and practices.

Contemporary African theologians, whether or not they are affiliated to ecclesiastical institutions, are more aware of and receptive to the critical need for a theological method that pays attention to present-day issues of concern to Africans.

For them a new methodology matters, as does a serious attention to context. I situate my theological activity within this framework.

As soon as a theologian in Africa begins to pay attention to method and context, he or she is confronted by the unsettling complexities of the African experience. To many outsiders, onlookers, and bystanders, Africa resembles an 'ocean of misfortunes'. But this epithet hardly defines the primary challenge of context. Africa means many things. With fifty-three independent countries and 700 million people spread across an intricate linguistic, cultural, social, and geo-political landscape, the continent defies any facile attempt to sketch a homogeneous picture of its fortunes or misfortunes. Africa represents a complex and complicated reality fully in evolution. What is true for Africa as a geographical entity holds true for African theology as an academic discipline. Thus theological activity in Africa can be construed as embodying a preliminary methodological caveat: that any reference to all things African would have to be partial, provisional, and contextualised. This methodological caution makes generalisations impossible and points up the need to define the context of one's theological activity with clarity and to clarify the issues at stake with precision. Where I stand (context) as a theologian in Africa carries implications for how (method) I go about conducting the activity of inquiring into the nature and meaning of God, human existence, and the way they relate to each other.

What factors determine the 'how' and 'where', the method and context, of theological activity in Africa and ultimately shapes the theological mind? Judging from recent experience the following factors and considerations appear to be pertinent.

Contemporary theological, sociological, and demographic surveys and statistics wax contentedly about the phenomenal growth of Christianity in Africa in the 20th and 21st centuries – so spectacular it tips global Christianity's centre of gravity southward. Several authors variously designate this phenomenal southward shift of global Christianity as the rise of the 'Third Church', 'Third World Church' or 'Two-Thirds Church'. With an optimism that borders on hubris, many declare the future of Christianity to be eternally willed to Africa. Yet, in Africa, analysis falls short if it overlooks the fact that the exponential growth of membership in organised religion is not a grace bestowed exclusively on Christianity; it also characterises the fortunes of Islam and traditional religion, neither of which is necessarily losing adherents to Christianity. Africans are giving more public expressions to their religious affiliations based on a triple heritage (Christianity, Islam, and Traditional Religion) that defines their contemporary worldview. A lengthy excursus on this phenomenon would be irrelevant here. This reality presents a set of challenges for theological activity in Africa, relating to the tension between Africa's dominant religions (Islam and Christianity) and the often violent struggle to control not only the religious, but also the economic and political space of Africans. How to understand the theological value of this battle for the soul of the African constitutes a pressing methodological concern for the African theological mind.

African Traditional Religion presents another set of methodological and contextual challenges, which the following personal example might help to clarify.

African Traditional Religion continues to play a significant role in shaping my theological mind. As a convert to Catholicism from African Traditional Religion, I face a constant challenge to account for the enduring influence of the latter on the former. This represents an even wider challenge, precisely because traditional beliefs continue to play an important role in the lives of many other African converts to Christianity. Whether one describes it in derogatory terms ('faith schizophrenia'), as some theologians are wont to do, or attempts to draw correlations and convergences between both, as others prefer, the fact remains that this tension cannot be wished away. One may take the African out of his or her religion, but this religion reappears in surprisingly potent forms irrespective of the depth of one's conversion and the tenets of one's newfound religious affiliation. Confronting this reality in order to integrate it into the Christian understanding of God, faith, and revelation shapes theological activity and defines a methodological concern of contemporary African theologians like myself.

There is yet another factor. Coming from Nigeria, a country of roughly 140 million people, almost equally split between Christians and Muslims, I am constantly intrigued by the various 'brands' of Christianity and their increasingly sophisticated mechanisms for marketing the 'goods' of Christianity to the populace. Implicit in this practice is the claim that religion offers concrete solutions to the needs of people. The kind of 'services' offered by some propagators of Christianity in Africa covers a wide gamut: health, wealth, business success, political power, rapid upward social mobility, etc. Here the intriguing methodological and contextual consideration concerns the timing of this 'religious boom' in Africa. Simply stated, the fortunes of religion seem to soar in inverse proportion to the disintegration of the socio-economic and political fabric of African societies. The signs and faces of this collapse appear in varying forms: poverty, hunger, deadly diseases, wars, civil strife, corruption, illegal immigration, etc. I myself have considered three such issues as paramount: HIV/AIDS, refugees, and poverty.[1] The reason informing my choice of these issues is not far-fetched. Beside the fact that Africa statistically leads on all three fronts, these are issues that theology and religion could not possibly avoid without completely bypassing 'where' faith matters for many Africans today. They challenge African theology with questions of methodological and contextual import: how does one theologise in this kind of situation? If tradition bears any relevance here, how does theology as faith seeking understanding make sense of this kind of situation? How does theology *work* for a theologian facing the disturbing complexities of the African situation? This is what I consider as one of the fundamental challenges facing theologians in Africa today.

In light of the foregoing, in keeping with my constant concern for method, I shall now describe one specific way in which *theology works* for me in Africa. It concerns the contribution of the social sciences to theological activity.

Because I am compelled as an African theologian to pay attention to social context and social issues, my approach opens up to the social sciences both as dialogue partners and indispensable resources for theological research. I do not pretend to overlook the possibilities of conflict between theological activity and the approaches of the social sciences. Nevertheless, I have found the combination largely beneficial. Again, the nature of the context influences my receptivity to the input of the social

---

[1]   See my *From Crisis to Kairos: The Mission of the Church in the Time of HIV/AIDS, Refugees and Poverty* (Paulines, 2005).

sciences. If theological activity focuses on understanding and interpreting ongoing human experience in the light of faith, the social sciences provide useful analytical and descriptive tools of research for this activity. Regrettably, only rarely have published materials appeared in Africa where the most critical tools of the social sciences have been brought to bear on theological scholarship. I myself have used this method extensively in my theological activities.

Since 2000 I have conducted ethnographic field research in various parts of Eastern Africa, notably Kenya, Uganda, and Tanzania. Although some methodologically conservative African theologians would dispute the validity of this approach, these research trips have proved beyond doubt the pertinence of a correct understanding of contextual reality for an appropriate theological method and reflection. To take but one example, it is one thing to account for the meaning and theology of the Incarnation by appealing abstractly to the scholastic categories of person and nature. It is quite another when one encounters, as I did in refugee camps in Tanzania, a re-appropriation of the Incarnation as the concrete, personal experience of God who journeys with the people of God in exile as the ultimate ground of their hope of return and reintegration into their home country. My conviction is that field research equips theology to appreciate correctly and appropriate intensely the density of human experience in a way that a purely speculative and metaphysical approach can neither penetrate adequately nor understand fully.

I hesitate to put a label on this approach. For the sake of convenience I call it a *generative contextualised* method of conducting theological activity. *Contextualised* because, as a rational discipline and activity, theology does not defy the laws of gravity to float above the human predicament; and *generative*, because the outcome of this insertion in human experience is neither predetermined nor amenable to dogmatic and doctrinal manipulation. It can spring forth surprises. The constitutive levels or stages of this approach are multiple, each with a defining question.

First is the *moment of encounter* of reality in its conditioned and conditioning potential ('What is going on here?'); second is the *interpretative moment* which draws upon a variety of sources and resources ('What are the different ways of understanding this present reality?'); third is the *synthesising moment* ('How do we image and re-imagine theology in the face of the complex reality?); and finally, the *generative moment* ('What practical models of faith, belief and action suggest themselves in this present context?'). At every stage in this multi-layered approach I have discovered the benefit not only of using and adapting contemporary resources (like the social science method), but also the rich and venerable resources of Scripture, Christian tradition of theology and Catholic social doctrine.

I consider this to be an experimental methodology in need of further refinement and precision. But my conviction remains unshakeable: theology is not an exercise in intellectual or speculative weightlessness. Nowhere would this assertion be truer than in Africa. As a theologian I cannot float blissfully above the conditions and complexities of life on a continent that is chronically religious and yet so tragically impoverished. The engagement in theological activity, whether in a professional or lay capacity, demands a radical descent into context, of the theologian and his or her community, in order to engage vital issues and questions at the interstices of faith and life.

The methodological trajectory sketched above relates eminently to the task of identifying and understanding the function, meaning, and theology of the community called church. In Africa, as in the rest of the 'Third Church', it is pertinent to inquire into the link between ecclesial reality and social context. For one thing *ecclesia* is a global phenomenon. Huge leaps in information technology and the present consciousness of globalisation make it impossible to treat the church as an isolated phenomenon. A *generative contextualised* approach is needed to explore and account for the various ways ecclesiality intersects with global social issues. To take but one example, in Africa, HIV/AIDS poses an unprecedented threat to Church and society. The pews of the Church, the prayer mats of Islam, and the shrines of African deities, gods, and goddesses are populated by people infected or affected by this deadly disease. I find the questions surfaced in this context for theological method extremely interesting: If Africans turn to religion *en masse* in the time of crisis, how does religion account for and meet their expectation without preying on their misfortunes or offering them a panacea? Here again the questions 'where?' and 'how?' intersect to create a rich terrain for theological inquiry in Africa.

If faith is construed as a constitutive dimension of the human person long before it is defined and circumscribed by institutional mediation, it remains a reality that is lived in a historical context. Paying attention to this context forms an important ingredient in the shaping of the African theological mind. If theological activity propels the theologian and the outcome of his or her analysis above and beyond concrete reality, then theology loses its raison d'être. I agree with those African theologians, like Jean-Marc Ela, for whom religion must have 'dirty hands'. What dirties the hand of theology and theologians in Africa are those critical issues which not only soil but menace the lives of millions of religious devotees and place their survival in jeopardy.

My theological vocation in a context such as I have outlined above is a risky one. Not that it exposes the life of the theologian to physical danger, but that it puts the authenticity and validity of his or her work to the test. There are those who consider theological scholarship in Africa a luxury, affordable only by those with guaranteed institutional or denominational support. This criticism is a function of how and where theology was done in the past – it was done in a disincarnate manner, within the closed walls of religious and ecclesiastical institutions. What relevance it had to real life situations was neither obvious nor deemed significant. A new brand of African theology is emerging, one that is not averse to the conditions and complexities of life on a continent that professes to be deeply religious, yet sorely tried by myriad socio-economic, political, cultural dilemmas.

My preferred method corrects the misconception that theology is a closed enterprise bordering on the arcane. In fact, dialogue and inter-disciplinarity count as key characteristics of theological activity. A dialogical and inter-disciplinary approach allows theology to address a wider variety of contexts that inform faith and life in Africa with a greater degree of credibility and confidence. I argue for and adopt this approach without claiming that it is the only valid method of doing theology. It does not, as might be feared, collapse theology into anthropology, sociology or religious studies. A generative contextualised theological method may raise questions that strain traditional categories; yet it neither abandons nor undervalues the rich resources of Christian tradition and Scripture. What direction this approach might take or the quality of the result it might yield in the future remains a matter for debate. It is enough to realise that unlike in the past, in today's Africa, *theology works*. To pay attention constantly to how and where it works appears as one of the major methodological considerations currently shaping the theological mind in Africa.

Chapter 15

My Theological Pilgrimage

C. René Padilla

I was born and reared in a poor – not extremely, but still quite poor – home in Quito, Ecuador. My father was a tailor who had learned his trade when he was thirteen years old. I remember him working long hours – sometimes deep into the night and mostly at home – with a great sense of responsibility to provide for the needs of the family. But I also remember him reading (mainly Christian) books, the Bible or the newspaper, sometimes in silence, sometimes loud enough for my mother and anyone else within reach to hear what he read while she prepared a meal. He had only studied up to third grade of primary school, but he was an avid reader. Undoubtedly, his reading habit was one of the legacies that all his children, including me, received from him.

My mother also did some tailoring, but she was mainly dedicated to taking care of their family of three girls and four boys. She had only finished primary school, but she excelled as a steward of the limited material resources that she had at her disposal. I remember her as a very intelligent and generous woman, always looking for ways to help people who had less means than we had. And how can I forget the times when she would pawn a valuable jewel she had, in order to feed her family?

When I was two-and-a-half years old we moved to Colombia. Those were the times of the Great Depression, and I suspect that my father found that his trade offered him better possibilities to support the family there than in his own country. Little did I know that this move would be for me in the end a sort of preparation for living as a stranger in a foreign land most of my life!

At that time Colombia had a concordat with the Vatican. There was no separation between Church and State, and the country, as was the case with several Latin American countries, was officially under the aegis of the Roman Catholic Church.[1] Accordingly, there was no religious freedom;[2] and schoolchildren were obliged to attend mass and to participate in Roman Catholic activities. My parents had become evangelical Christians in Ecuador, and we children experienced the resulting tensions and even persecution that were part and parcel of life for non-Roman

---

[1]   For a classical description of the Roman Catholicism that the Spanish conquerors brought to Latin America, see John A. Mackay, *The Other Spanish Christ: A Study of the Spiritual History of Spain and South America* (Macmillan, 1933).

[2]   The 1991 National Constitution of the Republic of Colombia instituted religious freedom and abolished the role of the Sacred Heart of Jesus as the protector of the Nation. It ruled that any person could establish a religious cult. Since then, the Protestant (mostly Pentecostal) movement has expanded in an amazing way.

Catholic Christians and others in pre-2nd Vatican Council days.[3] My older brother, Washington,[4] was expelled from high school because of arguing with a priest in a religion class, and I was expelled from third grade for not attending a Roman Catholic procession. These incidents led my parents to decide to return to Ecuador, with the addition of two sons and one daughter born in Colombia, a country where religious freedom had become a constitutional right in 1895.

Back in Quito, I finished primary school and then entered one of the very best government high schools in the country: *Colegio Mejía*. There my inherited Christian faith was put to the test for the first time. Several of my teachers were atheists and Marxists, and they seemed to delight in posing difficult questions to students in their classes. For instance, 'How can God be both good and powerful at the same time? If God is good, how can God allow so much injustice in the world? If God is good, God must not have the power to prevent injustice! On the other hand, if God is powerful, why does God not prevent injustice from prevailing in the world? If God is powerful, God must not be good, otherwise God would prevent injustice from prevailing in the world!' Or 'What do you, Christians, propose in order to eliminate injustice? Does your God care for the victims of injustice? If God does, what are you doing for the sake of justice?' In light of my home background, how could I deny the relevance of these questions?

Most of my peers were nominal non-practicing-Roman Catholics, and during the time that we were together as classmates several of them became atheists, some of them Marxists. As for me, as a boy fifteen or sixteen years old, I saw the need to personally decide whether I wanted to be a Christian or not. To that end, I read the New Testament from beginning to end. By God's grace, the result was that I committed my life to Jesus Christ and found myself longing to understand the meaning of the Christian faith in relation to issues of justice and peace in a society deeply marked by oppression, exploitation, and abuse of power.

Because of economic reasons, all through my high school years I was compelled to have a part-time job. Free time was very scarce, but I still managed to find time to read. I enjoyed literature – and that was my major in high school – and philosophy, but I also kept looking for books that would help me understand the social implications of the Gospel. That was not an easy task as the only Christian books that I found that pointed in that direction were the writings of Gonzalo Báez-Camargo, Alberto Rembao, and John A. Mackay – three pioneers of Protestant theology in Latin

---

[3]   There is no intention here to discredit the Roman Catholic Church. The religious intolerance toward non-Roman Catholic Christians and others is part of Latin American history and part of my own family history.

[4]   As an adult, this brother studied at Fuller Theological Seminary in Pasadena, California, and went back to Ecuador, where he worked with *The Voice of the Andes – HCJB* radio station and other Christian institutions, including the Bible Society of Ecuador, and became the first President of the Human Rights Commission in that country. He authored several books, including the first history of Protestantism in Ecuador, *La Iglesia y los dioses modernos* (Corporación Editora Nacional and Fraternidad Teológica Latinoamericana, 1989). He died on Good Friday, 1990.

America.[5] My reading of these authors affirmed in me the conviction that my total inability to articulate a Christian answer to the questions my teachers posed was due to the lack of a social dimension in the Gospel I had received at home – a Gospel for *individual* salvation by grace, through faith in Jesus Christ, and little more than that.

During my high school years, I had done a couple of correspondence courses on the Bible and Christian doctrine and had actively participated in street and prison evangelism. I had also been a member of a team in charge of organizing and leading a vacation camp for young people in Shell Mera in 1953 which was a team that included Jim Elliot and Peter Fleming. Who could have imagined at that time that these two young missionaries were to be martyred within the next three years?[6]

With this experience in voluntary service and with the encouragement of my brother Washington, who by then was studying at Rockmont College in Denver, Colorado, I decided to apply to Wheaton College in Wheaton, Illinois. My deep desire was to study the Bible and theology, but at the same time also to get the training in a profession, perhaps in Medicine. I was accepted, got an immigrant's visa, and traveled to the United States. I arrived in Wheaton in August of 1953 with my rather scarce high-school knowledge of English and what for me was a huge debt – the debt I incurred in order to buy my plane fare. I was supposed to start classes in the fall semester of 1953–54, but it did not take long for me to realize that I was not ready for that, even apart from the language problem. I had no money to pay tuition or room and board. I took courage and went to speak to Dr. Victor Edman, the President of Wheaton College at that time, and he kindly made arrangements for me to work washing dishes at the College dining hall and to start classes in January of 1954. By taking summer courses, I was able to fulfill the course requirements in three-and-a-half years and graduated with my BA in Philosophy in May of 1957.

The idea of studying Medicine or a similar career did not last very long. Once I got into philosophy, combined with several courses in Bible, theology and Greek, I became increasingly convinced that my next step was an MA in Theology. Further, at the 1954 Urbana Missionary Convention of InterVarsity Christian Fellowship, I had been challenged to prepare myself for Christian work among university students in Latin America. Accordingly, I applied to Wheaton College Graduate School. I was accepted and granted a fellowship, and I graduated (*in absentia*) with an MA in January of 1960.

I am deeply grateful for all that I received from Wheaton College. Far more than theological *contents* (of which there were plenty), what I received was a good acquaintance with diverse theological positions and tools for exegetical work, including the original biblical languages. Only later, after returning to Latin America in 1959, did I realize that Wheaton College had failed to give me a hermeneutical approach to enable me to answer the questions of justice and peace that had been

---

⁵ See, for example, Carlos Mondragón, *Leudar la masa: El pensamiento social de los protestantes en América Latina, 1920–1950* (Kairós, 2005).

⁶ Philip James ('Jim') Elliot and Peter Fleming were killed on January 8, 1956, by the Wuaorani Indians – more commonly known as 'Aucas' – in the Ecuadorian Amazon jungle, together with T. Edward McCully, Nathanael 'Nate' Saint, and Roger Youderian.

implanted in me during my high school years – questions that somehow during my Wheaton years I had managed to put in recess.

After finishing my studies at Wheaton College, I joined the International Fellowship of Evangelical Students (IFES)[7] as a staff worker and was appointed as a traveling secretary for four countries: Venezuela, Colombia, Ecuador, and Peru. My main task was to find Christian students in the main universities of these countries and to encourage them to be witnesses to Jesus Christ among their peers. It was then that I realized that I was ill prepared to wrestle with the questions that university students, both Christians and non-Christians, were asking – questions related to the relevance of the Christian faith to the Latin American socio-economic and political situation. The Cuban revolution had just triumphed and its leaders, including Fidel Castro and Che Guevara, had become icons of a new era: the era of social justice for the countries in the region. As a result, questions regarding Christian responsibility in society had become a serious concern and a recurring subject of conversation especially among university students.

In this context, time after time I found myself lacking a social ethic. My years of studies in the United States had not prepared me for the sort of theological reflection that was urgently needed in a revolutionary situation! My professor of hermeneutics at Wheaton College was Dr. A. Berkeley Mickelsen, who (a few years after I took his course) wrote *Interpreting the Bible*.[8] I could have hardly had a more brilliant expositor of the historical-grammatical approach to Bible study. I deeply appreciated his combination of sincere belief in the trustworthiness of Scripture, rigorous scholarship, and warmhearted commitment to biblical truth. For my beloved professor, 'the task of interpreters *is to find out the meaning of a statement (command, question) for the author and for the hearers and readers, and thereupon to transmit that meaning to modern readers.*'[9] Upon returning to Latin America as a staff worker with the IFES, the questions posed by university students and others forced me to see that the historical-grammatical approach to hermeneutics was a good and necessary step, but it was not enough.

The fact was that if I was to help Christian university students to witness to Jesus Christ in a context of injustice and poverty, it was not enough to teach them to study the Scriptures with the focus on the message in its original contexts. I had to help them relate biblical teaching to human life in all its dimensions. Necessarily, that meant going beyond the historical-grammatical approach to Bible study; it implied a rather different view of the hermeneutical task, an expanded view that in the interpretive process would keep the inextricable link between Scripture and the present-day context and between theology and social ethics.

---

[7]   The IFES is a worldwide fellowship of Christian university students who seek to witness to Jesus Christ among their peers. It was officially launched in Harvard in 1947, a year after a group of leaders of student movements in ten countries (Australia, Canada, China, France, Great Britain, Netherlands, New Zealand, Norway, Switzerland and the United States) had met in Oxford, England. At present the IFES is working in 150 countries. The InterVarsity Christian Fellowship (IVCF) in the United States and the Universities and Colleges Christian Fellowship (UCCF) in the United Kingdom are members of the IFES.

[8]   A Berkley Mickelson, *Interpreting the Bible* (Eerdmans, 1963).

[9]   Mickelson, p. 5, emphasis his.

Furthermore, I could not simply assume that I could extract myself from my own historical context, with all its conditioning socio-economic, political, and cultural factors, in order to interpret the text *objectively* or in line with the Subject/Object scheme inherited from the Enlightenment. I began to see myself and today's Church as actually participating in the story of the people of God which begins in the Old Testament and continues to unfold in the New and throughout the whole Christian era up to the present time. I realized that, without discarding the aim to understand the original historical context and the original meaning of the text, the task of interpreters had to be expanded to include, right from the start, the aim of articulating the biblical message for the sake of lifestyle transformation, for individuals and communities, according to the moral vision of Scripture.

Before I left for England (together with my wife Catharine and our two eldest daughters) for a period of study at the University of Manchester, *Cristianismo y Sociedad en América Latina* (Church and Society in Latin America)[10] had taken shape, and the writings of some of its leaders, Julio de Santa Ana, Rubem Alves, Hiber Contreris, and Julio Barreiro and others, had begun to circulate throughout Latin America. I fully agreed with their objective, which was to explore the socio-economic and political dimensions of the Christian faith, but I disagreed with their methodology.[11] From my perspective, their project was giving a great deal of attention to society, but not enough attention to Christianity. My feelings toward them, therefore, were quite ambiguous.

The research that I had to do in order to receive a PhD[12] in Biblical Criticism and Exegesis from the University of Manchester (UK) gave me the opportunity to do a lot of reading of biblical literature on topics related to social ethics. The resulting dissertation was to a large extent a Western style academic work, mainly focused on exegesis. After all, it was written in a Western academic context in the 1960s! Even so, the research provided me with a number of theological insights that later could be fueled into contextual theological reflection, such as the following:

- God's purpose of redemption embraces the whole of creation – not only individuals but all humankind and all things in heaven and on earth.
- The God of Israel is the God of all peoples, not only the God of Israel and not only the God of Christians, but the God of all.
- The prophetic announcement of a new era of justice and peace, the Kingdom of God, was fulfilled in the life and ministry of Jesus Christ.
- Christ's death is the means of reconciliation not only with God but also with

---

[10]   The first conference of this 'think tank' sponsored by the World Council of Churches was held in Lima, Perú, July 23–27, 1961. During the 1960s, *Cristianismo y Sociedad en América Latina* grew throughout Latin America, especially in Protestant circles. There is a good basis to claim that this movement laid the basis for liberation theology in the region.

[11]   For an elaboration of both my agreement and dissent with *Cristianismo y Sociedad en América Latina*, see my chapter, 'Iglesia y Sociedad en América Latina,' in C. René Padilla (ed.), *Fe cristiana y Latinoamérica hoy* (Certeza, 1974), pp. 119–147.

[12]   I finished my dissertation on 'Church and World: A Study Into the Relation Between the Church and the World in the Teaching of Paul the Apostle' in October of 1965, under the supervision of Prof. F.F. Bruce, and graduated *in absentia* in June of 1966.

one's neighbor to such an extent that through it every form of separation among human beings is abolished.

- Evil has a systemic nature. It does not only relate to individual sin but is structured in 'this world' dominated by the powers of darkness.
- The Church of Jesus Christ is the first fruits of a new humanity and occupies a central place in God's purpose.
- Although salvation is by grace alone, through faith, Christian discipleship is closely related to *participation* in God's mission and necessarily includes the practice of good works.
- Suffering is inseparable from mission.
- Because God is a God of justice, Christian concern for and action on behalf of the poor are an integral part of the Christian mission.
- True Christian spirituality is inseparable from submission to the Lordship of Jesus Christ in all areas of life and is possible by the power of the Holy Spirit.

Back in Latin America, I was thrust again into a situation that forced me to acknowledge my need to find 'a new way of doing theology' – a theology *faithful* to the Christian narrative witnessed to in Scripture, and at the same time *relevant* to present-day practical life in a world where injustice and oppression, corruption and abuse of power were rampant. A decisive contributing factor to satisfy that need was the IFES. Having been appointed Associate General Secretary of this student movement in Latin America shortly after my return, I found myself obliged to combine theological reflection – much of it clearly oriented to the shaping of national Christian university student movements throughout Latin America – with a great deal of administrative work, frequent traveling, public relations and staff training. Time for theological work as such was limited, but one can hardly exaggerate the importance that the IFES emphasis on the development of autochthonous national student-led movements had for those of us who were privileged to serve as student workers. We were given freedom to think and to creatively respond to the demands of the time without feeling compelled to conform to a ready-made imported program. As a result, the IFES in Latin America became a seedbed of a theology rooted in Scripture yet at the same time deeply aware of the need to spell out the practical social implications of the biblical message for the life and mission of Christians as individuals and as communities in the region.

The First Latin American Congress on Evangelism (or CLADE I in Spanish), sponsored by the Billy Graham Evangelistic Association, was held in Bogotá, Colombia, November 21–30, 1969, as a follow-up to the World Congress on Evangelism that had taken place in Berlin in 1966. CLADE I was 'made in the USA,' with very little by Latin Americans in the planning. It was supposed to be the launching platform for a thirty-year master plan to evangelize Latin America, but it offered an outstanding opportunity for the public exposition of the missiological reflection which was taking place in IFES circles. The spokesman for it was Samuel Escobar. No better choice of speaker could have been made! Samuel combined vast knowledge of and real passion for the subject with arresting eloquence, and a mellow spirit. As a result, his paper on 'The Social Responsibility of the Church'[13] provoked a standing ovation and threw into relief the fact that a significant sector of the evangelical leadership in Latin America was fertile soil for social concerns from a biblical perspective.

In light of the purpose of the organizers, CLADE I was a failure as the only concrete result was the unintended formation of what later became *Fraternidad Teológica Latinoamericana* (FTL). Its founding members met during CLADE I and decided to organize a theological forum that would facilitate an open discussion of the issues that Samuel Escobar had raised in his paper. The inaugural consultation was held in December 12–18 of the following year (1970) in Cochabamba, Bolivia.[14] Peter Savage, the son of missionaries in Peru (where he was born) was appointed the first General Secretary.

The timing for the formation of the FTL could hardly have been more opportune. The early 1970s turned out to be a time of major shifts in theology, strongly marked by two factors: (1) The stark reality of military dictatorships in several countries of Latin America – repressive regimes backed up by the United States government in light of the Cold War; (2) The flourishing of liberation theology, especially in Roman Catholic circles, which encouraged the recognition of 'God's preferential option for the poor' at the second General Latin American Episcopal Conference (CELAM), held in Medellin (Colombia) in 1968 for the purpose of analyzing the implications of the Second Vatican Council and of Pope Paul's encyclical *Popularum Progressio* (1967) for the region. Under these circumstances, how could people committed to God's revelation in Jesus Christ be satisfied with a theology devoid of social ethics? The FTL accepted the challenge and emerged as an attempt to articulate an evangelical theology both rooted in Scripture and relevant to life torn by socio-economic, political and ideological confrontation. A modest contribution to that end was the reflection that took place at the First Evangelical Consultation on Social Ethics, July 5–8, in Lima, Peru, which I organized as Director of *Ediciones Certeza* (the IFES publishing program for Latin America) for the purpose of producing a book that would encourage the reader to 'a life commitment to Jesus Christ – a commitment embodied in the Latin American reality.'[15] Even more important was the rediscovery of the centrality of the Kingdom of God in the life and ministry of Jesus Christ, which was the theme of the second FTL Consultation held in Lima, Peru, and became an axis for the FTL theology and ministry in the following years.

---

[13]   This historical speech was later published in English as 'The Social Impact of the Gospel,' in (ed.) Brian Griffiths, *Is Revolution Change?* (Inter-Varsity Press, 1972), pp. 84–105.

[14]   The proceedings of this conference were published in P. Savage (ed.), *Debate contemporáneo sobre la Biblia* (Evangélicas Europeas, 1972). On the first ten years of the FTL, see Daniel Salinas, 'The Beginnings of the *Fraternidad Teológica Latinoamericana*: Courage to Grow,' *Journal of Latin American Theology: Christian Reflections from the Latin South*, 2/1 (2007): 8–160.

[15]   The participants in this consultation were Samuel Escobar, Orlando E. Costas, Charles F. Denton, José Míguez-Bonino, C. René Padilla, Justo L. González, Pedro Arana, and Juan Carlos Ortiz. The proceedings were published in C. René Padilla, (ed.), *Fe cristiana y Latinoamericana hoy* (Certeza, 1974).

An unexpected event placed me within the orbit of what came to be known as 'radical evangelical' theology: the International Congress on World Evangelization (ICOWE),[16] which took place in Lausanne, Switzerland, in July 1974 and had as its motto 'Let the Earth Hear His Voice.' *Time Magazine* described it as 'a formidable forum, possibly the widest-ranging meeting of Christians ever held.' Perhaps never before or after have I felt so much at the center of, and so undeserving of the role given me in, what God was doing to awaken the social conscience of his people as when I delivered my plenary paper on 'Evangelization and the World'[17] in the morning of the third day of the Congress. Unpredictably, my speech was a lighted match that started a fire of open debate on a number of crucial missiological issues. A few days later, my good friend Samuel Escobar's paper on 'Evangelism and Man's Search for Freedom, Justice, and Personal Fulfillment'[18] added wood to the fire. Our main concerns, wrought in the context of the IFES in Latin America, were thus heard on a world stage and found a place (sometimes expressed in words literally quoted from our papers) in the well-known *Lausanne Covenant*.

My Lausanne paper was a synthesis of insights I had gained through my doctoral studies, combined with years of experience in university student work. To my surprise, four issues that I had touched on in that paper were included in the agenda of international theological conferences that took place in the succeeding years, in all of which I was invited to participate as a speaker:

The use of the 'homogeneous unit principle' as the basis for the missionary strategy of the church: In Lausanne I denounced the worldliness implied in the thesis that 'people *like* to be with those of their own race and class and we must therefore plant segregated churches, which will undoubtedly grow faster.'[19] This theme was debated at the Consultation on Homogeneous Units and Church Growth, which took place at Fuller Theological Seminary in Pasadena, California, May 30–June 2, 1977. I read in it a paper on 'The Unity of the Church and the Homogeneous Unit Principle.'[20]

The relation between Gospel and culture: In Lausanne I condemned the identification of Christianity with 'the American Way of life' and argued that 'the Church must be delivered from anything and everything in its culture that would prevent it from being faithful to the Lord in the fulfillment of its mission within and beyond its own culture.'[21] This topic was taken up at the Consultation on Gospel and Culture held in

---

[16]   The proceedings of the ICOWE were published in J.D. Douglas (ed.), *Let the Earth Hear His Voice: International Congress on World Evangelization, Lausanne, Switzerland* (World Wide Publications, 1975).

[17]   Douglas, pp. 116–146.

[18]   Douglas, pp. 303–326.

[19]   Douglas, p. 137.

[20]   This paper was later published in the *International Bulletin of Missionary Research* VI/1 (1982): pp. 23ff. and also in Wilbert R. Shenk (ed.), *Exploring Church Growth* (Eerdmans, 1983), pp. 285ff.

[21]   Douglas, p. 136.

Willowbank, Bermuda, in January of 1978. In that consultation I presented a paper on 'Hermeneutics and Culture: A Theological Perspective.'[22]

The relation between Gospel and lifestyle: In Lausanne I insisted on the impossibility, from a biblical perspective, to separate faith from practical life. 'Becoming a Christian,' I said, 'is not a religious change, in which one becomes the adherent of a cult, but a reorientation of the whole [person] in relation to God, to [one's neighbor], and to creation. It is not the mere addition of new patterns imposed on the old ... but a restructuring of one's whole personality, a reorientation of one's whole life in the world.'[23] This issue was examined at the Consultation on Simple Lifestyle, held in London, England, in March of 1980, at which I presented a paper on 'New Testament Perspective on Simple Lifestyle.'[24]

The relation between evangelism and social responsibility: In Lausanne I criticized the attempt to separate evangelism from social responsibility in the mission of the church. I said: 'I refuse ... to drive a wedge between a primary task, namely the proclamation of the Gospel and a secondary (at best) or even optional (at worst) task of the church. In order to be obedient to its Lord the Church should never do anything that is not essential, therefore, nothing that the Church does in obedience to its Lord is unessential. Why? Because love to God is inseparable from love to [people]; because faith without works is dead; because hope includes the restoration of all things to the Kingdom of God.'[25] This issue was taken up by the Consultation on the Relation between Evangelism and Social Responsibility held in Grand Rapids, Michigan, in June of 1982, at which I responded to Arthur P. Johnston's paper on 'The Kingdom in Relation to the Church and the World.'[26]

In the Introduction to *The New Face of Evangelicalism: An International Symposium on the Lausanne Covenant* (1976), which I edited shortly after the ICOWE, I stated that 'The Lausanne Covenant is little more than a detailed outline for an evangelical theology of mission.'[27] In a sense, because of the international consultations to which

---

[22]   The proceedings of this consultation were published in J. Stott and R. Coote (eds.), *Gospel and Culture* (William Carey Library, 1979). My essay was included in pp. 83–108. It was to a large extent based on a paper on 'The Contextualization of the Gospel', which I had presented at an international consultation on evangelical literature in Latin America held in June of 1975 held in Pinebrook, Pennsylvania, under the sponsorship of Partnership in Mission and the David C. Cook Foundation. This paper was included in the collection C. Kraft and T. Wisley (eds.), *Readings in Dynamic Indigeneity* (William Carey Library, 1979).

[23]   Douglas, p. 143.

[24]   The proceedings of this consultation were published in Ronald Sider (ed.), *Lifestyle in the Eighties:An Evangelical Commitment to Simple Lifestyle* (Paternoster, 1982). My paper was included in pp. 54–66.

[25]   Douglas, pp. 144–5.

[26]   The proceedings of this consultation were published in Bruce J. Nichols (ed.), *In Word and Deed: Evangelism and Social Responsibility* (Paternoster, 1985). Only a brief synthesis of my paper on 'The Church in Light of the Kingdom of God' was included in pp. 133–4.

[27]   Padilla, *New Face*, p. 15.

I was invited as a speaker between 1974 and 1982, more than by conscious choice, my theological reflections were to a large extent modest explorations of the issues included in that outline. Most of papers written in connection with these consultations were included in 1985's *Mission Between the Times: Essays on the Kingdom.*[28]

Already in November of 1979, the Second Latin American Congress on Evangelism (CLADE II), held in Lima, Peru, was a clear demonstration of the vitality of the theological thinking which, beginning in 1970, had been developing in FTL circles all over Latin America.[29] Entirely planned and carried out by Latin Americans, CLADE II strengthened the FTL as a movement made up of Christians committed to the task of articulating a biblical theology rooted in Scripture and relevant to their socioeconomic and political context.

As General Secretary of the FTL from 1984–92, I devoted much of my time to the promotion of this biblical and contextual approach to theology, especially among the younger generation. With little time to write myself, I invested countless hours organizing international and regional theological conferences and editing collective works on a variety of subjects related to social ethics. My period as executive officer of the FTL concluded with the Third Latin American Congress on Evangelism (CLADE III),[30] held in Quito, Ecuador, in 1992; a conference of which the distinguished Argentine theologian José Míguez-Bonino wrote: 'This ... meeting went beyond the limits of the Latin American Theological Fraternity to become a truly "Latin American Protestant Congress," as much due to the breadth of its representation as to the wealth of materials and the freedom of debate. We were there present as a truly "ecumenical event" – if the reader will forgive the use of this controversial term – of Latin American Protestantism.'[31]

This survey of my theological pilgrimage would not be complete without my making at least a very brief comment on each of two areas of reflection that have attracted my attention in the last few years. The first one is ecclesiology. Having served as a pastor in a Baptist church in Buenos Aires from 1976 to 1988, I became convinced that there is no place where contextual biblical theology has a greater possibility to display its transforming power than the local Christian congregation, called to be 'the community of the King'. My church experience, especially during those years, showed me the great potential that there is in the local church to become 'an agent of transformation.'[32]

---

[28]   The English edition was published by Eerdmans in 1985 and was followed by editions in Spanish, Swedish, German, Portuguese, and Korean. The Spanish version had as its title an expression that in the following years became the most common way to identify the main distinctive contribution of the FTL to mission thinking: *mission integral* (integral mission).

[29]   The proceedings of this conference were published under the title *América Latina y la evangelización en los años 80* (FTL, 1979). It includes the paper that I presented on 'Cristo y Anticristo en la proclamación' (pp. 219–231).

[30]   The proceedings of this conference were published under the title *CLADE III: Todo el Evangelio para todos los pueblos desde América Latina* (FTL, 1993).

[31]   José Míguez-Bonino, *Faces of Latin American Protestantism* (Eerdmans, 1997), pp. 50–51.

[32]   For an account of this experience, see 'Vignettes of a Servant Church,' in Tetsunao Yamamori and C. René Padilla (eds.), *The Local Church, Agent of Transformation: An*

The second area is the phenomenon of globalization. The dominant form of globalization at the beginning of the twenty-first century is the globalization of so-called neo-liberal capitalism, which Leslie Sklair aptly describes as 'driven by the TNCs [transnational corporations], organized politically through the transnational political class, and fuelled by the culture-ideology of consumerism, [which] is the most potent force for change in the world.'[33] The sinister consequences that this global economic system of institutionalized injustice is having on the poor around the world, including my own context, can hardly be exaggerated. That being the case, I am convinced that if the Church is to be relevant to the large majority of people in the world, she needs to learn what it means to communicate Jesus Christ's good news to the poor not only through what she *says* but also through what she *is* and what she *does*. Integral mission is not an option among many others – it is the only way for the Church everywhere, in the North and in the South, in the East and in the West. It means, among other things, practical solidarity with people in need – not only the sinners but also the 'sinned-against.'[34]

Ecclesiology for Integral Mission (Kairos, 2004), pp. 289–300.

[33] L. Sklair, *Globalization: Capitalism and Its Alternatives* (Oxford University Press, 2002), p. 47.

[34] For an elaboration of this topic, see C. René Padilla, *Transforming Church and Mission* (Forum for World Evangelization, 2004).

Chapter 16

A Life Story Intertwined with Theology

Andrew Sung Park

A Taste of Death

My theological journey started with a life crisis. During a summer camp, when I was a junior in high school, I tried to swim across a small bay. In the middle of the bay, I was exhausted but struggled to make it. After a desperate effort, I decided to let go of my dear life by letting go of my struggles. While sinking, within a split second I thought about the meaning of life. But, 'thanks be to God', the area was not deep enough and I was able to stand, keeping my head above water. This experience led me to ponder the direction of my life. I read part of *Meditations* by Marcus Aurelius and felt the vanity of life. The meaninglessness of life eventually directed me to finding the meaning of life in God.

A Mystical Experience

In 1970, when I was a sophomore in college, a group of students went to a country church for a week to help its vacation Bible school. On the Wednesday night, while I was doing a night vigil with others, I felt something unusual after midnight; an intense heat landed on my back. I thought it was a temporary summer heat overwhelming me, but it did not go away and it stayed with me while praying. Even in wintertime, the heat came back when I prayed in a cold empty chapel. Until I had this experience, my understanding of Christianity had been strictly as a moral/rational religion. After that event, I realized that Christianity was more than an ethical way of life.

That experience led me to read Christian mystical writings. Thomas à Kempis, Sadhu Sundar Singh, and Emmanuel Swedenborg were my favorite mystics. Their worldviews and theologies greatly influenced my young mind. They helped me draw a bigger picture of life in this universe and beyond. Sadhu Sundar Singh's life and thought have particularly challenged my life. His conversion process from Hinduism to Christianity is very similar to Saint Paul's. Unlike most Roman Catholic mystics, he did not pursue a mystical union with God. Rather God sought after him for communion. His life was not other-worldly and reclusive, but was active and transformative in this world for Christ's sake. His approach is Christocentric, yet inclusive. I was told, contrary to Singh and the others, that mysticism has a negative impact upon life by promoting a cloistered life and other-worldliness. That has not been my experience. The more I pursue the mystical side of Christianity, the more I get involved in the transformation of the world because I realize the eternal values of the present state of world affairs

Indebted to these mystics, I continue to love to explore other mystics and have taught on Christian mystics throughout my teaching at Claremont School of Theology (1987–1992) and United Theological Seminary (1992–the present).

Han[1] of the Family

When our family emigrated to the US in January 1973, we faced a tragic event in December of the same year as my parents were involved in a fatal automobile accident in Colorado Springs, Colorado. That was the darkest time of my life.

My mother's life was a series of *han*. Born under the Japanese occupation (1910–1945) and nurtured in a good Confucian family, she married a Christian, served an extended family, lost all the family possessions to the North Korean Communists after the independence of Korea and barely escaped to South Korea. She suffered the Korean War (1950–53), happened to be a refugee again with her extended family, became a poor country preacher's wife, supported the family through a variety of unskilled works, emigrated to the USA and was killed in an automobile accident. Since my youth, I had watched how she suffered her *han*-ridden life and physically collapsed a number of times because of unbearable *hans*. Because of my parents' life, especially my mother's, I have been keenly aware of issues of *han*.

Our family *han* was not an isolated *han*, but was connected with the collective *han* of Korea. In 1945, as soon as independence was restored, Korea was divided into North and South, against the people's will. It is incredible that Korea was divided. For example, after World War II, Germany was divided in two because of its crimes and its potential threat to the future world. In contrast, Japan committed the war crimes, but it was Korea that was divided.

Why did the division of Korea happen? South and North Koreans have spent 40% of their national budgets for military spending over the past 60 years in addition to the terrible cost of the Korean War. Our family's *han* is directly connected to the *han* of Korea.

In 1970, another significant event happened in Korea. Tai-il Chun, an uneducated Christian laborer, tried to organize a labor union in Seoul Peace Market for the first time in Korean history. As the Park regime hindered his labor union movement and blocked his street demonstration, he immolated himself to protest the exploitation of some 800 sewing machine shopowners against their 20,000 workers, most of them under-age workers. He ignited the *Minjung*[2] movement in Korea, which gave a birth to *Minjung* theology in the 1970s and later a civilian government in the 1990s. Because of my personal background and my background as a Korean, I was bound to focus on the issue of *han* in the world.

---

[1]   In Korean, *han* is a deep physical, mental, and spiritual ache responding to a terrible injustice done to a person, a wrench of all the organs, an intensely internalized or externalized anger, and the sense of helplessness and hopelessness.

[2]   *Minjung* in Korean are the common people who are politically oppressed, economically exploited, socially isolated, culturally despised, or religiously condemned.

Out of these backgrounds, I developed a theological method that focuses on *han* as a starting point. Sin causes hurt. If the hurt is not healed, it turns into *han*. Sin usually causes *han* in our moral life. *Han* can, in turn, cause sin or another *han*, perpetuating the vicious cycle of evil. How do we stop this vicious cycle of sin and *han*? An important task of theology is to locate the entanglement of sin and *han* and to find their solution.

In 1993, I dealt with the relations between *han* and sin in my *The Wounded Heart of God: The Asian Concept of Han and the Christian Doctrine of Sin.* It points out that without raising a question, there is no answer. Without diagnosing the real problems of people, we cannot unilaterally proclaim the good news of Jesus to them. Pastors and theologians have had only one tool to diagnose the problems of the world: sin. However, the theme of 'sin and repentance' has been overused for preaching and theological treatises. The sin-repentance model does not work for the *sinned-against*. Instead, my work suggests that sin and *han* be understood together to bring salvation to sinners and healing or liberation to the *sinned-against*.

In 2004, I took up this theme for further development in *From Hurt To Healing: A Theology of the Wounded.* I drew two distinctive routes of faith journeys for the *sinned-against* and sinners. For sinners, the Church has mapped out their journey: sin→ guilt→ guilt-anger→ repentance→ forgiveness→ justification→ sanctification→ full sanctification or Christian perfection (a map for the salvation of sinners). But for the *sinned-against* there has been no map showing their way to healing or liberation. For this reason, I developed a parallel map for the *sinned-against*, showing their way to liberation based on the Bible: *han* → shame→shame-anger→ resistance→ forgivingness→ justice→ healing→ jubilee/joy (a map for the liberation of the *sinned-against*). By juxtaposing these two journeys for contrast, I was really stressing the before 'uncharted' journey of the *sinned-against*. It is important, however, to understand that most people are sinners as well as the *sinned-against*, and thus need *both* journeys for their salvation and liberation.

The Claremont Years

As a student at Claremont, my old male-centered views began to disintegrate. Charlotte Ellen, spouse of the late Howard Clinebell, raised my consciousness. During the sessions of her consciousness-raising class, we did simulation games, in one of which I played a woman for a day. Through simulation games and class experiences, for the first time in my life I could see and feel the pain of women, particularly of my mother and my two younger sisters. When we grew up together, I tried to influence them to be 'good' young women, playing down their potential. Confronted by the course, I was turned around from my patriarchal ideas.

At Claremont, I also met John Cobb Jr. who changed the direction of my life. My interest moved from pastoral counseling to theology because of John Cobb. I had known theology as a narrow doctrinal discipline, but Cobb opened the horizon of my theological views, engaging me to study ecological, inter-religious, scientific, and process theology. Theology was not a dry, dreadful and dead discipline any longer;

it was alive! I thoroughly enjoyed learning theology. Like a sponge, I absorbed all the new learning into my heart.

Later, when I read Robert McAfee Brown's *Theology in a New Key,* I decided the direction of my study – to pursue liberation theology. He was teaching at Graduate Theological Union in Berkeley. Subsequently, I entered a PhD program at Graduate Theological Union.

Minjung Theology/Science and Religion

At Graduate Theological Union at Berkeley, I studied liberation theology/North American liberation theology under Robert McAfee Brown. With his encouragement I studied *Minjung* theology. There I also met Durwood Foster, a Tillich scholar. As his assistant, I taught the theology of Tillich with him for a couple of years. This teaching experience gave me an opportunity to be submerged in Tillich's theology. Robert Bellah also influenced me with his insights on the Sociology of Religion. All three guided me through the PhD program as my committee members and shaped me as a scholar.

In 1981, the Center for Theology and the Natural Sciences was established by Robert Russell at Graduate Theological Union. It was a great joy for me to learn from prominent scientists from UC Berkeley and Stanford University concerning the empirical and natural sciences – physics, biology, and Artificial Intelligence. Thus, at Claremont, my interest in the dialogue between theology and the natural sciences was formed and I was involved in the 1988 publication of John Cobb and Charles Birth's *The Liberation of Life: From the Cell to the Community.*

In 1985, I married a PhD chemical research scientist Sunok Jane Myong and since then, the dialogue between theology and natural sciences has really transpired at home. In 1997, Jane and I won a John Templeton Course Award and did team teaching at United Theological Seminary. It has been delightful for me to offer theology and science courses on a regular basis since then. I have never understood theology better than when studying it with the natural sciences. The natural sciences expose God's creation, the history of the universe, miracles, the future of humanity, and the end of the universe. But the natural sciences have their limitations. They cannot go beyond the boundary of the physical universe. Christian theology, particularly Christian mysticism, provides the meanings of creation and of our existence and our ultimate destiny.

I see these two ways complementing as well as confronting each other. These two ways are ultimate companions in searching for the meaning and direction of our lives, alleviating human suffering and offering a new horizon of hope. Theologians without the help of the natural sciences will turn theology into an irrelevant ideology. It is my hope to re-examine Christian doctrines in light of scientific theories and Christian mysticism.

Racial Conflict and Healing

After completing my doctoral program in 1985, I served Calvary Korean United Methodist Church in San Francisco with my spouse. We served the church with devotion and passion and the church had grown from twenty people to eighty regular attendees when we left for a faculty position at the Claremont School of Theology in 1987. It was delightful and humbling for me to teach at Claremont with my former teachers.

In 1992, racial conflicts erupted in the Los Angeles area after the verdict of the Rodney King trial. The angry crowd torched 2,500 Korean American shops in 'Korea Town,' prompted in part by an incident in which a Korean-American shopowner's wife shot and killed a fifteen year-old African-American girl in her store in 1991. The collisions between Korean-American communities and the African-American communities were almost inevitable because a number of Korean-Americans were store- owning middleman minorities in African-American neighborhoods. To resolve the racial tension, I was involved in the establishment of the African-American and Korean-American Clergy Coalition.

However, even before the 1992 eruptions, there were other incidents of conflict between these two racial groups in New York City. The 'Red Apple boycott' by New York African-Americans was headline national news in 1990. I was invited by the Multi-Ethnic Center of Drew Theological School to lecture on ethnic tensions in 1990.[3] Since then, I have endeavored to prevent ethnic conflict between African-American and Korean-American communities by raising racial consciousness. African-Americans have accumulated the deep wounds of slavery, part of which has been expressed through 'blues.' What I saw through the racial conflict of African-Americans and Korean-Americans was the collision between 'blues-filled' and '*han*-ridden' ethnic groups. To suggest a practical solution to racial relations in the United States, I published *Racial Conflict and Healing* in 1996. I contended that the sociological model of cultural pluralism inadvertently fueled the 1992 Los Angeles racial eruptions (and 1990 New York tensions) because the model promoted the isolation of ethnic groups, emphasizing diversity and plurality without unity. Seeing a need for a new theological model that churches should pursue, I worked on a mutual enhancement model. This mutual enhancement model suggests that we care for each other enough to celebrate each other's culture and tradition and to challenge each other's shortcomings with care and respect in place of violent and physical confrontations.

In 1998 Rosemary Radford Ruether invited several theologians, including me, to participate in the jubilee celebration of Palestinians. It was a memorable celebration where Edward Said, Ruether, and others spoke. I saw how unjustly Palestinians have been treated! On the one hand, I had a deep compassion for the *han*-ridden Palestinians who lost their land and homes to Israelis. On the other, I saw the fearful Israelis with the unhealed *hans* of World War II clinging to their false securities and oppressing Palestinians. The collisions and negative explosions

---

3   The Center published the lecture: 'A Vision of Overcoming Ethnic Conflicts,' *Multi-Ethnic Center For Ministry News*, Drew University, December 1990.

of *hans* have resulted in a vicious cycle of violence – military killings and suicide bombings. How do you cut off such a vicious cycle of suffering? The unraveling and healing of *han* only will alleviate and resolve their conflicts and will enable them to celebrate a true jubilee.

We do not need to develop an abstract theology, but we need to care for suffering people. In the process of questioning and answering about the suffering of life, a theology emerges. I teach my students to focus on the *han* or suffering of their congregants for weekly preaching. Then they will be *with* their parishioners in their faith journeys, walking with them toward the healing and graceful streams of Jesus Christ.

Chapter 17

To Give an Account of Hope

Gerhard Sauter

I was born on May 4, 1935, in Kassel (Hesse), in the middle of Germany. The ancestors of my father, Swiss Mennonites, emigrated to Southern Germany in the seventeenth century to 'seek the welfare of the city' (Jer. 29:7) by striving for truthfulness and keeping peace, at the same time guarding the integrity of their faith. I hope that something of this heritage is still effective in my genes. The father of my mother Adelheid was a Basel missionary in Northern China. He, his wife who came from a missionary family active in Africa, and their newborn child survived the Boxer rebellion in 1900.

My father, Hermann Sauter, served as a minister in a little industrial town near Kassel. He had been called there to reconcile the parish that was split into several factions, especially of rigid evangelicals and Pentecostals. Religious disagreement was intensified by political controversies in the 1930s. Many people were unemployed and economic exploitation for decades had caused social tensions, diseases, and spiritual impoverishment. In 1934, my father joined the Confessing Church, resisting the so-called German Christians who supported Hitler's policy. He was accused, for example, of insulting the German nation because he had preached about the guilt of the German people. Conducting a funeral on January 27, 1945, he died of a heart attack, worn out by the struggles he had faced in those troubling times, at age 45. At his burial service there were the first signs of a reconciled parish. Three months later, the parsonage was destroyed at the end of the war, and my mother, who had supported my father in his work, suffered from a lasting illness.

These early experiences molded my childhood and later formed my studies as well as my teaching of theology. The disunity between Christians has always challenged my perception of the unity of the church and its grounding. To become more acquainted with the social impact of Christian life, I wrote an essay about *German Protestantism Facing Social Tasks in the Nineteenth Century* in my last year at high school. During my later teens, Otto Salomon, a Jewish Christian, a poet, writer, and publisher, a friend of my father, introduced me into the life and work of Johann Christoph Blumhardt (1805–80) and his son, Christoph Blumhardt (1842–1919). The Blumhardts had been charismatic Swabian ministers who proclaimed the coming kingdom of God prefigured by signs of reconciliation healing body and soul. God's reigning power breaks in and simultaneously opens the suffering human being for faith and hope, for the outpouring of the Holy Spirit in unexpected ways, shattering the self-perception of human beings and of their views of the state of the world. Blumhardt father and son opposed the individualism and self-containment of the piety characterizing many of their contemporaries. The younger Blumhardt extended the proclamation of the coming kingdom of God to the social and political conflicts of his time. My father had learned from this message that 'God is with those who are broken and still growing.' Otto Salomon was married to a granddaughter of the younger Blumhardt and had to emigrate to Switzerland in 1938. In him the spirit of the prophets was alive. His sharp warning of any church's self-satisfaction remains with me. He used to say that 'only he who is shaken endures.'

Another crucial element of my father's small legacy was his evaluation of Rudolf Bultmann's program of demythologization (1941): the interpretation of the biblical, to a large extent mythological language, especially the talk of God's acting in a way that is comprehensible to the modern mind. The leaders of the Confessing Church in Hesse, of which Bultmann also was a member, had asked my father to look into the effects of this hermeneutical project on the tasks of the church. My father agreed with some intentions of Bultmann's work, but objected to what he considered its anthropological reduction. He concluded that Protestant theology is far behind other sciences and humanities in portraying the whole scope of human existence as it is called, justified, and sanctified by God in the context of God's whole work. After decades of participation in theological research and education, I am convinced that the task of a comprehensive theological anthropology is still unfulfilled, and I will try to contribute whatever I can to accomplish it.

In 1954–59 I studied theology and philosophy at the universities of Tübingen und Göttingen. Afterwards, the Blumhardt family provided me with sermons, documents of pastoral counseling, reports, and unpublished writings for my ThD thesis on *The Kingdom of God According to the Elder and the Younger Blumhardt* (1962). In 1961–62 I got my practical pastoral training in the Protestant Church in Kurhessen and Waldeck and was ordained in 1962. In the same year, I married Annegrete, a teacher, who later worked in a school for disabled children. Her experiences with suffering adolescents became an important influence on my theology.

In 1962–64 I wrote my second thesis to be qualified as a university professor (*Habilitationsschrift*), entitled *Future and Promise: The Problem of the Future in Contemporary Theological and Philosophical Discussion* (1965). Here I argued how the perception of 'future' depends on ontological as well as linguistic presuppositions to have critical importance. 'Promise' is the leading category of theology, opposing any kind of self-explanation of human beings who are only trying to stabilize their world. God is promising God's action, and God is acting in a promising way. It is a characteristic of God always to reserve further action for Godself, and yet to cast a hint of that future action into the present as a promise. I also tried to integrate biblical-theological insights about the relation of promise and fulfillment. Walther Zimmerli, my teacher of Old Testament studies, had told us that God works on God's promises in a surprising way, shaping our expectations, not confirming and closing them. Fulfillment does not mean the execution of something predicted by God. In contrast, fulfillment characterizes the very special way and manner God acts to pursue the divine will. Therefore, fulfillment often shatters expectations based on God's promises; it reshapes them and leads to a renewed hope. This constitutes a new perception of our 'being in time,' forming an *Eschatological Rationality* (1996).

Later, I often have been asked how my approach relates to Jürgen Moltmann's *Theology of Hope* (published in Germany in 1964). Independently from each other, we searched for the grounding of Christian theology that is always shaped by eschatology. We were both interested in *The Principle of Hope* of the Jewish and Neo-Marxist philosopher Ernst Bloch (1959, ET 1986). Bloch favored hope as vigorous, stimulating human energy to imagine possibilities and to anticipate their reality in order to put them into effect. Moltmann adapted Bloch's intention. He interpreted biblical promises as real-utopian goals that move us to grasp what is really possible in this world and to realize it towards the promised future of the justice, life, and kingdom of God. While Moltmann's work was and is related primarily to political hermeneutics, I concentrated more on the implications of 'hoping against hope' (Rom. 4:18) for Christian spirituality and the characteristics of Christian God-talk. Eschatology should be a touchstone for arguing theologically in general. In later writings, I emphasized that God confirms in Jesus Christ God's promises of everlasting life, justice, peace, rest in God, immediate vision of God. Everlasting life is prefigured in the communion with Christ, justice in the justification of the godless by faith, peace in the community of the justified sinners and in keeping the unity of faith, hope, and love. Resting in God is prefigured in the sharing of the body and blood of Christ, immediately seeing God in looking at Christ in prayer. These are only some signs of the dramatic reading of God's promises in the narratives of Israel in the light of the Christ-story, a reading that started with the New Testament and is going on in church history. Ethical tasks must be judged by the relation of promise and fulfillment. In this way, eschatology needs to be reconsidered as giving an account of hope, as being 'accountable to everyone who raises questions about the hope that is in you' (1 Pet. 3:15), questions caused by passions and actions, ways of life and preparations to die (*What Dare We Hope?* (1999)).

In 1965, I was called to teach systematic theology at the University of Göttingen. Three years later I succeeded Wolfhart Pannenberg at the University of Mainz. In those years, the so-called critical theory of the Frankfurt School, a Neo-Marxist social philosophy (Max Horkheimer, Theodor W. Adorno, Jürgen Habermas), influenced many theologians and intensified a crisis of traditional hermeneutics to be replaced by political analysis and sociological reconstruction of all areas of culture. I also became acquainted with representatives of the opposing philosophical party, the Neo-Positivists (Karl R. Popper, Hans Albert, and others). Both positions challenged me to ask again for the characteristics of arguing theologically, and they led me to studies in theory of science (*Wissenschaftstheoretische Kritik der Theologie,* 1973) – an opportunity to exchange some views with Pannenberg.

Theology as a discipline of reasoning is characterized by an intrinsic rationality that is valid whether its communication is internal or external. While theologians make themselves understandable to those who do not assent to what they argue, they cannot submit the rationality of their arguments to any vague universality, even to universal moral values. In the 1970s I could test this in a series of interdisciplinary debates on philosophy, sociology, and psychology of religion as well as in a working group discussing features of religious language with Emmanuel Levinas and Paul Ricoeur in Paris for many years. These studies resulted in a theological and philosophical essay on *The Question of Meaning* (1982; ET 1995).

In 1972, I received a call from the faculty of Protestant theology of the University of Bonn; we moved there in 1973. In 1976 I became Director of the Ecumenical

Institute. The interchange with Roman Catholic theologians, already begun in Mainz, was extended and deepened. I taught twice in the ecumenical studies program at the Dormition Abbey in Jerusalem. The encounter with Orthodox theology drew my attention to the interaction of liturgy and theology. In the following years I was able to establish some partnerships: with the Faculty of Theology of the University of Oxford, which made me an external member in 1990, with the Theological Academy in Warsaw, which educates all non-Catholic students of theology in Poland, with the Divinity School of Duke University, Durham, NC (USA), where I was visiting professor in 1979 and 2003, and with the Faculty of Protestant Theology of the Charles University in Prague since 1995. The exchange with English and North American colleagues and students enriched me enormously by their way of thinking, arguing and debating that is quite different from the German tradition. One of the fruits of the exchange with colleagues of Oxford was a research project on *Revelation and Story: Narrative theology and the centrality of story* (edited with John Barton, 2000). I am grateful that I could contribute something to improve theological education and training of graduate students in Poland. I also became a partner of a group of young Hungarian theologians led by my friend Ervin Vályi-Nagy, who had resigned his teaching position in Budapest because of political suppression. These experiences of doing theology under very difficult circumstances and often disturbed by misleading church politics cast a fresh and often exposing light on church and theology in Germany and in the Western hemisphere in general as well as on some tendencies of the policy of the World Council of Churches toward Eastern Europe. In particular, I regarded highly the theological thinking that developed in East Germany, less vain and interspersed with personal attitudes than in West Germany.

The participation in three consultations at the Ecumenical Institute in Bossey, Switzerland, in 1972–74 was instructive and formative (cf. the documentation *Doing Theology Today*, ed. by Choan-Seng Song, 1976). There I noticed both a readiness for a pluralism of different theologies that can hardly communicate with one another and the tendency to establish a new framework of doing theology by referring to 'contextual' preconditions. This led me to consider again the basic questions: What is truth in theology? How are substantial theological understanding and a forward-looking agreement possible which neither avoid inevitable conflicts by cheap tolerance nor rely on a common denominator found by an overarching worldview and by rigid moral intentions, for example, social justice and peace? If ecumenical discussion is confined to particular experiences, referring only secondarily to the Bible and perhaps, marginally, to confessional doctrinal traditions, how is theological significance of these experiences to be assessed? How are we able to distill genuine theological insights which are decisive to the whole Christian world family from historical or actual differences? How can we evade the temptation that theologians may merely depict their own biographical experiences and make themselves the subject matter of theology?

Here my analytical training helped me to distinguish between the context of discovery and the context of validation. The context by which we may discover perceptions to be addressed by theological arguments covers all the factors that in some way promote insights or contribute to significant findings. There may be different contexts of discovery: socio-cultural and economic conditions, gender relations, participation in the history of a church, of a nation or of a wider cultural setting, public affairs, etc. The context of validation (or justification) is the interrelation of statements that seek to follow the scope of God's work. Our theological integrity is precisely at this point at stake. Are we finally going to speak mainly of ourselves, of our feelings, of our wrestling with the conditions of life, of our social role, and of God only in so far as God enables and forces us to execute what we understand as God's will? The theological context of validation is a context in the strict and precise sense of the linguistic context in which we move. It is an open one, yet it is still coherent and consistent, so that it can support individual arguments and allow us to reject anything which may be said in disbelief. This specifically theological context is based on the interpretation of the Scripture and is continually nurtured by the art of reading the Scripture. It is developed by theological experiences in thinking that form dogmatics.

No fear of dogmatics! I am aware that the term 'dogmatics' is widely suspected today, even in some Catholic circles, of being outdated or repressive. A dogma seems to restrain and to hinder our freedom, it seems to be only a burden of tradition. Dogmatics is accused of closing all discourse instead of opening it. But carefully investigated, dogmatics relies on tried and tested experiences in thinking to be thought through again and developed further. It is a movement in thinking that is addressed by God's immense, tireless, and often disturbing actions and blessed with the abundance of God's promises. Therefore, dogmatics can encourage us to take seriously contextual relations of our doing theology. But it helps us to distinguish between the living source of proclamation and any derivation of theology from conditions that can be mastered by reflection on that situation, by its analysis, and by coping with its problems. Dogmatic statements assert who God is, what God has done, and what God has promised to accomplish. If these statements are linked with the freedom of faith and hope, they encourage us to be outspoken about what has been entrusted to us. This requires responsible reflection on what needs to be said under all circumstances, in a way that does not neglect the empirical context while not being determined by it either. The most crucial dogmatic statements were developed to clarify or to correct theologically church practices that had been distorted. Many statements were established as an explanation of the inner grounding and intrinsic rationality of church practices.

I hope to contribute more to this debate by two recent books: *Gateways to Dogmatics: Reasoning Theologically for the Life of the Church* (2003) and *Protestant Theology at the Crossroads: How to Face the Crucial Tasks for Theology in the Twentieth-First Century* (2007). I wrote most parts of these publications as a member of the Center of Theological Inquiry in Princeton, New Jersey, where I could stay for several times from 1988 until 2003. There I found dialogue partners from various parts of the world, theologians, philosophers, historians, and scientists. I was involved in the Pastor-Theologian program of the Center that drew attention to the ordained ministry as a theological vocation and to the church as a theological community. I also shared in two projects of the Center, reported in *The End of the World and the Ends of God: Science and Theology on Eschatology* (edited by John Polkinghorne and Michael Welker, 2000) and in *God and Human Dignity* (edited by R. Kendall Soulen and Linda Woodhead, 2006). The second topic inspired me to extend and to consolidate my studies on theological anthropology. The first combined my lasting interest in eschatology as well as in a dialogue with scientists, mainly because a serious examination of cosmology in German theology has been absent for a very long time, at least since A Ritschl, with the exception of Karl Heim.

In 1990, Princeton Theological Seminary called me to be the first Professor of Theology and Science there. This offer attracted me very much because the relationship between the natural sciences and theology is taken into account much more in the United States than in Germany. It would have been also challenging to work in a new context of discovery. But just after the unification of Germany and facing the new situation in Europe, my wife and I felt that we should stay in Bonn, among other reasons to continue the ecumenical obligations in a rapidly changing East Europe.

A grant made it possible to initiate and to supervise a three-year documentation and evaluation of the criteria of theological decisions of the Hungarian Reformed church in the period 1967–92. Many of these decisions were intended to overcome the guilty feeling of former wrong political judgments and of omissions in social life: Obedience of faith meant to refer to God's will as it is manifest in progress, often synonymous with the Marxist concept of history that promised to save humankind, and critical attitudes to it were suspected of lacking faith. After the political change in 1989–90, there was often the acclamation of the opposite political option. This justification of church politics by a concept of 'God in history' significantly differed from the efforts of some (not of all) German Protestant theologians and church leaders to confess the guilt of the German Protestant church, its complicity in the rise of National Socialism and the cruelty of World War II. In October 1945, the *Stuttgart Declaration* was presented by members of the Confessing Church to an ecumenical delegation. The German church leaders confessed to God, who judges and reconciles, as well as to brothers and sisters. The confession of guilt was used in public worship, hoping that a new beginning may be possible.

In 1985 I had published a theological interpretation about the *Stuttgart Declaration*, asking, How can Christians confess their guilt? How can they speak of a new beginning? Preparing this essay I often talked with Hellmut Traub (1904–94) who had as a student assisted Karl Barth during Barth's years in Bonn (1930–35), became a friend of Barth, suffered in a concentration camp and did pastoral counseling to imprisoned Nazis after the war. Traub helped me to understand more of the turbulences of the Third Reich, of the disastrous situation of Germany after 1945, and of the theological conflicts addressing this situation. He informed me about the life and work of Karl Barth much better than my theological teachers could. Traub was critical about Barth's move to an ethical attestation of theological insights since 1938.

When I began to study Barth's writings, especially the early ones, in the later 1950s, I was prepared by the theology of the Blumhardts, who had influenced Barth and his friends. In 1971 I was together with Nelly, Barth's widow, assigned to edit Barth's sermons of 1913. In 1982 I edited the first volume of Barth's *Christian Dogmatics in Outline* (1927). The lively dialogue with Traub and Hinrich Stoevesandt, the archivist of Barth's work in Basel, led me to revise some of my earlier difficulties concerning dialectical theology (Barth, Emil Brunner, Rudolf Bultmann, Friedrich Gogarten, and Eduard Thurneysen). It intensified my doubts about the criticism initiated, for instance, by Paul Tillich and Wolfhart Pannenberg, and it helped me to understand dialectical theology both in its own period and in its continued value. Besides these and other editions, I served as one of the editors on the journal *Evangelische Theologie*, where I still am a member of the editorial board, as well as the editor of *Verkündigung und Forschung* and of the series *Theological Library.*

An area of doing theology that always stimulated me is to write 'sermon-meditations' as developed especially by Hans Joachim Iwand, one of my predecessors in Bonn and a Lutheran theologian leading in the Confessing Church. Sermon-meditations are a link to the life of the church. They follow the lectionary and combine the exegesis of biblical texts with examples of the history of interpretation, theological reflection, and homiletic suggestions. From this task results a project that I hope soon to accomplish: a theology of the church year. The main dogmas of the early church were directed to the sequence of the ongoing story of Jesus Christ and to the structure of worship. They must be interpreted within this context. In celebrating the great acts of God through the church year we experience an awareness of time that is different from our adaptation to the cycle of the seasons. The rhythm of the church year permits us constantly to begin once again and yet to move forward, although even step-by-step we can never catch up with the fullness of God's acting. Therefore, the church year nourishes dogmatics. It invites us to accept God's creative acting and thus to be attentive to God's promises and their fulfillment. It trains us in memory and hope.

Chapter 18

On Belonging: Doing Theology Together

Dirkie Smit

Apartheid

It is impossible to reflect on the story of our South African theological generation without remembering the story of apartheid. We were the children of apartheid. The story of the Christian faith in South Africa during the second half of the twentieth century was too intimately interwoven with the story of apartheid and the struggle against it to be told without this backdrop – and therefore the same is true of the theology of our generation. Even those who thought they could practise the faith and do theology by ignoring the apartheid reality were deeply affected by its pervasive presence, precisely in their attempts to close their eyes, to minister and teach, study and write as though nothing were happening.

Apartheid (literally: apartness, separateness) refers to the official political system in South Africa between 1948 and 1994. Since the 1960s it was called 'separate development.' It sanctioned strict racial segregation and political and economic discrimination against all people legally classified as 'non-white.' Official apartheid was legitimated by an ideology and even a 'theology of apartheid' and the Christian faith (particularly although not exclusively the Reformed tradition) played a crucial role.

Apartheid was about separateness, about dividing people, keeping them apart, through legal, social, economic and political measures, thereby denying and destroying any form of *unity* between them, attempting to resist any form of belonging, solidarity, sharing, mutuality and caring.

Apartheid therefore led to separation, to estrangement, to alienation, to a deep lack of mutual understanding and acceptance, resulting in mistrust and suspicion, fear and hurt, even bitterness and hatred, in short, an urgent need for *reconciliation*, for acceptance and forgiveness, for building bridges over the deep divides separating people.

In this process, apartheid increased forms of social, systemic and structural *injustice* – all kinds of unfair treatment, of dramatic lack of facilities and opportunities for some, whether educational, medical, social or political, all kinds of violations of human dignity and human rights, the unjust denial of all kinds of personal and political freedom, eventually resulting in violent resistance and armed struggles, repressed by violent security and military power from the state. In short, apartheid built on and contributed to the fundamental absence of *unity*, *reconciliation* and *justice* in society.

According to many Christians and churches, from both outside and inside the country, the Christian faith was itself at stake in these developments. The truth of the gospel was being denied, the credibility of the proclamation and witness of the church was endangered, the very nature of the church was being betrayed, the message of the Bible, the integrity of Christian worship, the truthfulness of Christian life, all of these were threatened: in short, according to these believers the state of affairs constituted a *status confessionis*, a moment of truth in which the gospel of Jesus Christ was at stake. Church leaders and theologians like Archbishop Tutu, Beyers Naudé, Allan Boesak, Manas Buthelezi, Frank Chikane and Wolfram Kistner – with many others – became controversial public voices, but for many also deeply inspiring figures.

Our theological generation was part of those who were inspired to share these convictions.

Worship – Praying Together?

For most of us, Christian worship was crucially important. We were members of active congregations. We experienced weekly worship as deeply meaningful. Church attendance was high in the white Dutch Reformed congregations, as it was in most so-called black denominations in South Africa. Going to church, being involved in worship, was an integral part of life for us – and for many on the African continent, it is still true. Worship mattered and still matters.

Of course, we were to learn that lively worship is no guarantee of faithful worship, active and committed congregational and spiritual life, like flourishing religious activity and experience, not necessarily an indication of Christian discipleship. Learning to see that there may be a difference between religion, spirituality and even worship on the one hand, and Christian faith, life and obedience on the other, and then struggling how to discern between the two, became a crucial part of doing theology in the apartheid context – and it still remains a crucial challenge today.

After all, it is tragic but true that the story of apartheid in a way originated in the Lord's Supper, the heart of Christian worship. In 1855 white worshippers in a rural Dutch Reformed congregation refused to share the Lord's Supper with others. In 1857 the Synod decided that it was indeed 'preferable and Scriptural' that all believers shared the same worship and the same congregation, but granted that, where these measures obstructed the Christian cause 'as a result of the weakness of some,' worship could be organised separately, based on descent, race and social status.

Over many years, this historical concession became the common practice, and still later even the norm for the order and structure of the church. In 1881 a separate 'church' or denomination, the Dutch Reformed Mission Church, was established for Coloured people, and during the twentieth century several others would follow, all divided according to race or ethnicity. White believers were gradually made to believe that having separate churches for each nation was the norm and according to Scripture. This church policy of separate churches would later form the religious roots of the ideology and since 1948 the official political policy of apartheid. Since 1960, theologians, ministers and believers in the Dutch Reformed Church (DRC) who opposed this ecclesiology and pleaded for the unity of the church, were rejected as traitors of the *volk*.

The story is, obviously, much longer and much more complicated. The history of racial tension, discrimination and segregation reaches back to the beginning of colonisation. Many philosophical, cultural, social, legal and economic factors contributed to what became apartheid. However, there is no denying that Christian faith and theology also formed an integral part of that process. The DRC increasingly appealed to government to introduce different apartheid laws, and so-called 'Scriptural proofs' legitimated the ideology – so in a way it all began and was legitimated, sadly, in the heart of Christian worship.

In the *struggle* against apartheid, Christian worship would again play a crucial role, reaching a dramatic highlight again in the Lord's Supper. The decades after 1948 saw increasing opposition to the apartheid policy, ideology and theology in church circles, both inside South Africa and in the ecumenical movement. In 1982, at the Ottawa meeting of the World Alliance of Reformed Churches (WARC), representatives from the so-called 'daughter churches' in the DRC-family refused to participate in the official celebration, claiming that it would be false to do so in an ecumenical context, while they were excluded from the Lord's Supper in the DRC in South Africa. The WARC declared a *status confessionis* and back in South Africa the DR Mission Church did the same, regarding the theological justification of apartheid. A moment of truth had arrived – and this all began in Christian worship.

Theologically, many of us were therefore interested in understanding the complicated reciprocal relationships between liturgy, faith and life, between the so-called *lex orandi – lex credendi – lex (con)vivendi*. It is clear how worship can impact on life and ethics – through providing new ways of seeing, thereby subverting everyday perceptions; through liberating worshippers from fear and guilt and setting them free to love and serve; through establishing new forms of *koinonia*, of community and belonging; through the deliberate articulation of opportunities, issues and moral challenges; through experiences of divine calling, of vocation; through diverse processes of moral formation as well as personal transformation and renewal; through all kinds of comforting, encouragement and empowerment; through conscious acts of dedication and conscious commitment. Christian worship seems to involve all these, and similar processes of orientation and motivation.

We could indeed see this power of worship at work in the lives of many fellow South Africans suffering under apartheid. At the same time, we realised that serious worship was obviously not immune to deeply problematic developments – not only the history of Christianity, but our own experiences offered living proof. Under specific conditions, Christian worship can clearly become very ambiguous, captive to alien purposes, serving the ideological betrayal of the gospel. How does the church therefore discern the dangers inherent in worship?

Perhaps at least some help could come from worshipping together with others, we learnt, from sharing with them and learning from them, from an ecumenical spirituality of encounter, from a common Christian life – since the presence of the others could perhaps help us to see ourselves with new eyes, in different ways. Our generation had to learn that it was perhaps not without very good reason that precisely the issue of so-called *gesamentlike aanbidding*, common worship, praying together, became *the* most controversial practice in white Reformed church circles. We were denied the opportunity to pray together, because praying together might have threatened the matter-of-factness and power of the apartheid construction of reality.

Bible – Reading in Communion?

Perhaps even more important than worship and congregational life, however, to most of us, was the Bible – reading the Bible, studying the Bible, discussing the Bible. Perhaps this was a result of our Reformed tradition, or perhaps due to the strong evangelical influence in our particular Reformed tradition, but we loved the Bible. We grew up with the Bible and studied the Bible intensely. In the student congregation in Stellenbosch, about four thousand students gathered in the evenings during the week in hostels and houses to read and discuss the Bible in small groups. Many theological students of our generation were active in the students' Christian movement, where studying the Bible in groups was the main activity; reading the Bible mattered and still matters.

The reality was, however, that apartheid also impacted on these activities. Under the pressure of apartheid theologians and church leaders, Christian students were divided into separate associations for separate ethnic races and ethnic groups, even separate language groups. As a result, we read and discussed the Bible on our own, as white Afrikaans-speaking students, while English-speaking white students and so-called Coloured and black African students all read and discussed the Bible – only with themselves, separately! Such was the reality of apartheid, in church and society. Of the four thousand students in our congregation who met weekly to discuss the message of the Bible for our lives with such seriousness, all were white and almost all from Afrikaans backgrounds.

In fact, we were instructed and encouraged by our ministers to read the Bible by only listening to our own inner voices, our own intuitive understandings and immediate applications – since that meant listening to the voice of the Holy Spirit – and not to use any commentaries, study guides or theological material. In a very concrete way, we were thus isolated from reading in communion, from listening with others and to others and left to the subjective inspirations of our own inner feelings. As students, one of the important processes of liberation that many of us had to experience was therefore the seemingly simple process to read and to study while reading the Bible, expecting the voice of the Holy Spirit also to speak through others, and not only through our own inner convictions. In our South Africa, a contextual form of evangelical pietism and the contextual form of apartheid spirituality worked hand in hand to legitimate the *status quo* in church and society and reading the Bible in isolation played a crucial role.

Small wonder then that reading the Bible became very controversial during the apartheid history. The Bible was sometimes called 'a site of struggle' – and indeed a major ideological struggle. On the surface, the struggle was about the use of the Bible in socio-political and ethical reasoning, about the question of 'how it was possible to use the Bible in contemporary political and ethical controversies in a legitimate and responsible way?', or more specifically 'what are the implications of reading the Bible in apartheid South Africa?' Finally, we were debating questions such as 'what does the gospel say about racism, about apartheid, about political oppression and violations of human dignity and rights, about social and economic injustice?' What does the Bible say?

Underlying these debates, however, were more fundamental questions. At stake was the question whether it was legitimate at all to make any claims on behalf of the Bible, whether the Bible says anything at all in fact, whether there is anything like 'the Bible' in the singular.

At first, it was from the ranks of biblical scholarship that these questions were raised, rejecting – from their perspective – the seemingly naive and innocent misuse of the Bible by so-called ordinary believers, the seemingly sophisticated but in fact deeply misleading use of the Bible in official church documents, and of course the outdated doctrinal misuse of the Bible by theologians. The Bible might have been read this way in pre-modern and Reformation times, they claimed, but it was no longer acceptable, in the light of developments in the field of scholarly biblical studies during the last centuries. This criticism was particularly directed against their fellow biblical scholars who should have known better, but still participated in writing church documents actually using and quoting the Bible – whether defending or rejecting apartheid. The claim was increasingly heard that both apartheid defenders and anti-apartheid strugglers read the Bible according to the self-same paradigm. Their political values were opposed to one another, and yes, therefore their respective political readings of the Bible were directly contradictory, but their readings were also similar in that they all (still) believed that there is a Bible with a message and that this message was (still) relevant and could even be appropriated in contemporary theological and ethical arguments.

At least for our generation of Reformed theologians, this obviously raised extremely important questions. These debates continued in many forms, often under the rubrics of reception or reader-response theories, contextuality and contextual hermeneutics – and it is no wonder that so many Reformed scholars from South Africa have been deeply involved in developments in these areas.

It became increasingly clear that we do not simply read the Bible as individuals, but always as members of groups, of so-called interpretive communities. This brings the communal, the ecclesial, one could even say the underlying political nature of the debates concerning the reading of the Bible to the fore – if 'political' is taken in its original sense of referring to the *polis* or public. The questions are: 'to which community-of-interpretation, to which tradition or group, to which 'polis' does the Bible properly belong?'; 'where do we learn how to read and interpret the Bible responsibly?'; 'who are the real readers of the Bible – the church, the academy and biblical scholarship, or perhaps society?' And if the answer for some is the church, then which church, since they are also disagreeing over the message of the Bible?

Issues concerning the so-called rhetoric and ethics of interpretation were increasingly discussed. The focus of many biblical scholars shifted from hermeneutics to renewed interest in rhetorical studies. Black theologians and feminist theologians opened our eyes to the pervasive, albeit often unconscious, role of power and social interests in reading the Bible and in doing theology, through influential voices such as Allan Boesak and Denise Ackermann. They asked 'who are reading?' and 'for whom?' and particularly *'whose* interests are served by different readings?'

For us, the very heart of the Christian faith itself was here at stake in the apartheid struggle. Does the Bible have a message, and is it possible for us today to claim that the Bible says this, or that – or are we always and inevitably speaking on behalf of the Word, reducing its complexity and diversity and reconstructing it in ways that reflect and even suit our present purposes? Are we always speaking on behalf of the Bible? While some – like Itumeleng Mosala – cynically rejected and criticized their way of doing theology, since they claimed that the Bible is indeed the Word of God and that the Bible does have a message about God, church leaders like Archbishop Tutu and Allan Boesak continued to resist apartheid, appealing to and publicly and confidently proclaiming this message.

These issues were obviously not new. The apartheid history only demonstrated again in very dramatic fashion questions and challenges that had been present from the very beginning. Through the ages and in different cultural contexts and experiences, they have been addressed in diverse ways and this has always been integral to the theological task. During the last decades they have also been crucial to the ecumenical church. Christians from all over the world are facing precisely the same issues in what is often called 'ecumenical hermeneutics.' Coming from diverse communities and historical developments, from different doctrinal, confessional and liturgical traditions, from different cultural contexts, social and political experiences, these churches are also on a common search for their common apostolic faith and how to confess and practise that today, in one world yet in always changing circumstances; for their common message, which they hope to witness to and proclaim in their diverse cultural and social contexts, in spite of their many differences of understanding and expression. How do we read the Bible responsibly when faced with such a diversity of readings and interpretations, all claiming to speak on behalf of the Bible?

Again, for our generation at least, some part of the answer was given in the conviction that we needed one another, that we have to read together, to read in communion, with one another, with outsiders, with those on the margins – also and especially with those experiencing who we are and what we do precisely when we claim that we are doing what the Bible tells us what to do! We need others to help us to read responsibly.

Church – Not Our Own?

Central to these debates about worship and about reading the Bible was clearly an underlying debate about the church and about its nature and calling, and about its boundaries, in creedal terms, about its unity and its catholicity. In South Africa, the church mattered and still matters.

At the heart of apartheid theology was an apartheid ecclesiology. Apartheid theology argued that creation structures re-creation, that grace does not destroy creation but fulfils it, that the New Testament church of Jesus Christ should therefore be structured and organised according to the Old Testament reports about how God in grace and mercy divided and separated the peoples at the tower of Babel into different languages, cultures and communities, in order to experience the wonderful richness and diversity intended for them in original creation, but against which they revolted in their sinful attempt to unite and to bring together what God created differently – according to Genesis 11, the most often quoted pericope in apartheid theology.

At the heart of these debates was the question to whom the church ultimately belongs. Radically put, is the church the church of the *volk*, or the church of the Triune God?

Since Calvin himself, it has been a central claim at the heart of the Reformed tradition that we do not belong to ourselves, that we are not our own. This was the motto with which he described the Christian life. This was the thrust of the first question and answer of the *Heidelberg Catechism*, determining the structure and content of the whole document. Our deepest comfort is that we do not belong to ourselves, but in Jesus Christ to the Triune God, and in this comfort is hidden a powerful claim on our lives. This was the ultimate foundation of the *Theological Declaration of Barmen* and of statements of faith of Reformed and Presbyterian churches worldwide, including the World Alliance of Reformed Churches in Debrecen. We are not own own – and the church certainly does not belong to any *volk*, nation, country or social group.

Of course, in theory almost all Christians would agree, including apartheid theologians. The crucial test comes with our concrete ecclesiologies, with church life in everyday practice, in specific historical contexts. In South Africa, the 'acid test' came in the form of the question whether the church should be visibly one, and how.

Apartheid theologians fully agreed that the church is one – spiritually, invisibly, with one faith, one hope, one baptism, one bread and wine, one Lord. They denied, however, that this unity should become visible, at least in any structural or organisational form, which according to them belongs to the well-being of the church, and not to its being. Congregations could therefore determine who could become members and who could worship, even based on race and ethnicity, and denominations are merely congregations who freely organise themselves together because they have something in common, for example being part of and serving the same *volk*.

Hidden behind these – seemingly innocent – theological positions and these – seemingly timeless, theoretical and abstract – ecclesiological arguments, were of course different kinds of very real group interests, whether material and financial, cultural and nationalist, social, classist and elitist, political and economic. These theological viewpoints were ideologically used as powerful social weapons in a very real struggle about human life and death issues.

Ecclesiology became *the* controversial theological theme in apartheid theology. Many theologians in the Reformed churches in South Africa made major contributions arguing for the visible unity of the church, arguing that race and ethnicity should play no role in determining membership of the church of Jesus Christ, and arguing against the kind of *volkskerk* found in South African circles – people like Willie Jonker, Jaap Durand, Dawid Bosch, Allan Boesak, Welile Mazamisa, Daan Cloete, Hannes Adonis, Adrio König, Bernard Lategan, Andrie du Toit, Bernard Combrink, Flip Theron, Willem Nicol, Danie du Toit, Johan Botha, Francois Wessels, Coenie

Burger, and many others. They all rejected the apartheid ecclesiology, arguing that the church belongs to Jesus Christ alone and that this belonging to Him should also determine the visible structure and order of the church. The church does not belong to the *volk*. The *volk* does not determine who belong to the church.

Again, looking back from a distance, the specific developments in apartheid South Africa may seem so bizarre that it is tempting to think that they have no resemblance anywhere and that these serious theological debates at the time have no relevance for the rest of the worldwide church, but that may be short-sighted. Could it perhaps be that some fundamental flaws in Protestant ecclesiology and in what is today often regarded as innocent and normal Protestant denominationalism only became dramatically visible in apartheid South Africa?

Many from our theological generation think that this is indeed the case. Our context made us see and believe that seemingly innocent ecclesiologies may often be more problematic than many tend to think.

Christian Life – Embodying Belonging?

Were all these debates – about faithful worship, responsible reading of the Bible, the true nature of the church – merely about *adiaphora*, the many controversies about which believers legitimately hold different opinions? Or was more at stake? In South Africa, convictions were growing that we were facing nothing less that a *status confessionis*, a moment of truth in which the truth of the gospel itself was at stake.

In 1982 the DR Mission Church followed the World Alliance of Reformed Churches in declaring such a state of confession. They also decided to confess – to explain *why* the gospel was at stake, according to their understanding of the truth of the gospel for this historical moment and context. In this, they were following the tradition of Calvin and the early Reformed confessional documents, but also very consciously of Karl Barth and the German Confessing Church with the *Theological Declaration of Barmen*.

Over against the separation, estrangement and injustices caused by apartheid, the 'yes' of the confession affirmed living unity, real reconciliation and compassionate justice as the message of the gospel. These three are intimately related to one another. There could be no living unity amongst believers without real reconciliation, without addressing the painful legacies from the past, without healing the wounds of brokenness and separation, and there could be no living unity and real reconciliation without also addressing the blatant and crying social and economic divisions and injustices in society. Unity, reconciliation and justice all belong together as one, as together part of the truth of the gospel of Jesus Christ. Under apartheid, the good news that we do not belong to ourselves, but to the Triune God in Jesus Christ and therefore to one another, called for living unity, real reconciliation and compassionate justice, such was the conviction.

Hidden behind this decision were two important theological claims. The first claim of those believers and churches struggling against apartheid was that there exists an integral link between doctrine and *ethics*, between faith and life, theology and ecclesiology, truth and discipleship; in short, between witness to the gospel and a Christian life of unity, reconciliation and justice.

For a new generation of theologians, this link between theology and ethics became of crucial importance – people like Russel Botman, James Buys, Christo Lombard, Pieter Grove, Nico Koopman, Elna Mouton, Etienne de Villiers, Carel Anthonissen, Andrew Phillips, Piet Naudé, Robert Vosloo, and many others.

Specific examples of this link between theology and ethics include Russel Botman, who became President of the South African Council of Churches, who wrote his doctoral dissertation on Bonhoeffer's notion of discipleship as transformation, and was inspired by the convictions of *Belhar* that the confession involves a call to discipleship and obedience. Elna Mouton, the first woman who ever became dean of any faculty at Stellenbosch, likewise wrote her doctoral dissertation on an ethical reading of Ephesians, a rhetorical reading also aimed at visible embodiment in the real church. Nico Koopman, who became the first Director of the Beyers Naudé Center for Public Theology, wrote his doctoral dissertation on understandings of Christian ethics informed by the faith and taking form in real lives and the real church. All are examples of our generation of South African theologians enhancing the link between ethics and theology.

The second theological claim was that the credibility of this witness of the church that belongs to Jesus Christ calls for forms of discipleship, for practical and visible forms of Christian life and of being the church that visibly *embody* and practise these claims. Again, this was an important step for us.

For Reformed theologians, this should have been evident from the tradition itself. Theologians like Willie Jonker regularly argued during the apartheid years that Reformed confession calls for concrete embodiment. He described this confessional tradition as 'liberating truth' (*bevrydende waarheid*) and was convinced that it could and should liberate the South African churches and society from the ideological captivity to the *volk* and to take on new ecclesiological form as one church. He was convinced that there had always been three forces competing with one another in the DRC; namely, (1) loyalty to the nation, (2) faithfulness to the Reformed faith, (3) and the spirituality of pietistic evangelicalism. In his opinion, after the time of apartheid, a *volkskerk* ecclesiology was being replaced by subjectivist religiosity, while the liberating truth of the Reformed faith has never truly been practised and embodied.

The Reformed tradition was, of course, not alone in this opinion. It would be Bonhoeffer's ecclesiology, for example, as explained by Wolfgang Huber in his *Folgen christlicher Freiheit* that would open the eyes of many of our theological generation to this claim, that *Wahrheit* should take on *Existenzform*, that the faith confessed and the message proclaimed by the church should determine its own order, structure and life.

For those of us in the Reformed tradition, however, this should have been evident all along. Listening to the voices of the mothers and fathers could have helped us. At the end of his life Calvin recalled that when he came to Geneva there had been 'only preaching, no reformation.' That was the reason why he immediately wrote both a confession and an order embodying that confession for the congregation in Geneva, a practice that would continue in the Reformed tradition. Time and again, confessions would be accompanied by church orders, so that the witness of the community, through words, deeds and life, could indeed correspond to the confession.

Perhaps this second claim involved the most difficult aspect of the struggle against apartheid, namely to put these convictions into practice, to embody this confession – in the Christian life of those who confess, in new ways of ordering the church itself, and in public life. In post-apartheid South Africa, under the radically changed circumstances of a society transformed into pluralist democracy, this challenge to embody the faith publicly has taken on new forms and new urgency for our theological generation, and indeed for the next.

Christian life mattered and matters. The visible form of the church mattered and matters. The public witness of the church in the world mattered and matters.

On Doing Theology Together

Without the apartheid context, the theology of our generation would have been radically different. We responded to the questions and challenges of our time and situation. However, this does not mean that the context determined our theology, because it was indeed only too possible to do theology in completely different ways in the same context.

What then made any difference? Perhaps the question was in whose presence, in whose company we did our theology. Friends help one to see the world differently and to read the Bible differently, and therefore it is an important question for any theologian who one's friends are.

Living in apartheid South Africa meant living in different worlds, and the story of theology, and in particular also of Reformed theology, was a story of many stories. All depended on the others with whom we were doing theology, on how inclusive our circle of friends was.

It depended on the community – on the congregations we belonged to, on those with whom we worshipped together, on those with whom we read the Bible together, on those with whom we studied together, on those whose life-stories we heard and shared, on the community and the tradition we shared.

In short, we learnt that theology is something we do in communion, together – with the mothers and the fathers of the tradition, with the brothers and sisters of the ecumenical church, with the victims of our communities and our societies, with 'the destitute, the poor, and the wronged.'

Theology is the ongoing work of the church of Jesus Christ, and this church does not belong to any nation or to the arbitrary wishes, needs and interests of particular groups who may decide to form a congregation or denomination, but to the Triune God of the whole church, history and the world. It is in belonging to this community that we can do theology together.

Chapter 19

Catching the Post or How I Became an Accidental Theorist

R.S. Sugirtharajah

'What great teachers we were, when we didn't worry about our methods.'
— Daniel Pennac[1]

What follows is a somewhat haphazard attempt to re-arrange and reorder some important hermeneutical moments as an interpreter, and how I survived and tried to stay sane in the field of biblical studies. In doing this, I will be violating the idea that any theological articulation should be devoid of personal reflections. This academic dictum, some of us eventually came to realize, has a sub-text: namely, outside the sanctioned confines of theoretical frameworks you are incapable of thinking for yourself.

All was Quiet on the Eastern Front

Like most of my generation of Sri Lankans (at that time it was known as Ceylon), I went to study theology in India, at the United Theological College (UTC) in Bangalore. This was well before the escalation of regional and vernacular theological education. The mention of UTC evokes two images, the twin towers of ecclesiastical discourse – ecumenical and liberal. The label 'ecumenical' is easy to explain UTC probably being the first interdenominational theological college in Asia, and so the description, ecumenical was apt. 'Liberal' needs some explanation. It had a narrow application. In this context, it meant that students were exposed to what was, at that time in India, a new and contentious approach – the historical-critical method, then known as the higher criticism. Later, I will discuss what prompted the founding missionaries of the college, most of whom were products of evangelical theology, to grudgingly embrace modern criticism and expose us hapless students to what was xenophobically described as 'the German menace'. I will also point out the effectiveness and also tensions and traumas of applying the method in the sub-continent. Apart from this liberal element, in all other respects, and like most theological institutions, UTC was pretty conservative and not much more than pseudo-scholarly, and this image still persists.

---

[1] Daniel Pennac, *The Rights of the Reader* (Walker Books, 2006), p. 21.

Theological education at that time focused on two things – the Bible and Christian doctrine. The rest of the subjects were like the extra features we get in the current mobile phones. It is up to you to select and use the features that tickle your fancy. Indian Christian theology was unheard of at that time. Kaj Baago's *Pioneers of Indigenous Christianity*, introducing some of these hitherto neglected Indian-Christian writings, came out in the early 60s. It was nearly two more decades before Indian Christian theology was established as a proper discipline. Apart from an introductory course, there was no compulsion to study Indian religions. To paraphrase what Paul said to the Athenians – we lived and moved and had our being in these religions, but they were not seen as a theological priority. Indian Church History, too, was treated with disdain. Although the Christian Church has been in existence in India since the inception of Christianity, it was not included in the curriculum. The bits and pieces we came to know about Indian and Sri Lankan church history were introduced to us more or less incidentally through courses such as 'Early Church History' or the 'History of the Ecumenical Movement'.

Let me first say what really went on in our theology classes. Those were the days before 'indigenization' and 'contextualization' became buzz-words and were incorporated into theological discourse. Such ideas were not considered interesting or worthy to be addressed in systematic theology classes and were promptly consigned to the penal colonies of worship and liturgy classes. It was the theological writings of Aquinas, Barth, Brunner and Baillie, removed from their original historical contexts, which pervaded our classrooms. A considerable amount of time was spent not only on these difficult foreign authors and their books, but also on defending the universal validity of their methods and message. The prevailing view was that, like the word of God, these great theologians were speaking for all people and for all contexts. The classes assumed that one-theology fitted all contexts. Koyama's Northern Thai farmers were left on their own to flounder on with their water buffalos, cock-fighting and sticky rice.

This was the time when theologians were busy writing obituaries. Some obituaries made a great splash. *Time* magazine came out with a cover posing the question: Is God Dead? Although the imagined transcendental God of the West was dead, gods and goddesses in Asia were alive and thriving. While American theologians such as Van Buren, Altizer and Hamilton were proclaiming that God was dead, in India Raimundo Panikkar's *The Unknown Christ of Hinduism* was reviving the ancient thesis that God was very much alive and that the divine presence could be felt in other faith traditions – a thesis which K.M. Banerjea and T.E. Slater had espoused during the colonial period. It was all there to be seen. Rapid industrialization and the accompanying transport networks enabled people to travel and see for themselves busy shrines and temples of gods and goddesses.

In addition, at a time when the West was celebrating its new-found secular vision, most of the former colonies were gaining their freedom and undertaking massive redevelopment programmes, and the vigorously debated theological issues connected were going unnoticed in both the Western mainstream and our own sub-continental theologies. While we were struggling to enter the thought-world of Western theology, it was study-centres such as the Christian Institute for the Study of Religion and Society in Bangalore and the Christian-Buddhist Dialogue Centre in Colombo which were raising and addressing the issues connected with rapid development, urbanization, and religious resurgence in our newly independent countries. Unconcerned with Panikkar's book, the reinvigorated popular piety, and the issues of nation-building, we ploughed on with Barth, Brunner, Bultmann and Baillie.

The dominant theologies which held sway at the time were the secular theologies and biblical theology. Secular theology and its worst incarnation, 'the Death of God', was well past its sell-by date in the West, but its influence was palpable in Indian theological classes. This was the brief period when sceptics and doubters held sway, before the current God brigade began to assert their virulent version of Christianity. One of the texts that became almost a founding document of the time was Bonhoeffer's *Letters and Papers from Prison*. Written at a time when he was facing trial, these letters were complex, layered reflections on a variety of matters varying from the personal to politics to theology. Put loosely, one of his theological proposals, which became almost the slogan for the secular 1960s, was that one should live in the world as if God did not exist. This idea – and indeed the spell Bonhoeffer's entire life, work and death seemed to cast on his admirers – so mesmerized the theological fraternity that nobody cared to point out that his letters invariably ended with biblical quotations or a commendation of the recipient to the care of God:'God bless you and all of us each day and give us strong faith'. What such commendations demonstrate is that theologians are most appealing when they are most paradoxical and when they embrace ambiguity.

Now about the biblical classes – but before I come to that, let me recall a less serious matter which was nevertheless vital to my well-being. I was the only one doing Greek at the Master's level and the classes were held at Harold Moulton's house (son of the famous Moulton who wrote *the* Greek grammar). Harold, like me, was a serious student of cricket (read fanatic). This was before computers took over time-tabling and class-room booking. The date and time of the classes were fixed by Harold and myself with careful regard to the programme of cricket test matches between India and England, so that they did not clash with the broadcast commentaries. Live cricket telecasting, like Big Brother, was yet to hold the nation in thrall. Harold, like the Victorian amateurs, knew there was a world outside Greek syntax and the Markan Secret.

Needless to say, the critical principles and historical methods of the Enlightenment, which our missionary educators espoused, continued to be applied to study of the Bible. These were the halcyon days of biblical theology. Walter Wink was yet to come up with his startling claim: 'Historical biblical criticism is bankrupt'. Anyone in the discipline will know that historical criticism is a collective term covering a series of textual investigations which evolved gradually over the years in the West, as lower, higher, source, form and redaction criticism. These methods were introduced to us, though, as a single finished product, as if all these developments had happened simultaneously. It was as if carrier pigeons and emails were all bursting onto the scene together.

Unlike the current practice, where students are offered fast food-style ten-week modules, the courses tended to run the whole academic year. For instance, we used to start with Mark in June and expected to finish it the following April, though we were lucky if we got beyond chapter 8. This was well before the academic managers inflicted on us heavy-handed ideas like 'learning outcomes', 'personal transferable skills' and 'effectiveness of design and content of the curriculum'. Everything was done at a leisurely pace. This was the academic equivalent of forty years in the wilderness. We minutely dissected every single verse of Mark. We gazed upon small variations and minor contradictions until they were magnified into great theological propositions. Meanings were squeezed out of particles and conjunctions. The narrow quibbles of Vincent Taylor, C.H. Dodd, or Norman Perrin were noted with equal measures of awe, intimidation and boredom. The classes were a kind of mental torture which some future human-rights activist might care to refer to the International Court of Justice as a peace-time war crime.

The exegetical focus was far too narrow. Paul's *Letter to Romans* was restricted to chapters 1–8, and the pivotal parts where he deals with election and God's initiative in choosing other people – vital issues in a multi-religious context – were inexplicably left out. The Biblical Studies curriculum was vigorously laundered and scrubbed clean of the interfaith matters with which Paul deals, especially in 9–11. The fact that the curriculum framers failed to include this segment was an indication of the deadly grip Barth had on them. Most of the time was spent determining which were or weren't the genuine letters of Paul. The number of Pauline letters depended partly on what German biblical scholars (yes, it was German scholars) had pronounced at that time, and partly on the theological persuasion of those who taught the epistles. If the lecturer was liberal, the Pauline corpus was restricted to only five – Romans, 1 and 2 Corinthians, Galatians and 1 Thessolonians – and the rest were dismissed as tainted. The identification of the beloved disciple was another guessing game we used to play. The identity varied from John to Timothy to Philemon, again depending on the latest doctoral monographs from the Western academy. Later, I discovered through R.C. Amore that the idea of the beloved disciple was closely allied to and perhaps derived from Buddhist sources, with Ananda, the disciple of the Buddha, providing the prototype. Biblical Studies was essentially Eurocentric and the methods were Western, and there was no reference to any Indian way of reading the Bible. Any mention of *dhvani* would have meant the name of a fancy Indian curry. There was not even a hermeneutical circle for us to dance around.

The other hot methodological issue which reigned supreme at that time was demythologization – an off-shoot of the historical method. Bultmann become a patron saint or villain, depending on one's theological inclinations. The popular ditty at that time was :

> Hark! the herald angels sing
> Bultmann is the latest thing
> At least, they would if he had not
> Demythologized the lot.

Put simply, demythologization was an attempt to strip supernatural elements from the biblical narratives and so make the message applicable to a modern audience, specifically one of German Lutherans. No one bothered to ask how a discourse worked out in Germany to suit her theological needs was relevant to students in India. The whole discussion was marked by two absences. One that we were not told about was the Indian proto-Bultmann who had done a similar exercise during colonial times in the work of Raja Rammohun Roy. Roy's *Precepts of Jesus* (1820), which exemplified the spirit of the Enlightenment, was an attempt to cleanse the gospels of their narrow dogmatism and free the biblical God to be God of 'all living creatures, without distinction of caste, rank or wealth'.[2] I have shown elsewhere how Roy's agenda was larger than the one Bultmann had adopted. Second, in our tightly focused biblical classes, nobody was troubled by the abundance of myths and mythological figures which pervaded Asian cultures, and the various functions they performed in the lives of Indians and Sri Lankans. The demythologizing project led to the perception that anything to do with Indian myths was irrational, untrue and unscientific. Unlike German theologians fed on the diet of the Enlightenment, Indians took it for granted that myths were devised to deal with the human mess and to cope with a certain types of event, from natural disasters to personal tragedies. Ananda Coomaraswamy's definition of myth as the 'penultimate truth, of which all experience is a temporal reflection,' and myths as 'timeless and placeless' and 'true nowhere and everywhere', and that can be told 'with equal authority, from different points of view', hardly entered the culture-free zone of Biblical Studies. What was needed was not the debunking of biblical stories as myths, but encouragement to re-use and reconfigure old myths to meet the practical and political needs of the time. The writings of these German giants were imposed as the Gospel truth on generations of students in the former colonies, whose scholarly progress depended on being able to regurgitate their blinkered ideas, however inappropriate to our circumstances. As these were the days of pre-Saidian innocence, so we lapped up everything from the German giants. Before I describe how the scales started to fall from our eyes, a brief comment on the historical-critical method.

Troubling Tools and their Troubled History

The intellectual landscape of Germany which had produced higher criticism, as it was known at that time, was somewhat different from that of India. A mixture of pietism and rationalism contributed to the emergence of the method. The anti-dogmatic and anti-institutional stance espoused by pietism combined with scientific inquiry to create space for rational criticism to emerge, leading to the questioning of the veracity of biblical accounts of the creation and the patriarchal narratives. The emergence of science did not trigger off secularization in Asia, as it had done in Europe, nor did it pose a threat to Asian religious beliefs. India did not witness such a traumatic disturbance, and scientific inquiry as such was never seen as a direct danger to religion. Indeed, the contrary was true: 'The advancements in both science and religion went hand in hand from the ancient times. Scientific developments had

---

2   Rammohun Roy, *The Precepts of Jesus: The Guide to Peace and Happiness; Extracted from the Books of the New Testament, Ascribed to the Four Evangelists with Translations Into Sungscrit and Bengalee* (Baptist Mission Press, 1820), p. 1.

attained a significantly advanced level even during the Vedic age, and never had been in conflict with religion'.[3]

Historical criticism, as anyone who is familiar with it will know, is good at providing a close reading of the text and identifying problems surrounding the textual history of a narrative. Its weaknesses are many and these have been well-rehearsed: it breaks narratives into separate pieces, scrutinizes single words, deconstructs phrases, and exposes textual inconsistencies. What happens in historical criticism is similar to what goes on in a kebab shop. The meat is sliced and served in pitta bread. Like the chef, the biblical critic carves a large chunk of narrative into palatable *pericopes*. Instead of lettuce, the interpreter embellishes the *pericope* with his or her lexical wizardry. The distinctive Hellenistic and Hebraic influences are served up as a hot chilli sauce. The trouble with such a carve-up is that it doesn't help you to ask the big questions. Its focus is so much on minor details that the larger picture is overlooked. In its relentless quest for the constitution of the text and its narrativity, historical criticism misses the human story residing in the text.

The role of the historical-critical method in metropolitan centres and the colonial margins was an intriguing one. The greatest damage that historical-criticism did was not in its questioning of the veracity of the creation and flood narratives, or in exposing the inadequacy of biblical ethical codes, or undermining the biblical concepts of providence and prophecy; but, more worryingly, in making the contents of the Bible look primitive and uncouth alongside the march of modern progress. In the stages of human development and human thought, biblical narratives came to be seen as the literary product of tribal people and uncivilized times. As seen from the urbane, romantic and humane eighteenth-century Western perspective, the biblical myths and morality looked crude and in need of refinement and civilization. The decline in the West of the Bible as the definitive supplier of information pertaining to human development and knowledge began long before the advent of historical criticism. Historical criticism, nevertheless, provided the final nail in the coffin. Under the severe onslaught of the Enlightenment, biblical scholars found it difficult in the West to uphold the idea of the Bible as a uniquely distinguished book deserving special attention. When the Bible thus lost its moral and religious high ground, in order to traverse the ensuing morass it was re-conceived as another form of literature. With its images and poetry, it came to be regarded as radiating sublime truth. Cut loose from its doctrinal roots, it was refashioned as part of the secular narrative of the West. It came to seen as a human document and so the principle of *sola Scriptura* came to be regarded as an exaggerated claim. While in the metropolitan centres the Bible, which played a pre-eminent role in providing spiritual as well as legal guidelines, scientific knowledge and ethical principles, came under a severe re-appraisal, and in the colonies the Bible was projected hubristically as a culturally and theologically superior text.

One of the driving forces of historical criticism – the idea of linear history – proved to be a profitable ally for the missionaries in the colonies. The founding missionaries of the UTC at the beginning of the twentieth-century did not view

---

[3]   V. Indira Devi, *Secularisation of Indian Mind: A Study of Political Ideas in India from 1885–1914* (Rawat Publications, 2002), p. 60.

'higher' or 'modern' criticism as the work of the devil bent on destroying the basic biblical tenets, but as a collaborator in their missionary work. They were not deterred by the horror of a soulless tool being thoughtlessly applied to transcendental texts, nor were they dismayed by the spiritual damage that such a technical examination would cause. While the old theory of verbal infallibility offered confusion and contradicted some of the biblical claims, for these missionary educators modern criticism enabled them to place God's revelation in a chronological sequence and order, and to trace the growth of a people from a primitive and often cruel and barbaric condition to the glorious status of a chosen people. Missionary educators saw such a progression being replayed in India. Just as the Israelites had been extremely slow to apprehend the mind of God, a similar slowness among the Indians almost convinced the missionaries of their eventual enlightenment. One missionary educator, writing under the name XP, went on to defend the introduction of modern criticism in the mission field when many, including the British and Foreign Bible Society, queried it's application: 'The object of the present writer has been to urge that the increasing acceptance of the results of the higher criticism need be no cause of alarm to those who are interested in the spread of Foreign Missions. We as individuals may have to modify our views, and in some respects our methods of teaching'.

Such a notion of a teleological progress, as envisaged by historical-critical scholarship, is very much stacked against the colonized, always seen as falling behind in the imagined march of progress. Such a constrained logic not only provided a justification for 'redeeming' the incorrigible natives but also affirmed the righteousness of the imperial endeavour of the West. Historical-critical scholarship thus became an ally of imperialism, with the Bible masking the exploitation of colonialism.

When the Bible was introduced as a class text (in the Marquess of Tweeddale's phrase) in Indian schools, after much persistent lobbying by Anglicists against the religious neutrality of the British, as a way of luring upper-caste Hindus to Christianity, it was not promoted for its literary values but for its religious significance – more specifically, for its condemnatory potential. A book which generated so much religious uncertainty in the West was re-branded for India as a source text for religious belief, morality and, in particular, for its convictive capability. Whereas in the West its poetic images were seen as a pure and lofty form of spiritual aesthetics, in India the biblical images were seen as a way of exposing the spiritual inadequacies of Indians, and, as such, a vehicle for eventual conversion. As one of the missionary journals of the time put it, these biblical images would give the reader 'a shocking spectre of his own deformity, and haunt him, even in his sleep'.[4]

Despite reservations about historical criticism today, it is still a serviceable tool. One of the enduring results of source criticism is to demonstrate that sacred texts are not hermetically sealed entities. They often echo, however faintly, each other's ideas. Teachings which are strongly promoted as a singular characteristic of one religious tradition may, in fact, not be the exclusive property of that tradition. For instance, the ideas of heaven and hell, resurrection of the body, life after death, teachings on Satan, demons and angels, and apocalyptic beliefs such as millennial

---

[4]   Gauri Viswanathan, *Masks of Conquest: Literary Study and British Rule in India* (Columbia University Press, 1989), p. 55.

saviours, and the ending of the entire cosmos are found in both the Hebrew and Christian testaments, and may appear as typical of the Judaeo-Christian tradition, but actually have their roots in Zoroastrian sources. Initially entering and influencing the Jewish worldview, they were later borrowed, clarified or queried by Christianity and Islam. While Judaeo-Christian re-visioning of these concepts is recognized, the conceptual and intellectual roots are Iranian. Similarly, the New Testament ideal of 'non-violence, the concept of treasure in heaven, the quest for a pure mind' and the 'doctrines of the pre-existence of Jesus, the stories about his birth and infancy and the belief in his return to heaven followed the Buddhist model'.[5] At a time when the purity of a textual tradition is marshalled as a key weapon in the spurious war of religious certitudes, the considerable achievement of historical-critical scholarship has been to draw attention to the interrelatedness of different texts and demolish any claim for pure and unalloyed status.

The trouble with historical-criticism is that did not go all the way. Some of its targets, such as angels, miracles and unnatural incidents in the biblical narratives, were easy ones, as irritants to the modern mind. But its investigative incisiveness arbitrarily stopped at the claim that Jesus was exceptionally used by God. The method and its practitioners were tethered to its Christian roots and were reluctant to question one of the crudest manifestations of the Christian God as abusing and inflicting pain and punishment on his son, and then engaging in the most spectacular supernatural act of all, by raising him from the dead so that the world could be saved. Faced with the cruelty of this death and the accompanying images of savagery, even liberal theologians who employ historical-critical tools resort to mythological and pietistic defence which runs along the well-trodden argument that God's ways are inscrutable and humans are incapable of understanding the true meaning of the event. There is often a self-censorship and a refusal to pursue what Jacques Berlinerblau calls, 'the delectably blasphemous implications of its own discoveries'.[6]

Let me conclude this section with two characters, one fictional and one historical, whose words could be applicable to historical-criticism. In Harold Pinter's 'The Trouble at the Works', about a boss and a trade union official, the employee tells the industrialist that his workers were no longer interested in making a highly specialized machine tool. 'What do they want to make it in its place?', inquires the boss. 'Trouble', replies the union official.[7] This is exactly what historical criticism should do – make trouble and be an academic nuisance. The second is what Ed Murrow, the CBS journalist who fought Senator Joe McCarthy, said about the power and potential of TV, in the recent film, 'Good Night, Good Luck'. His closing words were: 'The instrument can teach, it can illuminate; yes it can even inspire, but it can do so only to the extent that humans are determined to use it to those ends. Otherwise it is merely wires and lights in a box'. To translate the last sentence,

---

    [5]   Roy C. Amore, *Two Masters, One Message: The Lives and Teachings of Gautama and Jesus* (Abingdon Press, 1978), p. 185.
    [6]   Jacques Berlinerblau, *The Secular Bible: Why Nonbelievers Must Take Religion Seriously* (Cambridge University Press, 2005), p. 10
    [7]   Stuart Jeffries, 'Playing it Straight', *Guardian 2*, 26.1.07, p.12. Note. In the televised version, the BBC deleted this scene.

historical criticism will be merely technique and weasel -words on a page unless its services are used for empowerment and emancipation. Our critical tools are by nature not defensive and are at their best when they are trenchantly offensive. They are designed not to sanctify the status quo but to be irreverently iconoclastic.

Orient and Career

What Germaine Greer calls 'the Samarkand moment' occurred when I came across two pieces of writing which came out in the 1970s but attracted my attention only in the 1980s. Importantly, both jolted the un-postcolonized world that I inhabited. The first was Jose Miguez Bonino's 'Marxist Critical Tools: Are They Helpful in Breaking the Stranglehold of Idealist Hermeneutics?'[8] It was my colleague, Bas Wielenga, who gave me the SCM pamphlet which carried the article. In it, Bonino lobbed in three incendiary bombs: ideological bias in interpretation; the need to place texts in their socio-economic context; and, theory and practice as an indivisible single function. To many of the present generation of interpreters, these may well be routine, familiar matters, but to those who were trapped in the academic gulags of neutrality, objectivity and methodological technicality, they were daringly refreshing at that time. The Bonino article, which I reprinted in *Voices from the Margin*, was, so far as I am aware, one of the earliest attempts to introduce 'ideological suspicion' into the flaccid world of biblical interpretation. Using Marxist analysis as a 'powerful instrument', Bonino was able to show how mainstream biblical scholarship, contrary to its claim to neutrality, had entrenched its own ideological biases. This supposedly 'scientific' exegesis was in fact aiding and abetting the interests of dominant classes. Bonino exposed the subjective, 'liberal bourgeois spirituality' deeply rooted in the writings of one of the revered masters of the time – Joachim Jeremias – demonstrating how even 'an honest and respectful exegete' like Jeremias could betray class bias. Later, when I came under the influence of Edward Said, I was alerted to detect and expose the Orientalist tendencies in Jeremias' writings. In his article, Bonino went on to show how biblical scholars ignored the historical and political significance of biblical events such as the death of Jesus and the *Parousia*, and turned them into 'individualistic and inward' looking experiences. Mainstream scholarship at the time focused chiefly on religious and theological aspects of the narratives and largely neglected the social and economic environment from which these emerged. Bonino widened and moved the hermeneutical goalposts in order to include the socio-economic context of the text, and expose ideological bias in biblical interpretation.

The other text was Edward Said's *Orientalism* – a text that has now achieved cult status. I really cannot recall who introduced me to Said, but I still remember where I bought my copy – in Birmingham at Hudson's Bookshop, which has now been turned into a designer-clothes emporium – a sign of post-book days. Said's *Orientalism*, like President G.W. Bush, coerces scholars to make polarizing choices – either you are with it or against it. When the book came out, it was attacked by

---

8   José Miguez Bonino, 'Marxist Critical Tools: Are They Helpful in Breaking the Stranglehold of Idealist Hermeneutics?', in R.S. Sugirtharajah (ed.), *Voices from the Margin: Interpreting the Bible in the Third World* (Orbis Books, 1995), pp. 58–68.

scholars both on the left and on the right. It has many faults, and Said himself has acknowledged and rectified some of these in 'Introductions' and 'Afterwords' to later editions, and has also answered his critics in subsequent works. In many respects, Said's work was much larger and more ambitious and thus went beyond Bonino. While both address the vital issue of economics and the link between politics and interpretation, engagement and reflection, Said widens the investigation to include culture, representation and, more significantly, colonial presence in fictional works and colonial impulses in historical documents. His perception of Orientalism became a model of how various European disciplines and institutions had come to construct knowledge about the colonized and used this to dominate them.

Apart from giving a complex new meaning to the word 'Orientalism', which until then simply signified serious scholarship in the field, his work made it clear that cultures and ideas of the colonized were available for examination largely in the form of imperial articulations. What, in effect, Said was trying to do was to challenge the unwillingness to acknowledge the presence and relevance of colonial experience in the scholarly and literary works of the time Said's book also launched a critique of the integrity of Western scholarship. It made scholars conscious of their starting points, sources and standing in the community at large, and was arguing for non-suppressive and non-manipulative forms of knowledge production. More personally, Said's theoretical framework gave those of us who work in the biblical field the confidence and intellectual wherewithal to question the exegetical articulations of Western biblical interpreters and write back.

After reading Said, at least two things became clear to me. One was the conservatism of biblical studies, not just in its theoretical outlook but in its intellectual and, more pointedly, its political conformity. Its style and tenor made it a closed discipline, a guild with strict rules, regulations and austere conventions. The other thing was the impossibility of taking any interpreter or interpretation at face value. Hermeneutical projects which claim neutrality often succumb to and display imperial attitudes such as racism and sexism.

Said's work was crucial for the development of what is now known as postcolonial theory, although Said himself advocated and continued to use the phrase 'secular criticism'. Postcolonialism as critical practice is an intensely contested project which has acquired different meanings and nuances depending on who wants to use it and for what purpose. Elsewhere, I have defined the term, narrated the history of its origins, described its method and provided examples of how it operates in biblical studies. I can only hint here at some possible directions it has taken for me. First, what postcolonialism does is to place 'empire' at the centre of biblical narratives. Biblical history was played out within the contours of various empires. Biblical texts are laced with imperial features such as subjugation, deportation, dispossession, exile and diaspora. The Hebrew Scriptures, for example, mention how the history and destiny of the biblical Jews and their neighbours were intertwined with the presence of Egyptian, Assyrian and Persian empires. The New Testament may be silent about the contemporary world order, but most of the New Testament writings were located within the Roman imperial context. What postcolonialism tries to do is to show how empire and imperial presence are pivotal to the biblical narratives. For instance, when looking at Matthew's *Gospel*, unlike mainstream commentators who are preoccupied with religious themes and spend their energies on the intra-theological rivalries between feuding local synagogues, postcolonial biblical criticism will set the *Gospel* within the imperial context. The aim of postcolonial biblical criticism in questioning the dominant way of reading Matthew and situating it within the imperial context, is to study how the writer was responding to the pressures of the empire – was he colluding with its imperial intentions, or was he offering a counter-narrative to the Roman power?

The second challenge of postcolonialism is to uncover colonial concerns which have shaped biblical interpretation. In spite of the alleged claim to neutrality, much biblical interpretation has its roots in various colonial projects of the nineteenth-century. Postcolonial criticism has shown how much biblical scholarship is riddled with Euro-American nationalism and racial overtones. Albert Schweitzer, famed for his search for the historical Jesus, is a notable case in point. At a time when everyone was disapproving colonialism, Schweitzer, who later became a missionary to Africa, asserted bluntly, for the sake of Africans, that the Europeans should continue to be in control of that continent and should say to Africans: 'I am your brother, but your *elder* brother'. Schweitzer was no exception. The work of key figures of the time such as Schleiermacher, Strauss, and E. Renan was driven by nationalism and imperialism. Recently, Halvor Moxnes has shown how these three, in their reconstruction of Galilee as the location of the historical Jesus, were influenced by the prevailing European cultural ideas of the time: colonialism, nationalism, ethnocentrism, and racism.[9] It has now come to light, also, how the nationalism and the racial bias of some of the leading German and French biblical scholars were regularly erased in translations of their work, leaving only a liberal hermeneutical agenda on show.

Another hermeneutical project which smacks of Oriental tendencies is social science criticism. Some of the methodological presuppositions of those who apply social science criticism to the Bible border on Orientalism and Occidentalism. Their articulations unusually emphasize and exaggerate the difference between the West and Middle Eastern cultures, and reinforce the notion that the West knows Middle-Eastern societies better than the indigenes themselves. They are reminiscent of Victorian travellers discovering for the first time the fauna and flora of the dark corners of the empire. What Said said on another occasion is equally applicable to the social science project: 'the Oriental become more Oriental, the Westerner more Western'.[10]

A third aspect of postcolonialism concerns the twin task of 'writing back', and 'listening again'. Writing back is a counter-discursive activity which aims at re-telling the story from the perspective of the Other. It is a hermeneutical attempt to clear away some of the defamatory and propagandist discourse of the colonizer which has painted the colonized in an unfavourable light. Re-writing is not a defensive, reactive exercise in which a set of disapproving images is replaced with an affirmative set. Rather, it is about re-examining the complex colonial contact to produce knowledge that is non-exploitative and does not domesticate. Equally important is to 'listen

---

[9]   Halvor Moxnes, 'The Construction of Galilee as a Place for the Historical Jesus – Part I', *Biblical Theology Bulletin* 31/26 (2001).

[10]   Edward W. Said, *Orientalism* (Penguin Books, 1978), p. 46.

again', detecting those voices which were submerged and neglected under the grand narratives of national independence and development.

A fourth aspect of postcolonialism is its method. Although it has been unashamedly eclectic and has borrowed critical practices from other disciplines, one reading practice – contrapuntal reading – could be claimed as its own. Contrapuntal reading is the interpretative reversal of the earlier dubious comparative method that put biblical texts and Western Christian discourse on the pedestal and castigated the 'other' texts for failing to measure up to Christian standards. By nature, comparative hermeneutics was antagonistic, adversarial and judgmental, whereas contrapuntal reading is an attempt to topple this hierarchy and to avoid the rhetoric of censure and slander. It is also a way out of the binaristic manner of thinking which makes claims for 'our' against 'your' texts. The operative principle of contrapuntal reading is that although sacred texts are complex and uneven, they are connected at some level however hidden or tenuous that connection is. The task of the contrapuntal reading then is to place these texts side-by-side and bring out the convergences, contradictions, discrepancies, oversights and omissions in them and to show that no one text has the finished and once-for-all meaning, and thus to challenge and to prevent claims of any text possessing the 'last' word.

One of the great benefits of contrapuntal reading is that it encourages one to read outside one's discipline. One may not be fully acquainted with the works of Appadurai, Bhabha, Derrida, Foucault, Spivak, Said or Zizek, but one must know something about them to grasp the dynamic of hermeneutics. Contrapuntal reading makes us, as Kermode said in a different context, 'smatters'. As he went on to say in the same interview, 'a certain amount of civilization depends on intelligent smattering'.[11] There is another advantage, too. In an age of increased specialization and niche thinking, contrapuntal reading tries to connect disparate disciplines and texts. It is a theoretical and pedagogical necessity.

Methods, Meanings, Manners

In current theological writing, methods and structure are so pervasive that creativity is stifled and replaced with programmatic and formulaic conventions. Working with a pre-planned method has advantages in that that one need not stray too far from the desired focus of study, but the flip side is that one ends with predictable and pretty dull stuff. To rephrase Mark Twain, methodology has become the last resort of the unimaginative. In the research-ridden academic world where most of us work, instinct and improvisation is treated with disdain and regarded as unscientific and emotional. Cleverly crafted methodologies alone will not make good writing. We like to think of theological writing as a battleground for ideas, methods and paradigms, independent of imagination and spontaneity. But once the methodological procedure has done its work, it is the inspired guess which enables the researcher to take the final leap. Listen to the words of anthropologist Oscar Lewis. When rattled by an unrelenting student pressing to know exactly what methodological procedure Lewis

---

[11]   John Sutherland, 'The Ideas Interview', *Guardian* G2, 29.8.06, p. 24.

had adopted when selecting one oral story over another, he was supposed to have said: 'maybe, sometimes, I hear a voice that says this is the way to go, here not there'. Biblical interpreters, too, who claim ruthless objectivity, have been known to fall back on intuition. A conspicuous example is Miller and Maxwell. In order to reconstruct the origins of Israel and Judah, they looked at both biblical and non-biblical literary sources, and at archaeological evidence, and brought into play various models derived from Middle Eastern cultural patterns and current social sciences. In the end they conceded that, in addition to all this, 'a considerable amount of intuitive speculation' went into their work.[12] It is an enormous relief to hear that inspiration and intuition play a role alongside ratiocination in solving profound and complicated issues. The message is that interpretation is not just about dense theories, and that there is room for the 'bathtub and Eureka' moment. It must allow for visions and taking risks and taking the plunge. Come to think of it, the two different responses by the shepherds and the Magi to the Nativity in *Luke* make helpful metaphors for what I am driving at – the shepherds spontaneously rush to see the new-born child after the angelic revelation, and the Magi studiously study the stars, taking time to weigh up the evidence in searching for the scene. One views interpretation as an intuitive, impressionistic activity, while the other sees it as taking time while the methodological procedure is selected, the facts tested and the evidence analysed.

Kosuke Koyama, who has a way with words, once asked whether a scholarly analysis of 'chopsticks' is more revealing than the experience of eating with them? That was in his pioneering 'waterbuffalo' days in Thailand, when he knew that making theology relevant to his Thai farmers required him to discard all abstract ideas in favour of their everyday interest, sticky-rice, cock-fighting and so on. Now, though, knowing that the context that prompted the question has changed, he would be the first to elaborate on the metaphor and say that his proverbial Thai farmer needs both an instinct for chopsticks and the ability to apply analytic skills to agriculture and the market if he is to continue to enjoy his sticky rice and his cock-fighting.

---

[12]   J. Maxwell and John H. Hayes Miller, *A History of Ancient Israel and Judah* (SCM Press, 1986), p. 77.

Chapter 20

On Being Radical and Hopefully Orthodox

Graham Ward

I have made choices, and they have been hard and yet, in a sense, I am still trying to grasp, they were grace to me.

At the age of fourteen I made what now I can see as one of the most decisive journeys of my life. In a cold December, when the snow blew about the streets and covered the ground, I piled my mother, three brothers, and myself into a taxi and headed for Salford. We sat crushed by all the things we could stuff into the cab, and silent, I in the front seat staring ahead. We had no money to pay the fare. We were living in the Pennines at the time, my mother was critically ill with what would later be diagnosed as Huntingdon's Chorea, my three brothers were all much younger and my father hadn't come home for several days. I have never seen my father since. The taxi bore us towards my grandmother's house, which she shared with her younger brother. This house was, and for many years remained, the only safe place I knew.

Salford and my grandmother are inseparable and the deepest shapers of my theological ideas. Salford is now a city subsumed under Manchester, a northern industrial city still riddled underground with the tunnels and shafts of coal mines. Every so often when the rain sweeps in from the North Sea for days on end, there will be a low rumble, the land will slip and Salford will shudder. It was a city of migrants because there was lots of cheap, if somewhat sad, housing. In my day it was home to the Jews, with the Scottish and the Irish still pouring into industrial cities looking for work. Today, it's the home also of peoples from India, Pakistan, Bangladesh, and new EU states like Poland, Hungary and the Czech Republic. Salford is a city of tongues. There have been summer nights when I have sat out in the backyard and heard arguments in Russian and domestic conversations in Punjabi. Up the road there's a whole area where only Yiddish is spoken. I still live in my grandmother's house; the house I came to at the age of fourteen.

My grandmother was one of thirteen children, and though not the oldest of those children by sheer force of personality the clan gathered around her. A small woman with dark hair and defined features, she was as intelligent as she was cunning; a master of knowing how to make the most out of very little. She was a hard woman with a tender heart. She had steered and sheltered the lives of her husband, father, mother, children and a whole host of related dependants through the scarcities of the Great Depression and the terrors of the Second World War. Until her seventies she threw an annual New Year's Eve party attended by tens of uncles, aunts, cousins and nephews, and refused all help with preparing the food. She was living on her state pension when the five of us arrived at her door on that December night. She paid the taxi driver and, without one question, took us in, put the chip pan on to heat, found us beds to sleep in and, in the days ahead, clothes to wear.

Had I not come to Salford, had I not come under the honed and powerful love of my grandmother I cannot say where I would be, but certainly not a theologian and probably not even educated beyond the age of sixteen. For adolescents still could leave school at fifteen and sixteen when I grew up, though already Salford's industrialism was weak and exhausted. I remember a teacher saying to a class of sixteen-year-old boys most of whom left school to find work: 'This is a lost generation.' There was little employment to be found and most of it for a youth at that time was illegal, cash in hand, without insurance, casual, and tax-dodging. I knew this world intimately. In fact, I left school at sixteen with the thought of getting a hospital job. My best friend at the time was a Scottish lad evading a court order in Glasgow who worked for a garage re-spraying cars. He smoked, and one day when he threw the red end of his stub away it set fire to the paint. In minutes, his trousers were on fire and he had to be rolled in a blanket. He suffered major burns to his legs that kept him in hospital for almost a month. His employer gave his mother a hundred pounds and said there was no more work for him. They paid no insurance for their workers. I didn't get my hospital job. I couldn't get any job. So my grandmother sent me back to school.

I was not interested in theology; that came much later. Over the summer when I'd left school and was looking for work, I discovered a passion – for writing. I wrote my first novel on an old office typewriter made from wrought iron that I found in a junk shop. The passion for writing was closely connected to a second passion, for reading. Taking something, I think, from my grandmother's resolve, when I returned to school it was with a determination to study literature and become a novelist. And from someone who had not exactly been a high academic achiever, I also decided that since so many of the writers I admired either went to Oxford or Cambridge then I would do so also. So from a schoolboy leaver who couldn't get work, over that summer I became a budding intellectual, and my grandmother bullied the city council into giving me a monthly annuity.

I came to theology then through literature. Much later I was to become the editor of the Oxford University Press journal *Literature and Theology*, and remained editor for eight years. The two disciplines indulge in and develop what, to my mind, is one of the most vital and human of faculties: the imagination. The imagination is that faculty which makes alarmingly new connections, intuits new possibilities, probes in an inchoate, half-blind manner into territories less than half known. To a boy and an adolescent in a grey, damp and impoverished landscape, the power of the imagination was world-defying. Every word, to my mind, conjured from nothing an image, a context, a colour, a sound. I knew instinctively the power of spells and enchantments – the weaving from language of geographies unsurveyed, of domains of dreams and wishes and nightmares. Great imagination needs great courage, maybe even hubris; the courage of conquistadors like Dante's Ulysses, or Columbus, Frobisher, and Pizzaro. The courage and maybe even the hubris, not only to conceive something new but to dare to create it. George Steiner wrote thousands of words describing this artistic emulation, even envy, of God. And one knows, as intimately as knowing one's calling, that to materialise any true conception will take you down ginnels and gutters, byways and pathways, sniffing in a panic for the Spirit of truth like a man in a dark cave fighting for fresh air and the way out. To explore a theological theme, like the incarnate flesh, and to delve into the inner thoughts of a character in a novel being written, a plot being unfolded, is a very similar experience: the end is not known, the potential connections are there but not yet discovered, made. Freud knew this in his groundbreaking voyage into the subconscious. Rothko, after finishing a painting, would sit back mesmerised by what had been achieved, groping to understand just where he had been.

I read English and French at Cambridge and my third year undergraduate dissertation was on the seventeenth century writer John Bunyan. This is a strange tale. I type now in the bedroom where it all took place. In many ways Bunyan was an unusual choice. My father was a Catholic, my grandmother a nominal Anglican, though at school and later college I associated with a number of Christian evangelicals. I was deeply divided about my dissertation, already having thoughts that I would try for a career in television, with the BBC, as a scriptwriter or director. I wrestled one night about who I should chose for the subject of my dissertation, again somehow sensing this was a life choice – a decisive direction. My love was the erotic poetry of Christopher Marlowe, my fascination was the exotica of Andrew Marvell, through a rather dull and I thought snobbish teacher, Professor Gillian Beer, I had been introduced to the heady delights of structuralism, but in my bedroom that dark night I sensed very clearly that Bunyan should be the subject of my dissertation. In particular, I was drawn to examine the allegorical world of *The Pilgrim's Progress*, its topography, its creation of an alternative theological *topos*. At heart, I think, I was drawn to the relation between language and imagination, word and image; a strong and seductive combination. And it was through Bunyan that I became interested in theology. When I graduated I moved to doctoral research on Bunyan, specifically the nature of the Puritan uses and conceptions of metaphor. One of the first essays I published was an analysis of the way Bunyan had to move beyond the literal sense of Scripture to maintain his psychological health.

Metaphor cannot be separated from a host of rhetorical tropes such as simile, analogy, synecdoche, and metonymy. When I began to study for a degree in theology I was very fortunate to have as teachers and mentors both Dr. Janet Soskice (whose work on metaphor had recently been published to great acclaim) and Professor Nicholas Lash. It was Lash who led me beyond Saussure, Levi-Strauss, Jacobson and Greimas to Wittgenstein. He annually taught a seminar at Cambridge on analogy. I had, by this time, moved away from literature; mainly, I sense, because the thrill of thinking about language itself has never left me. The way a word can conjure a whole world; the way writers can skilfully create such worlds and populate them, the way the reader transposes those worlds and populations into his or her own suspension of disbelief – this continues to fascinate me. I enjoy textual analysis, my work is littered with close readings of Scripture, of films, of images, paintings, pop videos, and theological discourses, but what I am always attempting to grasp a little more deeply is the way language is working, exercising its control over the reader or listener. In Lash's seminar we read Aquinas and Barth and Wittgenstein, and being the great teacher that he is, he made age-old problems about God-talk into something I would spend the next decades fathoming.

'If a lion spoke how would we know?' This is a footnote in *Philosophical Investigations*, but it reintroduced me to the question of otherness from a theological perspective. I say reintroduced because, from my days researching in literature at a time when the Cambridge English Faculty was going through civil wars concerning the teaching of structuralism and poststructuralism, otherness had been a key concept to understanding Heidegger, Levinas and Derrida. Each of them had related otherness, or alterity, to difference and it was this connection that now I began to examine with respect to theology. What nature or natures does theological difference take? How do we *understand* the otherness of God? How do we understand the *otherness* of God? What is the relationship between ontological difference and theological difference? The focus for these questions came to be Karl Barth's reflections on the spoken Word of God, *Deus dixit*, for here too was a man obsessed with language and how it operated. Listening to Lash and discussing ideas with other people in his seminar, including a fellow theologian, David Moss, a project began to take shape. It could take shape at all only because the American reception of Jacques Derrida's work underwent a major shift around this time: he was starting to be read by a handful of theologians, many but not all emerging from the 'Death of God' school, and he was being left behind by the literary doyens. While this shift was taking place, Derrida himself began to write more overtly about a comparison he had alluded to in one of his early essays, but never until now developed: the relationship between *differance* and negative theology.

Students will bear this out: most of learning is quite routine, but occasionally you come across a voice, the hearing of which, you will never forget. Today, when I teach the history of philosophy, I know the students will be intrigued by Plato, Augustine and Descartes, and slightly bored by what seem the mechanics of reasoning in Aristotle and Aquinas. But they never forget the first words they hear of Nietzsche. When I teach systematic theology, the same can be said of those who read the opening paragraphs of Barth's *Romans II*. You may agree with these writers, you may disagree, but no one can remain indifferent to the sheer power of their declamations.My first reading of Karl Barth has never left me. Whenever I write about Barth (or Hegel or Derrida) I think 'this time I will be rid of him.' I always want to get to the other side of Barth, put him in the past, but I wrestle with him continually – as with a great mind which had already seen the moves you will make and weighed their shortcomings. Since so much of Barth's theology is a theology of the Word, I wanted to examine what he had to say about language and the cultural context in which such depictions of language were current. The research question began to take shape under Lash's guidance: how does Derrida's understanding of logocentrism (and his critique of its pretensions) speak to Barth's ruminations on the Word of God that is always mediated? And how does Barth's understanding of Christ as the Word, speak to Derrida's investigations into *differance* and negative theology? How, with these two people, might we approach the perennial philosophy of religion question of the language of theology in a new way? *Barth, Derrida and the Language of Theology* (1995) began with these questions.

In the meantime I had been ordained and was working as an Anglican curate in a large civic church in Bristol; by day I visited the bereaved and couples wanting their child baptised, and by night I was trying to clarify how Barth's *Redephilosophie* differed from that being advocated by the Patmos Group (with which he had passing acquaintance). But that double practice – of practising theology and writing it – became very important. It lies, I think, behind my concerns about much systematic theology – its idealism, its levels of abstraction, a forgetting that it arises from a context and is related to a praxis that continually negotiates as it performs concepts like 'salvation', 'forgiveness' and 'grace'. My time at Bristol as a curate also raised for me an abiding question: what is the task of theology, for whom is it speaking and to whom? I recall sitting with a couple with a new baby. They were not married and the woman's mother did most of the talking. They were living with her in one of the flats overlooking the church. It became obvious, as I was going through the forms, that the father was unemployed but believed this would be held against him because the baptism form required specific answers to the father's 'occupation'. He was profoundly embarrassed when his false information became evident, and I was profoundly sorry the forms I was completing made it seem necessary for him to lie. But throughout the whole event, and later when I actually baptised the child, my question was why they wanted to put themselves through such trials, such embarrassments with an institution with grandiose visions of its own importance and which they rarely attended. 'We have a right', I remember the mother telling me. 'He was born in the parish, we have a right to have him baptised.' These were the kind of people I knew from Salford: determined, willing to submit themselves to the game of having the well-spoken curate round for a chat, if they could get what they wanted. This baptism was of the utmost importance to both of them (and the mother-in-law) but they could not explain why. There was genuine faith here though very little understanding. The theology I write I doubt they would ever read or think of reading. But that is not the point, to me the incident raised, in its first guise, what the significance of theology is that time should be taken being a theologian. When I moved to a secular university the questions this incident raised, returned to me again, in another guise: what role does a Christian theologian have in a university with no commitment to train people for a church; no commitment to the explication of Christianity as such at all?

I finished *Barth, Derrida and the Language of Theology*, having become Chaplain and Tutor in Theology at Exeter College, Oxford. The fact that Derrida was perceived to be a postmodern thinker was incidental to my thesis; that I was groping towards writing a postmodern theology of my own was very far from my thoughts. I was trying to understand something for myself about the power of language and its relationship in Christian theology to the Word of God. I only began to realise how contentious the move was towards investigating a systematic theologian through a contemporary philosopher, and a contemporary philosopher through a systematic theologian, when the book fell among the 'Barthians'. There have been two incidents in my professional career to date in which I have been caught up in the cultural politics of Christian theologians and different theological factions. The experiences had profoundly affected my thinking and led to my most recent work on religion and political culture. The first was this brush with the Barthians and the interpretative monopoly they seem to claim and the second was the reception of Radical Orthodoxy (RO). On the other hand, through my encounter with the Barthians I came to the attention of what might be called the new 'Yale School': some of the people taught by Hans Frei and George Lindbeck who had now themselves established themselves as independent theologians. With these people I began a very fruitful and influential conversation. In fact, one of them, Walter Lowe, was himself working on a correspondence between Barth and Derrida while I was studying with Lash. Another, Serene Jones, was reading French feminist theorists like Kristeva and Irigaray and also thinking through the reading of Barth. For me two key positions crystallised through the reception of my first book among the Barthians. First, my belief that modern Protestant systematic theology, that wished, as I wished, to eschew liberal correlationalism, could become tediously circular and idealist unless it sought critical interventions beyond its own purlieus. Despite the Yoders and the Hauerwas's such theology was still far too apolitical, acultural and asocial. Second, there was a need to introduce theologians to the number of contemporary continental voices, interested in discussing religious issues, who might provide conceptual tools for such critical interventions.

The Postmodern God (1997) and *Theology* and *Contemporary Critical Theory* (1996) were edited (in the former case) and written (in the latter case) to fill this perceived gap. This was a time also when I became very interested in the work of one thinker in particular, the French Jesuit Michel de Certeau. De Certeau's work, more than Foucault's or Bourdeau's, enabled me to think through issues related to cultural politics and the role of religion. His book *La fable mystique* charts the theological changes that led from a communal understanding of the mystical, in the church, to the individual cries of both the mystic and the demonically possessed. Always de Certeau keeps his eye on the political, social and cultural changes within which such changes in religious practice and thinking took place. De Certeau taught me not only the meaning of, but something of the methodology for doing, contextual theology. Out of this interest came my edition of *The Certeau Reader* (2000) and a number of essays on de Certeau's thinking.

The reading of de Certeau's work came at a time when I was also reading the theology of another Jesuit, Hans Urs von Balthasar. I had come across von Balthasar when researching Barth's understanding of analogy. Now I began to work through von Balthasar's understanding of analogy, being drawn to his immense indebtedness to the Greek Church Fathers. His voice, like Barth's, I will not forget. They are such different theological minds. Not because one is Protestant and the other Catholic, but rather because Barth's mind is forensic and von Balthasar's poetic in character. If Barth posed an intellectual challenge for me, then von Balthasar posed a spiritual challenge (as, a little later, did his French confrere Henri de Lubac). As I began my reading of him the doctrine of kenosis seized my attention and imagination and likewise his critique of liberal culture. I recognised links with old friends, such as George Steiner – particularly the end of Steiner's *Real Presences* and the appeal to the silence of the Word on Holy Saturday. But it was only as I began to write about von Balthasar that the politics of doing so became apparent. Few Roman Catholics of my acquaintance had much time for him, mainly because of the popularity of his theology for Pope John Paul II and Cardinal Ratzinger. The Roman Catholics who were interested in him tended towards exposition rather than critical engagement, although several Anglicans, including Rowan Williams, had begun some excellent critical appropriations of his work. Eventually, in a beer garden in

Oxford, discussing the issues with my close friend, David Moss, we conceived the idea for a collection of essays examining the connections between von Balthasar's theology and postmodern theory. Along with Lucy Gardiner and Ben Quash, David and I developed *Balthasar at the End of Modernity* (2001), with my own essay on von Balthasar's doctrine of kenosis in relation to the work of Julia Kristeva, Jean-Luc Nancy and Gianni Vattimo. In a sense, in what I regard as one of my more important essays, I was returning to a method I had worked out with the comparison between Barth and Derrida; revealing the way theology can operate therapeutically on postmodern thinking, whilst postmodern thinking could assist in gaining a critical perspective on theological discourse. Although I was to go on and examine other postmodern thinkers, and revisit those I had become familiar with in the French continental tradition, from this time I began to distance myself from theory as such because I was becoming interested in the development of a culturally engaged systematic theology. I was developing a sense of my own vocation as a theologian with a philosophical and literary-hermeneutic bent.

There is no doubt in my mind that highly influential at this point in my life was the decision to return to Cambridge, this time as Dean of Peterhouse, and my conversations there with theologians like Janet Martin Soskice and John Milbank. This was the moment Radical Orthodoxy was formed. Much has been written now about Radical Orthodoxy and its origins. It remains mistaken, to my mind, to see either John Milbank's *Theology and Social Theory* or Catherine Pickstock's *After Writing: The Liturgical Consummation of Philosophy* as providing the theological foundations for Radical Orthodoxy. John's book was well known to me and its thesis chimed with critiques of theological liberalism in the work of British theologians like Donald MacKinnon and Rowan Williams and American theologians of the Yale School or Hauerwas inspired. Catherine's book was, at the time Radical Orthodoxy was conceived, still a doctoral thesis awaiting examination. Nor can the 'Introduction' to the opening volume of the book series, *Radical Orthodoxy: A New Theology*, be read as a theological programme. I would concede the 'Introduction' was something of a manifesto insofar as it set out a theological agenda: to read western culture in terms of the Christian gospel and, in so doing, disrupt western culture's own evaluation and self-understanding. The Christian tradition became a standpoint for reading contemporary culture back to itself, and indicating the ways in which such a culture has sold itself into a superficial and nihilistic consumerism. But that 'Introduction' did not set out a systematic theology. Though there are theological lines of genuine affiliation, what I called a shared sensibility, between some of the major voices in Radical Orthodoxy, there was no agreed dogmatics. In fact, one of the weaknesses of the enterprise theologically was its ecclesiology – although I would contend this is a weakness of Protestant theology *tout court* and the reason why ecumenism is so important a Protestant pursuit. And Radical Orthodoxy was certainly ecumenical – as the conferences to date on RO and Roman Catholicism, RO and the Reformed Tradition, RO and the Orthodox Tradition and RO and Process Theology testify. But what the three editors of the Radical Orthodoxy did plan was nothing less than a frontal attack on a contemporary secular culture that had come to dominate certain intellectual terrains: philosophy, art, music, sexuality, the body, the city etc. Radical Orthodoxy did not name a dialogue partner, it named an enemy:

secular liberalism, and in subsequent volumes it took up arms against this enemy as it manifested itself in liberation theology (Daniel Bell), economics (Stephen Long), philosophical nihilism (Conor Cunningham), Catholic detraditionalisation (John Milbank, Catherine Pickstock and Tracey Rowland), discourse (James Smith) and debates around science and religion (Simon Oliver). My own contribution was a first attempt at a systematic theology.

From my earliest theological training systematic theology made sense to me. Dogmatics was like a wheel – wherever you began, with the Word of God in Christ, with human nature, with the Church, with the Scriptures etc., the same ground would have to be covered: a doctrine of God, a doctrine of creation, ecclesiology, eschatology, soteriology, theological anthropology, etc.. The question was where to start, the order that would follow and the consequences of beginning in this place rather than that. At the same time I reacted against what seemed to me the abstract even idealist levels towards which most systematic theologies were pitched. In part this was a response to the intense spirituality of von Balthasar. But even Barth, despite his continuing interest in the political situation (and the work of exegetes like Marquardt, Hunsinger and Gorringe) often seemed to be building a great cathedral that hovered above our heads (as Richard Roberts observed). His theology lacked that incarnationalism I wanted to emphasise and the sacramentalism that rooted von Balthasar's understanding of analogy. I wanted to develop a systematic theology that issued in a specific cultural context and posed a critical intervention with that context, like the liberation theologians, like liberal theologians, but which took the revealed origins and materialism of theology seriously. This is what I mean by 'culturally engaged'. This theology would negotiate both the top down approaches of Barth and the bottom up approaches of Tillich, avoiding the theological abstractions of the former and the existential reductions of the latter. I began several essays on various aspects of this systematics that unfolded from a major turn to the body and examinations of desire in contemporary critical theory: transpositions in the body of Christ that gave rise to meditations on the Church and sacraments. But I still lacked a starting point.

I found my starting point when I made the decision to move from Cambridge back to Manchester and when I made my first visit to the States, to New Orleans. I rediscovered the city. I still recall coming over the freeway at night towards my first experience of an American city. New Orleans emerged from the plain like an insistent prayer for something and I spent my five days in that city trying to decode what kind of a theological statement the city was making. That the statement it was making was theological I could not deny: everywhere, from the postmodern skyscrapers to the sports arenas and the art deco mouldings, spoke of a transcendence, of a communal aspiration and ambition that was both terrifying and inspiring. The book that emerged from trying to make theological sense of the city was *Cities of God* (2000); a book self-consciously attempting to return to Augustine's experience of cities like Carthage, Milan and Hippo Regius and his theological politics. Unfortunately, Routledge decided to put an end to the Radical Orthodoxy Series before the other two volumes of that project were written. So the second, methodological volume, *Cultural Transformation and Religious Practice* (2005) was published by Cambridge University Press, and the third volume, which explores the dogmatics of Cities of

God through negotiations with sites of intense urban attention (the crisis of liberal politics, globalisation, the re-enchantment of contemporary western cultural, virtual kingdoms, and what I call cultural sadomasochism) will be published by Oxford University Press in 2009.

Meanwhile, as I have been working on this culturally engaged systematics my theology has been taking a further turn. This turn has always been embryonic in the work I have done to date on micro-political issues, such as gender and the cultural politics of what makes any belief believable at any given time. It began to come into focus the more I studied Augustine and Hegel's *Philosophy of Right*. But it consciously came to dominate my thinking when I teamed up with a younger colleague in my department of Religions and Theology at the University of Manchester, Dr. Michael Hoelzl. For the last four or five years I have felt the need to engage more directly in the relationship between religion and political science, particularly political theology. In part, this new development in my theological work resulted from accepting the critique that Radical Orthodoxy needed to address questions concerning ecclesiology. But ecclesiological thinking is never undertaken in a cultural vacuum. It issues from reflections upon a tradition and it is thoroughly informed by what Charles Taylor has recently called 'social imaginaries'; that is, conceptions and contemporary practices of social organisation and sovereignty. With Michael Hoelzl, I embarked on a four-year project sponsored by the British Academy to examine the new visibility of religion and its impact on democratic cultures in Europe. With him I have also edited a Reader in Religion and Political Thought and we will publish next year a translation of Carl Schmitt's *Political Theology II*. I am still at the stage of learning another discourse, while simultaneously developing certain dogmatic foci. For example, *Christ and Culture* (2005) is an attempt to bring together various strands of my thinking on Christology and its profound relation to ecclesiology.

The overall aim remains the exposition of an engaged systematic theology that can act as a cultural critique; that can be understood as *Kulturkritik*, albeit one which deepens, metaphysically, the earlier work of Horkheimer and the work of Adorno. Benjamin's concerns with the messianic and the eschatological point something of a way here. And I don't read Benjamin as a secularist. To be engaged is to have a standpoint and to name an enemy – that was Schmitt's understanding of the concept of the political, though Schmitt saw the political with respect to the nation-state not the Church. But theology is a political act; that is what the new turn in my work boils down to recognising. The extent to which this is understood brings apologetics closer to polemics. But as polemics theology avoids being a placebo; it is radical, and today we are coming to see ever more clearly how socially and culturally dangerous are people with faith convictions. Nevertheless, unless we confront these convictions, rather than control and privatise them (the move liberalism makes), unless we genuinely strive to negotiate the potential violences of these convictions and the social visions they embody, then we are not taking multiculturalism and religious truth-claims seriously, and we are constructing pictures of world peace on liberal (often now economic) illusions. There are values in this world that transcend money, liberal democracy and even individual rights; there are sovereignties in this world that need to be challenged and struggled with;

and only with those challenges and struggles will sectarian violence be avoided. Human beings cannot afford to be naïve, least of all about themselves; and there is no such thing as a neutral party. To this extent the theological vision I maintain remains faithful to the early conversations that led to the development of Radical Orthodoxy and to the recognition of the profound capacity of human beings to err. This was so important to the three most important theological influences upon my work: Augustine, Barth and von Balthasar.

Chapter 21

Between the Local and the Global: Autobiographical Reflections on the Emergence of the Global Theological Mind

Amos Yong

What is the 'global theological mind'? Is such a thing even feasible? Accessible? Producible? Legitimate? In the following pages, I reflect on this set of questions by looking back at the shape, structure, and evolution of my own theological work, focusing chiefly on my book publications.[1]

I was born in West Malaysia as the eldest child of parents who were then (and remain) Assemblies of God ministers, both of whom converted to Christianity during their teenage years. When I was 10, they moved our family (now three boys, including Ebenezer and Mark) to Stockton, California to take a pastorate among Chinese Christians, most of whom were also first generation immigrants to the USA and I spent the rest of my growing up years trying to fit into the mould of a 'model minority' Asian American. Then, during my young adult years, I went on to complete an undergraduate degree in theology at a denominational school (Bethany College of the Assemblies of God in Santa Cruz, California), met a beautiful Mexican-American woman while I was there and married her shortly after my graduation. I worked as a youth pastor in a denominational church in the San Francisco Bay Area, attained two master's degrees (in historical theology from Wesleyan Evangelical Seminary and in intellectual history from Portland State University) and received into the world three children of my own.

In the summer of 1996, we moved from the Pacific Northwest region to the Boston, Massachusetts, area where I matriculated into the PhD program at Boston University (BU). I already knew what my dissertation topic would be as a result of my graduate studies: a Pentecostal perspective on theology of religions and on inter-religious dialogue. My studies at a Wesleyan Holiness seminary raised the intra-Christian ecumenical question for me with great force, challenging me to confront the very sectarian and exclusive form of Christian self-understanding which characterized the Chinese-American Pentecostal churches of my upbringing and which went relatively unchallenged during my undergraduate education. Further

---

[1] My thanks to editor Marks for the invitation to participate in this volume. I have taken this opportunity to reflect autobiographically on the topic under discussion.

graduate studies expanded the ecumenical question; namely, if it was possible that those who I before considered as outside the pale of Christianity (e.g., Catholics, Orthodox, even Lutherans) did indeed have a saving relationship with God, then what about others also categorized as pagan, heathen, or non-Christian (e.g., Jews, Muslims, Buddhists and so on)? In addition, I had joined the Society of Pentecostal Studies during my seminary years, a move which not only salvaged for me the possibility of being a 'Pentecostal intellectual' (still considered oxymoronic even within Pentecostal circles), but had begun to open me up to the vitality, diversity, and charismatic face of world Pentecostalism in particular and of world Christianity in general. While early during my seminary studies I had struggled with the question of whether or not I could remain within the Assemblies of God and pursue advanced theological study, by the time I went to Boston I was convinced that part of my vocation involved a stance of critical loyalty toward the denomination and movement which had nurtured my Christian faith. So, the driving question for my dissertation written in 1998 was how Pentecostalism, given its primary self-understanding as a Christian missionary movement, should posture itself in a world of many faiths.

Hence two global horizons intersected in the dissertation which was later published as *Discerning the Spirit(s): A Pentecostal Charismatic Contribution to Christian Theology of Religions*.[2] The first global horizon was that of my own religious community, the modern Pentecostal-charismatic movement, and the second was the emergence finally in the twentieth century of religious traditions as worldwide phenomena. As an aspiring Christian theologian, I had come to the conviction that theology was in part a public activity which engaged in conversation any and all those interested in its topics. In a post-foundationalist world, of course, how *theology* itself was defined would depend on who was involved in the discussion to begin with. If we agree that there was a place at the table for all who were engaged with the questions which most ultimately concerned human life and destiny, then we could not arbitrarily bar persons from other faiths from framing the questions and presenting their own perspectives in response. Hence, part of the driving force of this early volume was to provide an apologetic for expanding the theological conversation to include the world's religious traditions. Christian theology in the twentieth century could not ignore, much less avoid, the pervasive presence of other faiths.

But I was also a theologian concerned with the question of relativism. If I was indeed going to take the perspectives of those in other faiths seriously, did I not have to be willing to change my mind if I was convinced that their view was more compelling than my own? Did I not have to 'relativize' my own theological convictions to very particular social and historical experiences? But then again, did not my dialogue partners from other faiths also see things from their own limited frames of reference? If none of us could claim superior vantage points, whither our truth claims, and why our conversations?

It was this realization which drove me back to the tradition I knew best – Pentecostalism – and I found in the worldwide movement a much more global set of perspectives than I previously knew existed. I knew, for example, that the

---

[2]   Amos Yong, *Discerning the Spirit(s): A Pentecostal-Charismatic Contribution to Christian Theology of Religions* (Sheffield, 2000).

phenomenology of Pentecostal-charismatic spirituality was both quite diverse and shared some characteristics with a wide range of indigenous religious experiences. Related to this was the challenge of defining Pentecostalism: if we opted for a *phenomenological* approach, then what counted as Pentecostal would include all kinds of groups whose Christian identity was under question; or, if we opted for a *doctrinal* approach, there could be no possibility of agreement about the boundaries of Pentecostalism. I intuitively opted for a theological approach focused on the presence and activity of the Holy Spirit, long central to my Christian experience. But having made this commitment, the question quickly turned to how to discern the Holy Spirit from any other spirit, especially since the discernment of spirits relied upon phenomenological categorization which in turn muddied the task of discerning other faiths. I embraced this challenge because it seemed to me to accomplish three objectives which I thought indispensable to Christian theology in the twenty-first century: (a) it was theologically driven (with the focus on pneumatology), but in a way which did not discount the contributions of other disciplinary perspectives; (b) it allowed me to pursue the task of developing a Pentecostal theology (remember that Pentecostal scholarship is still a relative newcomer to the theological academy); and (c) it opened up theological space to take seriously the perspectives of those in other faiths on their own terms. My theological path seemed clearly charted out when *Discerning the Spirit(s)* was released at the dawn of a new millennium.

As should be clear from the preceding, my attempt to formulate a Pentecostal perspective on theology of religions raised a host of methodological, epistemological, and philosophical issues. Could theology actually take phenomenology or any other discipline into account without compromising itself? Why did similar phenomenological manifestations across the world's religious traditions have pneumatological implications, and, from the other side, did the theological assumption regarding the universality of the Holy Spirit's presence and activity actually have anything to do with the diversity of religions? Isn't perspectivism in theology still a problem, or how does adopting a pneumatological approach ameliorate the partiality of our theological starting-points? Could world Pentecostalism and the charismatic experience of the Spirit sustain a robust theological vision? These questions quickly pushed me to write a sequel theology of religions and, more importantly for our purposes, a book on theological hermeneutics and theological method.[3]

Spirit-Word-Community: Theological Hermeneutics in Trinitarian Perspective was my attempt to wrestle more deeply with some of foundational philosophical and theological questions. The primary problematic was how to understand the universality of the Spirit's presence and activity in a postmodern world. To make claims to universality (in effect, all truly theological claims) was the challenge for theology in our time. How could the Christian confession of the universal work of the Spirit be sustained as coherent and plausible in the public square without finally lapsing into fideism? If not, then what differentiated Christian fideism from any other kind of fideism?

---

[3]   See Yong, *Beyond the Impasse: Toward a Pneumatological Theology of Religions* (Grand Rapids, 2003) and *Spirit-Word-Community: Theological Hermeneutics in Trinitarian Perspective* (Ashgate, 2002).

My response in *Spirit-Word-Community* cut across three domains in metaphysics, epistemology, and anthropology, each of which has implications for our quest for understanding the emergence of a global theological mind. First, any robust answer to my questions could not avoid the classical topics of metaphysics (the nature of reality) and ontology (the nature of being). Universal claims have to come to terms with metaphysical and ontological discourses. Saying the Holy Spirit is universally present and active in the world without providing some kind of account of this presence and activity leaves us with the kind of subjectivism which has long plagued Pentecostal-charismatic piety and spirituality. Having said this, of course, classical metaphysics had corrupted the Christian theological tradition to the point that the God of Abraham, Isaac, Jacob, and Jesus was no longer discernible after onto-theology. Hence, I needed to articulate a metaphysics and ontology which was recognizably theological.

But what epistemological point of view could suffice for such claims in a post-metaphysical world? To simply say, 'The Spirit told me so' (quite prevalent in Pentecostal circles, actually) helped neither the cause of Pentecostal scholars in the wider Christian academy nor of Christian theologians in a world of many religions. I therefore had to articulate an epistemology which could chart a middle way between absolutism and relativism, between objectivism and subjectivism, and between modernism and postmodernism. Such an epistemological posture need not shy away from making claims, but had to be humble, provisional and vulnerable to correction.

Finally, I needed a theological anthropology which could begin to address the question of how human beings could encounter, respond to and reflect upon the divine. I began to see that understanding human beings as communal, interpersonal, and inter-subjective realities helped me to respond not only to the anthropological question but also to the epistemological one. The pneumatological motif helped me tie the pieces together, leading to a foundational pneumatology (sketching a metaphysics and ontology of divine presence and activity), a pneumatological imagination (human knowing as emergent from our imaginative engagement with the world), and a pneumatological anthropology (humans as social creatures bound together by common needs, interests, and purposes). The result was a theological hermeneutics and methodology featuring a dynamic epistemology that recognized human knowing as an inter-subjective enterprise. Put succinctly, Christian theological reflection occurs in communities of faith that are continuously shifting, that overlap with innumerable other communal perspectives, and that are each constituted by material practices directed toward the creation of a better world.

Such a theoretical formulation enlarged the global horizons of *Discerning the Spirit(s)*. In addition to world Pentecostalism and the world's religions (both of which were present in *Spirit-Word-Community*, but in the background rather than at the forefront), theology now not only could provide a preliminary account for but also needed to draw from the diversity of perspectives derived from the multitude of communities that constitute humankind. Here, we have ideological communities, ethnic communities, political communities, communities of inquiry, religious communities and the like. Theology could no longer belong to a few elites. Rather, a truly global conversation was already well under way, enabled, of course, by modern (!) technology, so that any responsible theological articulation had to find some way to engage the multitudes. For me, however, this move was driven not by political correctness or identity politics, but by the theological axiom of the universal presence and activity of the Spirit of God.

Shortly after *Spirit-Word-Community* was published (2002), I reconnected with a colleague, Peter G. Heltzel, who was entering the PhD program at BU at the time when I was on my way out. In renewing our friendship, we landed on the idea of putting together a *festschrift* for our *doktorvater*, Robert Cummings Neville (to whom I had previously dedicated *Spirit-Word-Community*). My views regarding theology as being at least in part a public enterprise were developed during my BU years in dialogue with Neville's *oeuvre*. Neville's own philosophical and theological work was deeply informed by engagement with Eastern traditions, specifically Confucianism. Further, he had also contributed to revising the BU theology program to include the study of foundational texts of the world's religious traditions in the core curriculum, and, during the years I was there, was leading in a comparative theology study group associated in part with the Boston Theological Institute to rethink Christian theology in a world religious context.[4] Finally, as first and foremost a systematic philosopher, Neville has long been concerned about the plausibility conditions for philosophical and theological reflection in the late modern (not quite post-modern, but not un-chastised modernism either) world. Hence Heltzel and I sent out invitations to Neville's colleagues and former students who had worked on issues related to modernity, on the inter-religious dialogue and theology of religions and on systematic theology.

The result was an exemplary kind of global theological conversation, and that precisely because it was rooted locally in concrete communities, projects, and conversations.[5] *Theology in Global Context* suggested that theological reflection in the twenty-first century could not but be ecumenical, multi-disciplinary, and inter-religious, even as it engaged voices from North and South, East and West. Some of the contributors approached the task of theology in our late modern world by wrestling with issues such as global citizenship, political terrorism, ecological ethics, racism, and violence in African-American communities. Others wrote on Christian doctrines and themes (e.g., atonement, apocalyptic, theology of religions) utilizing resources drawn from the history of Christian thought, the philosophical tradition, and the ecumenical and interreligious dialogues. And, of course, voices from the world's religious traditions were also present, such as Islamic views on modernity, a Daoist theology of religions, Advaita Vedanta and religious non-dualism, Mahayana Buddhist insights on the doctrine of creation and Hindu-Christian readings and interpretations of religious texts and ideas among others. *Theology in Global Context* turned out exactly as intended: a 'snapshot' of a global theological conversation already in full gear.

The success of the *festschrift*, in my estimation (and this notwithstanding my biases as one of the volume's editors), was due in large part to Bob Neville's embodying

---

[4]   See Robert Cummings Neville (ed.), *The Comparative Religious Ideas Project* (3 vols., Albany, 2001).

[5]   See Amos Yong and Peter G. Heltzel (eds.), *Theology in Global Context: Essays in Honor of Robert Cummings Neville* (T. & T. Clark, 2004).

in his own life and work the kind of global awareness that is emerging in our time. It was by following after, disputing against, engaging with, and even attempting to go beyond Neville's work that each of the essayists were themselves cultivating the global theological conversation. To be sure the different contexts, different conversations and different dialogue partners at work in each essay produced the wide range of chords struck by each author. Yet this shows that whatever the global theological mind might be, it is dynamically fluid, pluralistically informed and polyphonically constituted. While there will always be a place for theology produced by the church and for the church, the horizons of twenty-first century Christian theology are necessarily global, brought about by the ever-expanding communicative technologies, socio-economic (ex)changes, cross-cultural fertilization and political trans-nationalism.

While the Neville *festschrift* was making its way through the publication process, I was writing and revising *The Spirit Poured Out on All Flesh: Pentecostalism and the Possibility of Global Theology*.[6] In many ways, this work encapsulates what I had been doing over the past decade. First, it presents a systematic theology, albeit one reconceived from a distinctively Pentecostal perspective. Not so modestly, it brings Pentecostalism into the heart of the academy, signalling the arrival of the 'Pentecostal mind' at the theological conversation table. Second, the central theological motif driving the book's argument is the universal presence and activity of the Holy Spirit. Hence I propose in its pages a pneumatological soteriology, a pneumatological ecclesiology, a pneumatological theology of culture and a pneumatological theology of the creation, among other loci of Christian theology systematically reconceived. Last but not least, the horizons of *The Spirit Poured Out on All Flesh* are thoroughly global, drawing into one conversation historic Christianity, the entire range of the ecumenical dialogues, the inter-religious encounter (as sifted through the lens of Muslim-Christian dialogue), the science-and-religion interchange (harnessed toward the formulation of a theology of environment), social justice issues, and feminist perspectives. Still, the framework within which these disparate voices are held together is the broad spectrum of worldwide Pentecostalism.

Methodologically, *The Spirit Poured Out on All Flesh* fleshes out what was presented much more abstractly in *Spirit-Word-Community*. In a post-foundationalist world, Christian theology cannot proceed ahistorically, but is grounded confessionally in a community of faith, and concretely in the various tasks which bring together the broad range of human communities. My work here is unabashedly Pentecostal, but it is an expression of Pentecostalism that is informed, engaged, and chastened by the global realities of our time. Further, my understanding of historic Christianity is sifted through my Pentecostal lens, with each providing leverage on and corrective to the other. Finally, however, I am still a theologian rather than a cultural critic, comparativist, or socio-political scientist, etc., and this shows in the robust pneumatological theme running through the book. As a pneumatological theologian, however, I am attempting to ride the fine line between preserving that which was once and for all handed down to the saints and receiving the new things which the

---

6　　Amos Yong, *The Spirit Poured Out on All Flesh: Pentecostalism and the Possibility of Global Theology* (Grand Rapids, 2005).

Spirit is doing in the world. Is this not central to the task of doing theology in global context today?

I am hopeful that this volume will continue to inspire Christian theological reflection along each of these lines: Pentecostal theology, pneumatological theology and global theology. For me, completion of this book only anticipates future work. James K.A. Smith (Calvin College) and I have launched a project on Pentecostal theology and the sciences which will result in a book with contributors drawing from many disciplines in the humanities, the social sciences, and the natural sciences. I have already begun work on the Buddhist-Christian dialogue which I hope will see the light of publication soon, and I hope to begin turning my scholarly attention to the topic of religion in China and sustain that research for the next few years. In the longer run, I hope to return to a multi-volume reformulation of Christian theology in a global context which is framed pneumatologically (once again), interdisciplinary (engaging with the natural and social sciences), and informed by the inter-religious dialogues (especially the Chinese religious traditions).

In the mean time, however, I have just completed a sabbatical project funded in part by the Louisville Institute's Christian Faith and Life. The final product is titled, *Theology and Down Syndrome: Re-Imagining Disability in Late Modernity*.[7] In some ways this might be seen as a detour from the theological trajectory on which I have been set. In other ways, however, it is a project emergent like all of my other books: from the local circumstances of my own life, specifically my relationship with my youngest brother Mark who was born with a triplication of the 21st chromosome, more commonly known as Down syndrome. A few years ago, I mentioned to my parents that I felt compelled to write an account of our lives with Mark and Down syndrome, as well as to provide some theological perspective on it. As with my first book – *Discerning the Spirit(s)* – personal biographical and autobiographical vignettes will centrally shape the argument. As a systematician, I cannot but think about Down syndrome in light of the entire theological spectrum: the doctrines of creation and providence, theological anthropology, ecclesiology, soteriology, eschatology, and the doctrine of God. Once again, the pneumatological motif will run through the book. In our late modern world, our understanding of Down syndrome must also be interdisciplinary, drawing from the neuro-biological, social and educational sciences. And, finally, thinking theologically about Down syndrome and intellectual disability cannot but occur in a global context, taking into account international developments, cross-cultural perspectives and the views on disability of those in other faiths. In each of these senses, *Theology and Down Syndrome* will represent the application of the theological methodology formulated and fleshed out in my earlier works to the complex but still relatively delimited topic of intellectual disability.

How then would I summarize my responses to the questions with which I opened this essay? I would simply say that the 'global theological mind' is that emerging orientation to theology which recognizes that theological reflection and argumentation in the twenty-first century must proceed in dialogue with the concerns, questions and perspectives of any and all who are interested in the conversation.

---

[7]   Amos Yong *Theology and Down Syndrome: Reimagining Disability in Late Modernity* (Waco, Tex.: Baylor University Press, 2007).

Hence, global theology in our time must be multi-perspectival, interdisciplinary, cross-cultural, inter-religious and, finally, thoroughly dialogical. Seen in this way, global theology cannot be something we do in addition to doing theology, but must be understood as intrinsic to the theological task itself. This does not mean that what we produce is not theology unless these aspects are taken into consideration. It is to say that theological treatments of any topic will remain incomplete until the global theological mind is engaged. Further, as I have described it, the global theological mind cannot be monolithic or homogenizing and that precisely because it is constituted by the multitude of confessional commitments, concrete historical projects and local perspectives. Finally, then, the global theological mind is dynamic and fluid, shifting according to the winds of the Spirit, whose tracks we continuously attempt to track: 'Come Holy Spirit ....'

Index

Ackermann, Denise, 158
Adams, James Luther, 60–61
Adorno, Theodor W., 147, 185
Aikman, David, 22
Albert, Hans, 147
Altizer, Thomas J.J., 164
Amin, Idi, 92
Anselm of Canterbury, 82n6
Apartheid, 6, 35, 37–8, 119, 153–62
Appadurai, Arjun, 3, 174
Aquinas, Thomas, 164, 179
Athanasius of Alexandria, 16, 18
Augustine of Hippo, 19, 180, 184, 185, 186
Aurelius, Marcus, 139

Báez-Camargo, Gonzalo, 128
Baillie, John, 164, 165
Barth, Karl, 7–8, 29, 33, 35, 74, 150, 160
        164, 165, 179, 180–84, 186
Bauer, Angela, 84
Beck, Ulrich, 3n12
Bediako, Kwame, 71
Beer, Gillian, 179
Bell, Daniel, 184
Bellah, Robert, 142
Benjamin, Walter, 185
Berlinerblau, Jacques, 170
Berman, Harold, 75
Bhabha, Homi K., 174
Birth, Charles, 142
Blixen, Karen, 113
Bloch, Ernst, 147
Blumhardt, Christoph, 145–6, 150
Boesak Allan, 154, 158, 159
Boli, John, 1n3, 3n13
Bonhoeffer, Dietrich, 35, 36, 38, 161, 165
Bonino, Jose Miguez, 8n18, 133n15, 136,
        171–2
Bourdeau, Jean Ovide, 182
Brahman, 10–12, 73
Brubaker, Pamela, 84
Brunner, Emil, 150, 164, 165

Bulgakov, Sergei, 18
Bultmann, Rudolph, 28, 150, 165, 167
Bunyan, John, 179
Buthelezi, Manas, 154

Calvin, John, 159
Calvinism, 52, 54, 56, 59
Cannon, Katie Geneva, 84
Castells, Manuel, 3n11
Castro, Fidel, 130
de Certeau, Michel, 182
Chiang, Kai-Shek, 74
Chikane, Frank, 154
Chomsky, Noam, 2n7
Chun, Tai-il, 140
Chung, Hyun Kyung, 84
Churchill, Ward, 60
Civil Rights Movement (USA), 35, 77, 80,
        81
Cobb, John Jr., 141, 142
Cone, James, 51, 52, 84
Confessing Church, 145, 146, 160
Congar, Yves, 5
Contextual Theology, 5, 10, 18–20, 32, 36,
        72, 95, 97, 99, 100, 105, 118, 119,
        122, 126, 131
Coomaraswamy, Ananda, 167
Cosmicity, 55, 57
Crisis Theology, 6
Cunningham, Conor, 184

Da Xue (The Great Learning), 66–7
Dalit theology, 95, 100
Deiros, Pablo A., 46n12
Derrida, Jacques, 174, 180, 181, 183
Descartes, René, 69, 180
Devanandan, Paul, 99
Devi, V. Indira, 168n3
Dionysius the Aeropagite, 19
Discipleship, 48, 49, 104, 106
Dodd, C.H., 166
Dogmatics, 8, 30, 33, 124, 149, 151, 183, 184

Driver, Tom, 73, 84
Dualism, 67–8, 70, 72, 102
Dutch Reformed Church, 37, 154, 155, 160

Edwards, George, 115
Ela, Jean Marc, 93, 125
Ellen, Charlotte, 141
Enlightenment, 30, 69, 72, 76, 165, 167, 168
Erickson, Victoria, 84
Escobar, Samuel, 19

Falwell, Jerry, 4
Farley, Edward, 6
Feigl, Herbert, 28
Florovsky, Georges, 17, 18
Foster, Durwood, 142
Foucault, Michel, 174, 182
Francis of Assisi, 142
Frei, Hans, 182
Freire, Paulo, 78, 84
Freud, Sigmund, 179
Friedman, Thomas, 2n5
Fukayama, Francis, 1
Fundamentalism, 2, 46n12, 67, 103

Galeano, Eduardo, 42n3
Gardiner, Lucy, 183
Genocide, 92
Giddens, Anthony, 2
Ginés de Sepúlveda, Juan, 42
Gitari, David, 71
Globalization, 1, 2, 3, 4, 41–4, 47–50, 53,
    58, 92, 96, 103, 104, 105, 137
Gogarten, Friedrich, 150
González, Justo, 82, 133
Gorringe, Timothy J., 184
Gramsci, Antonio, 61, 82n7
Greer, Germaine, 171
Greimas, Algirdas Julius, 179
Grove, Pieter, 161
Guevara, Ché, 130
Gutierrez, José Ángel, 57, 81

Habermas, Jürgen, 147
Hamilton, William, 164
han, 140–41, 143, 144
Harrison, Beverly, 83
Hauerwas, Stanley, 91, 92, 182, 183
Hegel, G.W.F., 180, 185
Heidegger, Martin, 180
Heim, Karl, 150

Hick, John, 4, 27
Historical Criticism, 163, 165, 167–71
Hoelzl, Michael, 185
Hooks, Bell, 119
Horkheimer, Max, 147, 185
Huber, Wolfgang, 161
Hume, David, 69
Hunsinger, George, 184
Huntington, Samuel, 2

Ignatius, Loyola, 19
Incarnation, 5, 47–9, 124, 184
Inculturation Theology, 5, 47–9, 124
Indigenous Theology, 100, 106, 107
Individualism, 3, 5, 7, 36, 48, 56, 57, 67,
    68, 75, 102, 103, 107, 110, 111, 112,
    129, 145
Irigaray, Luce, 182
Isaac of Nineveh, 16, 19
Iwand, Hans Joachim, 151

Jacobson, Eric, 179
Jaspers, Karl, 25
Jeffries, Stuart, 170n7
Jenkins, Philip, 4, 29, 32, 124
Jeremias, Joachim, 171
John Damascene, 16, 17
John Paul II, 182
Johnston, Arthur P., 135
Jones, Serene, 182
Juarez, Benito, 58
Jüngel, Eberhardt, 6

Kähler, Martin, 29, 72
à Kempis, Thomas, 139
Kennedy, Will, 84
Kermode, Frank, 174
King, Martin Luther, 52, 56
Kistner, Wolfram, 154
Knitter, Paul, 27
Koyama, Kosuke, 71, 74, 164, 175
Kraemer, Hendrik, 70
Kristeva, Julia, 182, 183
Kuomintang, 65

la lucha (the struggle), 79–80, 87
de Las Casas, Bartelomé, 65
Lash, Nicholas, 179, 180
Lausanne Covenant, 67
Law, John, 2
Lechner, Frank, 1n3, 3n13

Levinas, Emmanuel, 147, 180
Levi-Strauss, Claude, 179
Lewis, Oscar, 174
Liberation Theology, 63, 78, 79, 86, 99, 131, 133, 142
Lindbeck, George, 182
Lonergan, Bernard, 52
Long, Stephen, 184
Lossky, Vladimir, 18
Lowe, Walter, 182
de Lubac, Henri, 182
Luther, Martin, 29, 30, 48, 56

Maathai, Wangari, 117–18
Mackay, John A., 127n1, 128
MacKinnon, Donald, 183
Mandela, Nelson, 38, 117, 118
Marlowe, Christopher, 179
Martinez, Antonio José, 59
Marvell, Andrew, 179
Marxism, 2, 8, 76, 128, 150, 171
Maximus the Confessor, 16
Maxwell, J., 175
Mayman, Margie, 84
McAfee Brown, Robert, 142
McCarthy, Joseph, 170
McFague, Sallie, 7, 44n9, 93, 109–12
Merleau Ponty, Maurice, 28
Meyendorff, John, 18
Meyer, John, 4
Mickleson, A. Berkley, 130
Milbank, John, 183, 184
Minjung Theology, 95, 100, 140, 142
Moltmann, Jürgen, 146–7
Mondragón, Carlos, 129
Mosala, Itumeleng, 158
Moss, David, 180, 182
Moulton, Harold, 165
Moxnes, Halvor, 173
Murlenburg, James, 83
Murray, Edward, 170
Mysticism, 15–16, 19–20, 20, 139–40, 142

Nancy, Jean-Luc, 183
Naudé, Beyers, 37, 154
Neal, S. Marie Augusta, 51
Neo-Marxism, 147
Nicholas, Colin, 96n1
Niebuhr, H.R., 32
Niebuhr, Reinhold, 83
Nietzsche, Friedrich, 180

Oliver, Simon, 184
Orientalism (Said), 2, 6, 171–3

Padilla, René, 71, 133n15, 135n27, 137
Panikkar, Raimundo, 164
Pannenberg, Wolfhart, 147, 151
Parades, Tito, 8, 9, 71, 73
Pellauer, Mary, 84
Perrin, Norman, 166
Phelps, Jamie, 80
Philosophical Model, 98
Pickstock, Catherine, 183, 184
Pinter, Harold, 170
Plato, 180
Pobee, John, 116
Polanyi, Karl, 1n2
Popper, Karl R., 147
Post Colonialism, 41, 45, 104, 172–4

Quash, Ben, 183

Radical Orthodoxy, 181, 183–6
Ratzinger, Joseph (Benedict XVI), 182, 184
Reconciliation, 26, 27, 28, 68, 76, 87, 90, 93, 131, 145, 153, 160
Reformation, 30, 36, 75
Reformed Theology, 37, 153, 155–6, 157, 159, 160, 161
Rembao, Alberto, 128
Renan, E., 173
Ricouer, Paul, 147
Ritschl, Albrecht, 150
Roberts, Richard, 184
Robertson, Roland, 2
Rothko, Mark, 179
Rowland, Tracey, 184
Roy, Raja Rammohun, 167
Ruether, Rosemary Radford, 44n9, 86, 143

Said, Edward, 2, 143, 167, 171–2, 174
Salinas, Daniel, 133n14
Samuel, Vinay, 68, 72
Sánches, Ricardo, 61–3
Sankara, Adi, 10, 11
de Saussure, Ferdinand, 179
Sauter, Gerhard, 8
Savage, Peter, 133
Schaeffer, Francis, 67
Schmitt, Charles, 185
Schweitzer, Albert, 173
Seagrave, Stirling, 65n2

Singh, Sadhu Sundar, 139
Sklair, Leslie, 137
Smith, James K.A., 184
Social Gospel, 66, 67
Socolow, Susan Midgen, 43n7
Song, C.S., 74, 99
Soskice, Janet Martin, 179, 183
Spivak, Gayatri Chakravorty, 174
Steiner, George, 178, 182
Stoevesandt, Hinrich, 150
Strauss, David, 173
Sugden, Christopher, 68
Sung, Jung Mo, 42n5
Sutherland, John, 174n11
Swedenborg, Emmanuel, 139

Tarando, Yolanda, 81, 82
Taylor, Charles, 185
Taylor, Vincent, 166
Thurneysen, Eduard, 150
Tijerina, Reies Lopez, 52
Tillich, Paul, 28, 29, 83, 142, 151, 184
Tinker, George (Tink), 101
Todorov, Tzvetan, 45n10, 117
Togba, George, 117
Trapasso, Rose Dominie, 78
Traub, Hellmut, 150
Trible, Phyllis, 84
Troeltsch, Ernst, 29
Tuite, Marjorie, 80
Tutu, Desmond, 37, 154, 158
Twain, Mark, 174

Urry, John, 2

Vályi-Nagy, Ervin, 148
Van Buren, Paul, 164
Vasconcelos, José, 55
Vatican II, 77, 128
Vattimo, Gianni, 183
Viswanathan, Gauri, 169
von Balthasar, Hans Urs, 8, 182, 184, 186

Wagner, Peter, 72
Wahl, Jean, 28
Wallenstein, Immanuel, 3, 4n14
Walton, Janet, 84
Warren, Karen J., 44n9
Webb, Pauline, 117
Wesley, John, 72
West, Cornell, 83
Westhelle, Vitor, 49n14
Wielenga, Bas, 171
Wilken, Robert, 72–3
Williams, Rowan, 182, 183
Wink, Walter, 165
Wittgenstein, Ludwig, 28, 180
Womanist Theology, 83, 95
World Social Forum, 49

Yoder, John Howard, 182
Yu, Carver, 67

Zimmerlie, Walther, 146
Zizek, Slavoj, 174